Jessica Lofthouse

LANCASHIRE'S OLD FAMILIES

Three Rivers
Off to the Lakes
Off to the Dales
Lancashire Landscapes
Lancashire's Fair Face
Lancashire—Westmorland Highway
The Curious Traveller Through Lakeland
West Pennine Highway
The Curious Traveller: Lancaster to Lakeland
Lancashire Countrygoer
Countrygoer in the Dales
Portrait of Lancashire
Countrygoers' North
North Wales for the Countrygoer

Lancashire's Old Families

JESSICA LOFTHOUSE

Illustrated by the author

ROBERT HALE · LONDON

© *Jessica Lofthouse 1972*
First published in Great Britain 1972

ISBN 0 7091 3330 8

Robert Hale & Company
63 Old Brompton Road
London, S.W.7

PRINTED IN GREAT BRITAIN BY
CLARKE, DOBLE & BRENDON LTD
PLYMOUTH

Contents

Illustrations

Foreword

When I was working on the *Portrait of Lancashire* the present heads of old Lancashire families gave me so much rich material that, had I used it all, instead of writing a balanced book about all sorts of Lancastrians against assorted backgrounds, this would have been top-heavy with landed gentry and country seats.

Another book was called for, concentrating on family histories; on families surviving the centuries—as do the Stanleys, Asshetons, Blundells, Shuttleworths and Towneleys—and those who made their impact on county history though—like the Butlers, Norrises, Radcliffes and Pilkingtons, Southworths, Sherburnes and Tyldesleys —they no longer occupy their ancestral halls.

Most rewarding were hours I spent browsing through family archives in libraries—what wonderful private collections there are —looking up from letters and journals to the portraits of their writers there on the walls—Tudor gallants, Cavalier and Round-head ancestors and frail ladies of the eighteenth century whose hands penned the faded pages.

More halls than one hopes for retain fragments of medieval and Tudor work. A great many were rebuilt in the seventeenth and eighteenth century and some over-exuberantly restored and improved by Victorian owners. Of these still standing I made my sketches from the life. Fortunately I had sketched most of the derelict buildings before demolition gangs moved in, but where I had no record of the homes of the families included in this book I borrowed from the prints and water-colour drawings of eighteenth- and nineteenth-century topographers. Way back in Tudor times topographers and antiquaries foretold doom for the old families, as did Camden, confessing to little enthusiasm for barbarous Lancashire and small encouragement to meet the natives or seek out family seats: "Time has completely destroyed original names everywhere, but that I may not seem to neglect Lancashire, I must attempt the task, not doubting but Providence

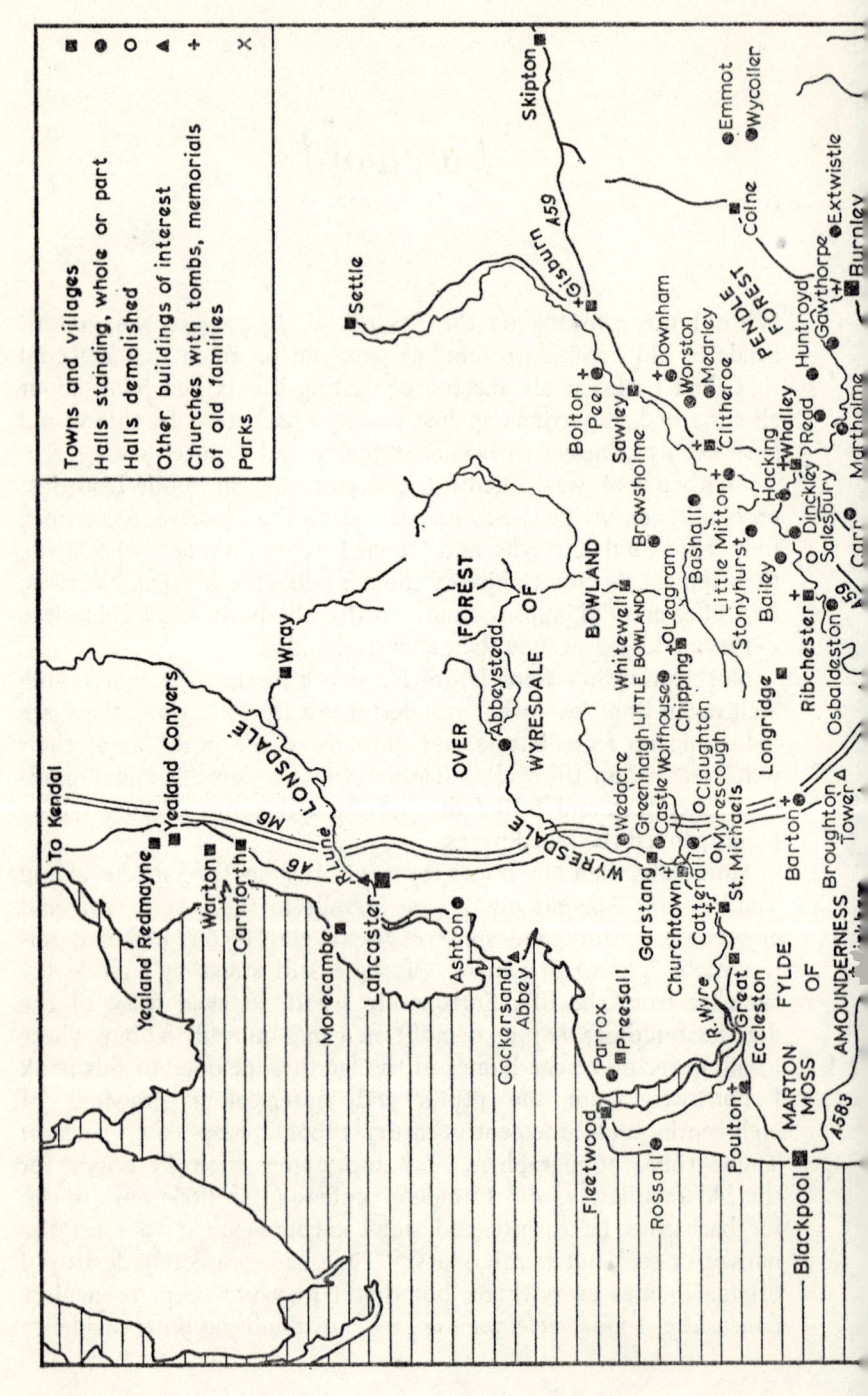

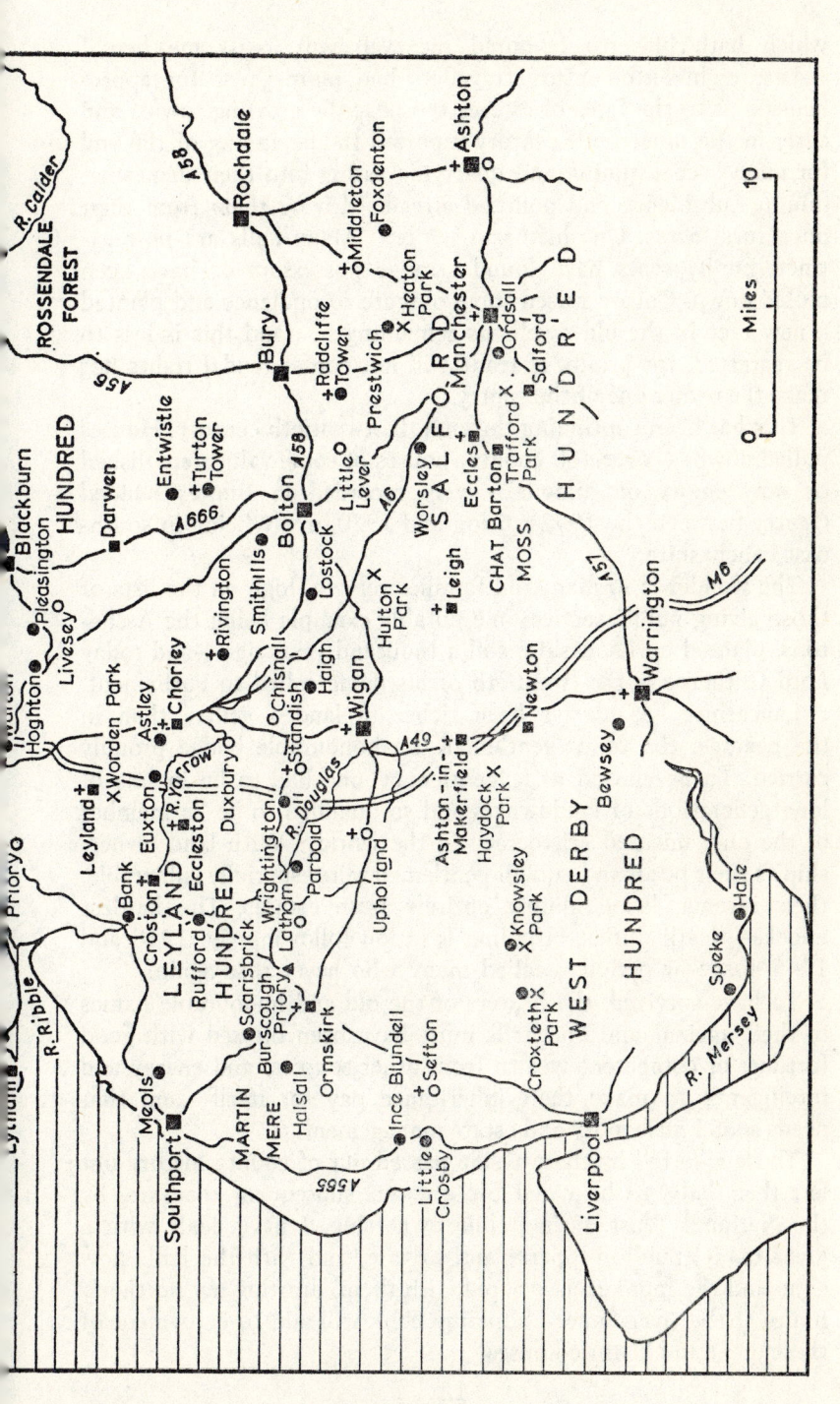

which hath hitherto favoured me well will assist me here."

Late eighteenth-century travellers had more cause for apprehension as to the fates of estates too near the growing towns, and early in the nineteenth century reported the beginning of the end for many—coal mining and quarrying eating into their demesnes, mining subsidence and polluted streams driving them from their once rural acres. One historian wrote: "Many halls are now extinct, family seats have found strange possessors or have been pulled down. Cotton raised some obscure to opulence and planted a new race in the old dwellings remaining . . . and this is less to be regretted, for profits of trade will not confer feudal rights nor make the owner one of the gentry."

This has been continuing through the twentieth century. Houses pulled down—"over 400 country houses of some value demolished or now empty or ruinous"—were recorded in *Burkes Landed Gentry* between the 1952 edition and 1970, many being in southeast Lanchashire.

The wonder is so many old families remain, high on the lists of those giving public service, one notable example being the Asshetons, planted on Lancashire soil a thousand years ago—and today Lord Clitheroe is the twentieth of his name called to Parliament.

Lancashire has always been richer in landed gentry than in the peerage, the term 'gentleman' an honourable badge proudly carried. To be classed as a 'gentleman' one had to be in line of long generations of landowners and so qualified to be "a member of the only untitled aristocracy in the world." With land ownership as their be all and end all gentlemen were especially vulnerable, their revenue being almost entirely from estates. The hardest knocks—death duties, crippling taxation following the 1918 and 1945 post-war periods—felled many who never rose again.

To have survived, the bearers of the old and honourable names in their ancient and fine halls must have been blessed with good fortune, or competent wealth from other sources, and energy and intelligence to make their inheritance pay for itself—and that needs sound husbandry and estate management.

Those who fell by the wayside passed out of county history but left their halls to be cared for, for our subsequent pleasure, by the National Trust or in public ownership. I have dealt with a great many, public property and private, and with the halls now gone and the families associated with them, drawing my northerly limits at the river Lune. I hope my book will add to enjoyment of these great and historic houses.

PART ONE

South-East Lancashire Families

Asshetons of Ashton and Middleton

Which family has about the longest claim on Lancashire, here a hundred years before the Conquest and as Anglo-Norse 'natives' dispossessed by the Conqueror's henchmen, Nigel and Roger de Poictou? The Asshetons are certainly among the founding fathers. Ralph Assheton in 1613 signed his name at the end of a pedigree covering fifteen generations.

According to the family historian the family tree begins with Aylward (or Edward) and Orm, Vikings who drew up their longships on Duddon shores at Kirkby Ireleth in A.D 900. "So, 'on the spear side' we can make no claim to have come with the Conqueror." On the distaff side yes, for the son of Orm robbed of his lands by Nigel, had a son Ormus Magnus who wed Aliz daughter of the powerful Hervey Walter. Their Anglo-Norse-Norman grandson Orm Fitzeward, Ormus Normanus, received with his wife Emma—daughter of the great Albert de Greslet, one of the barons at Runnymede—one caracute of land at Ashton on the Tame; also he was handed lands in Dalton, Parbold and Wrightington. The head of the family chose Ashton, built a fortified hall watching the river Tame, its ford and bridge and inroads from the Cheshire plain and forests. From this he took his name.

Clerks spelt it "indifferently, a source of considerable embarrassment to the genealogist". Robert of Eston, Robertus Asheton, Robert of Assheton, Sir Rafe Ashton, Radulpho Esheton—and when Ralph was first choice of name for eldest son, this appeared as Rafe or Raphe also. Assheton is now the accepted form for the family, Ashton for the hall and modern town.

According to the Reverend Richard Orme Assheton, from the eleventh to fourteenth centuries the Ashton Hall family were out of the public eye, "not one on the front row, so far as we know not one joined the Crusades, persecuted Jews, assassinated archbishops, fought neither French nor Scots nor even put in an

15

appearance off Magna Carta island". Content with their lot on the wide airy heights above the west Lancashire plains they dwelt at Parbold, Dalton and Wrightington, and occasionally at the Ashton stronghold where they hunted on the demesne of neighbours and friends, the Byrons. Then Sir Roger, returning from Clayton Hall, thought of asking the King for a free warren at his own Lyme Park, a glaring omission by his forbears? So with royal leave he imparked, and kept out poachers too fond of his "lepores, cuniculos, phaisanos and perdices".

Ashton Hall before demolition

Now Asshetons begin to come to the fore. Sir Robert, his brother Sir William and the five generations to follow in the thick of English history. "There was hardly a public event without Sir Robert in it," in Ireland as Chancellor, Admiral of the Coast west of Thames, and in France where he was at the taking of Calais and Guynes, sharing the victories of Edward III. Sir Robert was Edward's Chancellor of the Exchequer, head of the royal administration during the warring years, and later, as the King's Chamberlain, a position of greatest trust, at the King's elbow. When Edward was near to death he was royal spokesman to the mayor, sheriffs and aldermen of London. He was Richard II's Household Treasurer too, and Executor of the King's Will. Sir Robert had an exceptionally long innings, from 1324, when he was of Edward II's Great Council, to 1384, when as Warden of the Cinque Ports he died and was buried in Dover Castle. An earlier Assheton, Sir John, was in the 1324 Great Council.

Three Asshetons were among the 'brave and the wise' when

Lord John King of Castile—John of Gaunt—made his unfortunate expedition to Spain to claim his wife's throne, and plague and dysentry caused so many deaths that the forces were disbanded and formal renunciation of Spain and Leon forced upon him. Present at the gathering of the nobles and princes was Sir William Assheton, Chancellor to John of Gaunt, Receiver to the Duke of Lancaster.

From this time the family was close to the House of Lancaster; Sir John, who shared John of Gaunt's campaigns remained loyal to his son Henry Bolingbroke, throwing in his support when the young King Richard II turned bitterly against his cousin. Ashton men met Henry's forces at Ashton and continued with them to Wales and the eventual capture and submission of the King at Flint Castle. In 1428 on the eve of his coronation Henry IV made forty-six new Knights of the Bath, "three of his own sons, Sir John Ashton and divers others", after confession, shriving, a night in prayer and a thorough purification.

When an uncle of the Asshetons, Piers de Legh, was summarily executed by Henry, the family ceased to trust him and were thereafter "indifferent adherrants". But they were all behind Henry V. Sir John he called to his first Parliament, made him governor of towns in France and chose him as a go-between on diplomatic missions with the Duke of Burgundy. He was at Agincourt with men of Ashton and after the victory and truce was left behind as 'Conserver of the Peace' which followed. He had followed in his father's footsteps. According to Froissart, 16-year-old John Assheton defeated twelve French knights singlehanded in Picardy!

At Agincourt knights received £113 15s.; archers 6d. a day. They returned home to Lancashire to a joyful reception. This date "ever after", as stated in the fascinating *Custom and Rental of the Manor of Ashton-under-Lyne 1422*, became one of two annual rent days "ton half at the Feast of St. John the Baptist [Midsummer Day], tother half at the Feast of St. Martin in Winter [November 11th]", when tenants delivered to their Lord of Ashton at the Hall Mote all moneys and dues.

The Asshetons had their manor from the kings for feudal service and, like contemporary manorial lords, had to observe custom. Everyone knew exactly what was due. Free tenants were held by "honourable obligations", gave personal service in war, often paid nominal rents—like John of the Highrode, Thomas of Staneley, a penny, a red rose, or 7s.—annually, and often took their names from ancestral land holdings. Tenants at Will were well down the feudal ladder, their payment was not in military service, but manual labours in agriculture on set boon days (days appointed for work for the lord of the manor), ploughing, harrowing at seed time, carting turves from the peat beds (turbaries) to Ashton Hall, "shearing 4 days" in harvest. Their obligations were servile and lowly.

As well as on rent days they thronged to the hall 'to give their presents at Yule' and stayed to dinner, the Lord "bounden to serve only the gud men and the gud wyf". Gatecrashers not allowed! Widows came too, like "Alys that was Pole wyf, Syssat that was wyf of Dicon Hoggerson, the wyf of Peryn and Margret that was wyf of Hobbe the Kynge." The last-named's spouse was king in some Yule mummery or play-acting and the name stuck. Women had their place in the manor, and recognized a clear-cut order of rank and precedence for forms (seats) in the Kirk of Ashton, to end squabbling, unseemly haste and pushing aside.

But whence came the manorial lord's revenues? From tolls of fairs, from fines at his courts. From seasonal feasts and gyst-ales, yearly jollifications and guisings when Hobbe the Kynge and his like strutted around. In heriots, the best beast of a deceased tenant's stock. Income from rents, and gifts paid by tenants at will. And so on, these being usual with variations throughout feudal times. The rich man in his castle, the poor man at his gate, each knew on which step of the feudal ladder it had "pleased God" to place him.

The fortified Hall of Ashton in those days had a formidable aspect with its donjon towers (not dungeons) impregnable, whilst bows and arrows and short-range weapons were the only ones known. The townsfolk looked towards it with some apprehension, for therein dwelt men who had undeniable rights and power over them. Traditions were repeated and exaggerated by succeeding generations of infamous Asshetons who "kept the dungeons full" and the gibbet on Gallows Field never without dangling bodies. Bedtime stories for Ashton infants for centuries to come!

Sir John III had two or three wives and at least thirteen children, the eldest Sir Thomas the heir known as The Alchemist because of experiments practised with his friend Edward de Trafford —and with King Henry VI's willing consent, the royal coffers being woefully inadequate for his finances. When the folk saw lights at midnight in high towers they crossed themselves, believing devil's work was being done by Sir Thomas.

Sir Ralph Assheton and Margery de Barton

The youngest of the sons was Ralph. His father was very fond of his 'Benjamin', handing 1,000 marks to the Whalley abbot to hold for the boy's use. He was page to the young king and at court until he married a very rich heiress, Margery de Barton, and gained control of Middleton and estates in Yorkshire. No one who married so much money was over-popular with less fortunate relations, or with early friends. Ralph for twenty-three years absented himself from court and public life, lying low during the opening stages of the Wars of the Roses.

The King seemed to have forgotten him. His allegiance to the House of Lancaster—to which all the other brothers were committed—wavered. His eldest half-brother, head of the family and too involved with his alchemy, gave him unpleasant work to do. Long remembered were his spring visits to Ashton to perform the Guld Riding, a perambulation of land where the golden weed, ragwort or corn marigold grew too freely. Tenants who neglected to control the weed were fined or clapped in the Stone Rings—or worse still flung into the dungeons, according to old tales. He had to do many unpopular deeds. Folk scowled, muttered against the impositions, and started a hate campaign. He became known as 'The Black Lad'. Brother Thomas, wrapped in his studies, was most popular. Folk repeated a litany:

Sweet Jesus for thy mercy sake and for thy bitter Passion,
Save us from the axe of the Tower and from Sir Raufe of Ashton.

In fact, Sir Ralph, once Constable of the Tower of London, was "of Middleton", a more difficult rhyming word! The Asshetons, none having any fondness for Ralph, condemned his high-handedness. Sir Thomas repudiated his actions and abolished the annual Guld Riding, retaining only the spring ceremonial to provide money for the 'black knight' who led the procession. This continued into living memory.

Dodd, in 1840, was shown Ashton's 'donjon keep', then tolerably perfect with its flanking walls. He saw 'gallows field' and heard of 'wicked' Sir Ralph "annually commemorated by a singular custom of riding the black lad, a straw figure of the tyrant paraded round the town," and then ignominiously destroyed. "His cruelty was occasioned by his zeal for agricultural improvements." It would seem that Ashton's celebrations were a mixture of their ancestors' pagan ritual, rejoicing at the return of spring and light, the banishment of black winter and death—the lean black figure destroyed by many blows, relics of the original Guld Ridings— and remembered hatred of Ralph of Middleton, as well as of triumphal returns of two 'black' knights, both local heroes. One brave Assheton bore home from Durham the royal standard after the battle of Neville's Cross, fighting with Queen Eleanor, and was knighted by Edward III for his valour. Another won the sword of the Scot's king's standard bearer at Flodden Field. In Middleton Church he laid down his own standard and black armour in a service of dedication for safe return from Flodden.

As the family historian points out "Sir Ralph would have been more than human had his conduct been absolutely flawless". In the 1460s he was back in royal favour, acting from the first year of the Yorkist King Edward IV's reign in a score of capacities. He arrayed all the King's Yorkshire subjects for defence against the Scots, arrested and imprisoned traitors in Derbyshire, arranged wool transport in Durham county, surveyed the sea and land

20

transport of Kingston-upon-Hull and the Humber. In the 1470s he was High Sheriff of York, took possession of the Harrington castles and lands in Yorkshire for the King, and for his pains was granted three Cornish estates of the 'traitor' Earl of Devon. He was commissioner of peace in Yorkshire, fought with the Duke of Gloucester at the siege of Berwick and for outstanding bravery in battle was made a knight banneret.

So the infamous Black Knight coin had two sides! Richard III, who had been most popular in the North, could not do enough to honour Sir Ralph, who rode in the knights' procession to his coronation; he was awarded for his attachment by three manors of "king's rebels" and several properties in Kent. The City of London gave him a tun of wine annually in token of civic appreciation!

Sir Ralph was an old man when the King lost his life and his crown after Bosworth Field. Of his numerous children two sons were to establish two strong branches, the eldest Sir Richard, heir of Middleton, and a younger Sir Ralph, by marriage with the heiress Margery, founder of the line of Lever. As for the sons of his brother Sir Thomas, Lord of Ashton, they too proliferated, the eldest taking Ashton, Edmund as husband of Joan Radcliffe founding the Chadderton line, Geoffrey with another heiress Jane Shepley starting the Shepley line—and a descendant of theirs sailing with Admiral Sir William Penn, his uncle, on his second voyage to Pennsylvania, hence the New England Asshetons. A fourth brother Nicholas had for his wife a daughter of Lord Willoughby de Broke; his home was Callington in Cornwall, afterwards the seat of a remote branch of the family.

Great Lever Hall before demolition

So does one old family spread its wings and travel away from its place of origin. I can write only of a few descendants, the main Lancashire lines.

Sir Thomas's grandson, Thomas also, fought at Flodden but died soon after his return, leaving three heiresses. Their third shares came to a young Richard de Hoghton, who married Alice; to Sir William Booth, the husband of Margaret; and to a kinsman Ralph Assheton of the Middleton-Rydale line, who married Elizabeth. This marked the end of Asshetons of Ashton, Elizabeth the last survivor dying in 1553. There was much dissension and argument over the inheritance, the three husbands or their families fighting for ownership. For many years Hoghtons held on; then the Booths, Sir George of Dunham Massey handing over £5,500, became owners. Each surviving branch has its own history, each going its own way, not at all unanimous in their loyalties.

The present-day Asshetons of Downham are direct in descent from Sir Ralph of Middleton and Margery de Barton through their son who married the Lever heiress. From this alliance in Elizabethan times came two brothers, a younger falling on his feet when he first began to practise at the Bar in London.

Though no early Assheton halls have survived—Ashton, Middleton and Lever gone—family memorials in stained-glass and church brasses are outstanding. In Ashton parish church are priceless panels—once in the east window but now at the west end of the south aisle—best seen when late morning sunlight streams through them patterning the place with the clear colours only York's best stained-glass artists could produce. In Middleton church, as well as the Flodden memorial window, with every safe returned archer portrayed and named, there are some extremely fine brasses, one to Sir Richard and his wife, and numerous epitaphs in stone.

The Assheton windows are of the same date, Sir Thomas of Ashton, the donor, before his death in 1516 commissioning these windows with the life story of St. Helen in minute and fascinating detail. Helen, or her son Emperor Constantine, appears in each panel: in one the little princess entering the convent in company with her father King Coel, that merry old soul, and a curious peeping nun at a window; in others the betrothal and wedding of Helen, the birth of a son, a babe in swaddling clothes, but because he was to be the great emperor portrayed as a grown man complete with beard and crown on head. The 'silver window' is of great beauty and shows ranks of victorious soldiers who shared with Constantine the victory over Maxentinus—recalling maybe the recent victory of Flodden? One incident shows Helen's meeting with Pope Sylvester, his powerful magic which restored to life a bull with very sharp golden horns, which a so-called magician had slain—Helen was thereby converted to Christianity. Was Sir Thomas showing to local doubters, who had talked of the strange occult activities of an earlier Sir Thomas the Alchemist, that magic was respectable?

*Sir Richard
Assheton and
his wife*

Family groups are included in the panels: Sir Thomas and ten of his brothers and sisters, and their father Sir John and his three wives; the earlier Sir Thomas, who died in 1456, with Elizabeth Byron his wife, and of course Sir Thomas III himself with the three he married, Elizabeth, Anne and Agnes Harrington. One 'portrait' of the earlier Sir Thomas is of great value according to one historic glass expert, for his collar has upon it the unique SS, a combination of the Order of the Garter with the Souvrain Order introduced by Henry IV; if a sum can be put on what is priceless, it is worth near £10,000! One grows apprehensive realizing what is imminent, the great gash across the churchyard when a bypass is engineered through, not far from these windows. If a bulldozer ran amok, or an explosion occurred too near! *

Radcliffes of Radcliffe Tower and Ordsall Hall

Who were these Radcliffes whose name appears as territorial landowners in places as scattered as Clitheroe, Tockholes and Todmorden, the Smithills, Ordsall, Wythenshawe, Foxdenton and Radcliffe town? They were descendants of an eleventh-century Nicholas Fitz Guilbert de Tailbois granted for his military service to his feudal overlord the Manor of Radecliffe. Having an English heiress as bride helped him to come to terms with his tenantry. His Anglo-Norman grandson wed Baron Montbegon's daughter, which was a leg-up for the family too.

Odd references on ancient documents show the family having fingers in many pies, and sometimes burning them. One unwisely joined Prince John against the absentee King Richard; he was fined and paid up. Another prospected for "minera" on his common pasture without royal permit; he was cautioned and forbidden. William Radcliffe was called by the King to bring the local Doomsday survey up to date with current thirteenth-century land valuations. His sister Eugenia for leave to remarry, as King's Gift, had to pay 40s. for the privilege. His sons and grandsons rode out to fight the King's wars in Wales and Scotland, Edward I showing his appreciation when Richard was granted leave to hunt small game in Radcliffe and Quarlton warrens, the same terrain over which James I in 1617 gave Holcombe Hunt its charter.

Things began to look up in Sir Richard's time, his sons branching out from the parent home. The heir stayed at Radcliffe, one brother settled in Salford and became 'of Ordsall'. A third son, Margaret Barton's favourite great-nephew, was her heir, so beginning the first of six generations of Radcliffes of Smithills Hall.

Like their Assheton neighbours they decided Henry Bolingbroke's cause was likely to succeed; and in return for loyal service Henry IV allowed James to "crenallate, embatell and make a certain fortalice" of the old manor house by the clear Irwell's banks, and to surround the open country beyond to contain his deer park. Overcome by such royal favours James decided to rebuild the nearby church. Look for the fine nave arcading, decorated capitals, and one small roundel of old stained glass whereon is the crowned head of a king—Henry IV?

* The windows were dismantled in 1972.

Radcliffe Tower in 1840

Radcliffes were with Henry V in the French wars, but with the weak Henry VI as king they could have toppled. James' wife was Sir John Tempest's daughter, her Talbot in-laws seriously involved in the king's betrayal, in Yorkist good books, and inevitably on Henry Tudor's black list. It chanced the male line was soon to end, so none appear to have been implicated, or their possessions forfeited.

History here is vague, tradition filling blanks, true or no. We are told in an old ballad that the last Radcliffe of the Tower had an only child the Fair Ellen, the poor girl hated by a jealous stepmother who prevailed upon the master cook to 'do her in', speaking in riddles. "Go kill a milk white doe and bake her in a pie". Such was the girl's horrid end, despite a little page's pleas:

> Oh save her life good master cook
> And make your pies of me.
> For pitys sake do not destroy
> My lady with your knife.
> You know she is her father's joy,
> For Christ's sake, save her life.

The ballad describes the cook's death, plunged in boiling lead, and the stepmother's, burnt alive at the stake; as for the loyal lad, the bereaved father "gave him all his lands"! The tale is untrue, for the manor passed to a kinsman—fortunately a Yorkist so he took the estate intact. He was Baron FitzWalter.

One November day we went in search of the Radcliffes, first to the old church which is well away from modern Radcliffe town,

25

then through the churchyard to the tower. I had read of Dodd's visit in 1840, "an agreeable walk from the Bury-Manchester highway to find the village and in a meadow the church . . . disappointing outside but its antique interior inducing feelings of solemnity." The sexton led him to the tomb of Fair Ellen, lying in alabaster effigy by her father, and as he gazed upon the cold white features Dodd was told how parishioners believing there was virtue in the very stone covering the pure maiden, had made a habit of chipping off scraps as charms. We approached the church, expecting that so venerable a fabric must contain what we looked for. We met the verger who could tell us of Sir James the builder's tomb now under the sanctuary, but nothing of Fair Ellen's grave. There were drastic alterations early this century.

What of the tower, the adjoining hall and the deer park? A visitor of 1790 saw remains sufficiently grand to describe as "oak roof principals fine, carvings wonderful, moulded cornices and Gothic tracery of the windows impressive", but by 1830 one antiquarian was depressed to see the ancestral hall of the Radcliffes "reduced to a hayloft and cowshed". Dodd in 1840 was too late to see anything more than foundations of hall and the noble ruins of the strong, many-arched tower—which in 1970 was still strong enough to edure the last stages of degradation. There has been much talk locally of attempts to preserve the ruins, valiant members of archeological societies have done their best to rouse public interest. But we stood, ankle-deep in trampled grass and mud, in acres of black ooze extending across the ancient park—a scene devoid of any hope, so it seemed. As for the tower, gone—roofs, floors, window tracery—only imperishable walls, window openings like tunnels within them, and broken stairs climbing to nowhere!

"Why did not the new manufacturing classes at little cost take measures to preserve for coming ages such precious monuments of the past?" asked Dodd in sorrow. Why not indeed! And why this neglect? Radcliffe passed to a distant kinsman and absentee owners, three Earls of Sussex, the last selling the tower to provide his daughter's dowry on marrying Sir Thomas Wharton, the Border defender. He sold to Middleton Asshetons for whom it had no appeal, except for hunting. Finally the Assheton heiress, wife of Sir Thomas Egerton later Baron Grey of Wilton, lost all interest in it. Who could blame her for she now had two homes, the fine mansion of Oulton Park and the Hall of Heaton.

Next we tracked down Ordsall Hall, finding our way from the

26

Seaman's Mission, the 'Flying Angel' at the heart of Salford's dockland, ship's funnels and derricks at the street end, and women gossiping at doors of red-brick Victorian houses facing a brick wall and a yard filled with parked lorries and cars. Over the wall, the coal-black hulk with boarded windows was Ordsall Hall. Queen Elizabeth had once been there, said one woman, and another, "Guy Fawkes hid in the cellars." We could not enter the hall, a woman living in the occupied seventeenth-century brick wing told us, but we could get the key from Mr. Shaw of Peel Park Art Gallery. The inside was still worth seeing, a raised dais where Radcliffes dined, screens, speres and passages to kitchens and buttery. There was a minstrel gallery too—all much better than one might think. Fifty thousand pounds had already been spent on stopping further decay and damage; £5,000 more was promised to help "put it back on its feet". Visions of restoring past glories, recreating something of its golden past, comfort for returning ghosts—of Radcliffes who sang the praises of the Virgin Queen and sent a daughter to be her maid-in-waiting, who sheltered and plotted with Fawkes and Catesby, who fought for King Charles, losing thereby freedom and life! With memories of brave and noble Radcliffes: a sad end, alas!

By 1972 the hall was splendidly restored.

Ordsall Hall in 1840

Old Names in the Salford Hundred

Although it was an inhospitable region of swamps, called mosses by the mixed bunch of native Angles and Danes who had filtered into the Manchester Barony from Cheshire and south Yorkshire, the bully boys of the Conqueror seemed very eager to stake claims therein, arriving on the bandwagon of the Barons de Greslet, and Roger and Nigell who received the lion's share.

They claimed their land grants, married heiresses of native stock and eventually, as did Asshetons, Radcliffes and many kinsmen, became Lancashire Englishmen.

What land grabbers they were, and on the ball when estates were changing hands. The Le Byrons endowed with Rochdale and Milnrow acres in Norman times, in the Tudor period made a profitable land deal in monastic property and thereafter were Byrons of Newstead Abbey. Lord Byron the poet parted with his Lancashire estates in 1823. John Byrom the Jacobite poet and political rhymester, who gave his daughter as Christmas gift "Christians Awake", was of the same family. So in early times, was Sir Hugh le Byron who, returning from the Crusades and anticipating a joyful meeting with his young wife, met her funeral cortège crossing the drawbridge of his home, Claydon Hall. After which, overcome by grief, he retired to Kersall Cell.

The Prestwich family were settled at Hulme Hall for generations and considered rich enough to be asked for a free gift "for the necessities of state"—£50 towards Elizabeth's finances. A century later Sir Thomas offered his money, without being asked, for the cause of Charles I, and was assured by his mother, an ardent Royalist, that when that was used she had a secret treasure chest waiting for him. Unfortunately she alone knew the hiding place and when a fit of apoplexy took her speech she died without divulging the secret. All Sir Thomas's attempts to find the wealth was in vain, even occult agencies failing. He was obliged to ask Sir Edward Mosley's help mortgaging his property to pay fines to Parliament. Later the meagre left-overs, and the title, came to a Prestwich cousin who bewailed his penury. "Without riches or lands, to be heir is nought but vanity", was his plaint.

The Mosleys, possessed of lands at Ancoats, Collyhurst and Hough End, through the misfortunes of the Prestwich family took their holdings in Manchester Barony and later gained more—and kept them intact in spite of dangerous times.

The De La Warres were early on the local scene and remained important for centuries, until they considered it expedient to sever all links with Manchester and emigrate to America. They gave Delaware, the river and the Indian tribe their names.

It was a fortunate alliance to the Baron de Greslet's heiress that brought young John De La Warre to the fore, the couple taking over the Baron's Hall. There the family remained for eight

The gateway to Barons Hall, Chetham's Hospital, Manchester

generations until Baron Thomas, priest and rector, received from Henry V a charter which made his church collegiate, and forthwith handed his hall to become a college of priests where "they might keep hospitality together". We know it as Chetham's School now, a tranquil place near the old heart of Manchester, its inner places—the great refectory, the cloisters and the enclosed Fox Court—belonging to the time of the priests and the De La Warres.

At times the peace was disturbed. As in the 1420s when Booths picked a quarrel against a young clerk in the church, sprang upon

29

him during the service and would have misused him had not the congregation rushed to his aid. Whereat the Booths scattered into the streets, gathering support until five hundred partisans had mustered—including Byrons ripe for a fight—and all made for the Hall, swept into the Warden's House and there in revenge "seized many documents".

These Booths were early 'booths-men' who dwelt near Barton Moss in the thirteenth century, until a son made a break by finding a bride of English noble and Norman blood, a step which gave him a push in the right direction, into the list of landowners destined to wield power in the Eccles parish.

Sons did very well. William, Bishop of Lichfield and Coventry, was raised later to the Archdiocese of York, into which See a younger brother moved after him. He had occupied the bishopric of Durham, had been Chancellor of Cambridge and was to be trusted as Lord Chancellor by Edward IV. This Lawrence, second Booth to be archbishop, had his own Mint whilst at Durham. One bishop raised the splendid nave roof over Eccles chuch, about 1450.

The heir meanwhile was concerned with home affairs around Barton, Booths and Eccles—the role of eldest son.

A third brother married the last heiress of Ashton, thereby coming into vast estates, holding those in Lancashire and acquiring new in Cheshire. He began the Booths of Dunham Massey, the most outstanding of that branch being George, a keen Parliament man in the Civil War, who had change of heart in the Commonwealth and attempted a coup in 1658 to bring back the exiled king. The Booth Rising failed, but when Parliament decided time was ripe to restore the monarchy Booth was their mouthpiece at Charles II court. The restored king showed his appreciation by bestowing the title Baron Delamere of Dunham Massey, and later the family added that of Earl of Warrington. The end came soon when the male line ended, three daughters conveying their third shares to husbands of Trafford, Legh and Molyneux stock.

Traffords filled the local scene around Chat Moss in early days —before the Conquest they claim. Their shield bearing a red griffin on a white field was seen in the forefront of many battles, and their badge on tunic and sleeve of retainers progressing to Parliament or royal court. One Trafford had built Ancoats Hall; another, with his Booth wife's inheritance to help, erected a grand mansion in Trafford Park—which Manchester golfers know well. Though Roman Catholics they long claimed right of burial in Eccles church.

The north-east chapel was Traffords', the south-east for generations belonged to the Workesleys and their descendants, this being home ground from Norman times. Eliseus, a Workesley warrior, chose the losing side when Duke Robert of Normandy rebelled against Brother William Rufus and went with him out of England. Their energies were devoted from then on to the Crusades, where apart from overcoming giants and exterminating fire-breathing dragons, Eliseus still had time to exterminate Saracens. A great serpent got him in the end, on the Island of Rhodes. After which the exploits of later Workesleys as Knights Hospitallers seem tame, but more credible.

Associated with Worsley (the name of the town and the estate of the Workesleys in old records) was the main branch who long held court here at their "manor place with moat chapel and great barn", receiving as feudal dues for their land tenure pence, or iron spurs, or iron arrows from their tenants. They held much power locally. Some over-exceeded themselves, as did Sir Richard Brereton who gained on marriage with Dame Dorothy Egerton of Ridley, Tatton and Worsley, which she had inherited from her father. As an active upholder of the New Faith he carried out to the letter the penal laws against Papists, ransacking suspected houses, winkling out hidden priests—and making himself thoroughly hated. He and Dame Dorothy lie in alabaster effigy in Eccles church, their titles cut deep; but the toy-sized cradle containing the doll-sized babe is evidence of what was deep grief to both. They say Dorothy walking in the Worsley woods was frightened by a bear—or was it a boar?—so that her child was born prematurely and died.

In widowhood Dorothy married Sir Peter Legh of Lyme. And Sir Richard's ghost began to walk through Worsley, consternation and terror left behind. Exorcism was tried in vain, appeasements offered and dead chickens as sacrifice. Finally the ghost was chased to the mosses—to Ringing Pits, they say—and forced to promise to return no more in frightening form. If he must return let it be "one day in summer, as a swallow".

I saw many swallows the other day when I wandered from the highway below Worsley's St. Mark's church along Old Hall Lane to where beyond great barns and sheltered by great trees, the black and white timbered hall looked most pleasant in the sunlight. Anyone so inclined can enjoy Georgian fare, candlelight and appropriate eighteenth-century music at the banquets now held here. Much changed since Dame Dorothy's heir decided he had no use for Worsley Old Hall.

Dorothy had a half brother, Thomas, whose bastardry proved no impediment in his progress at the courts of Elizabeth and James I. He was Keeper of the Great Seal and at the death-bed of one, and much trusted as Lord Chancellor by the other. After he bought Ashbridge, Brackley and Ellesmere, his son had no use for his Aunt Dorothy's home. Younger sons sometimes lived at the old hall, however.

To track down Worsleys now it is to Yorkshire one goes, to Hovingham from whence Thomas Worsley in the seventeenth century won a bride and took possession of a goodly estate. The Duchess of Kent is of this line—a junior branch of Worsleys, formerly of Booths Hall and Boothstown.

To find the Egertons, Tatton Hall is the place, full of family possessions, and family portraits, including that of Sir Thomas, Elizabeth's and James' trusty servant, keen-eyed, with high crowned hat. Another Thomas, of Heaton and Oulton, got added wealth with his heiress bride, an Assheton, and gathered greater titles. In 1784 he became Baron Grey of Wilton—and proceeded to employ fine architects to design what was to be Heaton Hall and a fitting home for his heirs. Great hopes, but in two generations all came to a grandson on the female side, the Duke of Westminster.

The Duke of Bridgewater and the Earl of Ellesmere

The canal-building Duke and his selftaught genius of a surveyor, James Brindley, have had their share of notice in Lancashire history books. We are not told that the third Duke of Bridgewater, a fifth son, was so mentally retarded as a child that moves were made to debar him from the succession as an 'idiot'. They sent him to Eton, where his masters did what they could for him —which was not much. Fortunately his sister and her husband Lord Stafford, saw to his affairs. Through them John Gilbert their able agent was sent to look over the Worsley pits in 1757.

Gilbert believed a canal could be made to move the coal— cheap easy transport, and financial rewards certain. The 21-year-old Duke on being consulted—at the time he was preoccupied with horses and women—was quite agreeable. So Gilbert, having the 'go ahead', asked Brindley to come to Worsley to survey for the canal project—paid on a day-to-day basis. The work went on during the summer of 1759. Brindley was here but a short time. He was responsible for routing 400 miles of canals in other parts of England.

The Duke, being capable of thinking of no more than one thing at a time, when he began to 'think canals' was obsessed by the idea. Gilbert was a really great man and the Duke did well to entrust him with so much. He farmed the Worsley demesne; he tackled draining of nearby Chat Moss, tipping there tons of coal pit spoil, and finally started planting trees where bog had been, transforming the landscape—"waste, wilderness" from the beginning of time. He also reclaimed other swamps in West Lancashire, and engineered with immediate success the 46 miles of underground canal at Worsley pits, on the absent Duke's behalf.

When the Duke died in 1805 his sister's nephew inherited, young Leveson-Gower (pronounced 'Looson-Gore') marrying the Duchess of Sutherland. The Duke's will made it clear their second son should inherit Worsley if his elder brother inherited the title. In 1833 Francis the second nephew took the name Egerton and the estate of Worsley which he found quite appalling, "a God-forsaken place full of drunken, rude people with deplorable morals". He remedied the cruel conditions of his workers, taking women hauliers and little children out of his pits and finding alternative work for them. He introduced new methods to improve agriculture, and made of this a 'civilized region'. He presided dutifully at the Easter and Michaelmas Courts-baron held at Worsley. The Court House was restored by him—and is well used now by many local societies.

He built the new Worsley Hall in 1845, the ancestral Old Hall being rescued from long neglect when Lord Algernon Egerton took up residence in 1855. The new mansion, the work of Blore, standing in a spacious park was worthy of entertaining royalty, both Victoria and Edward VII being received there.

In 1846 he was created Earl of Ellesmere. What a pleasant transformation he made of the Worsley landscape, with parkland, tree-planting, spacious roads and avenues, the fine new St. Mark's Church he caused to be built—one of G. G. Scott's best— and the graceful 'Eleanor Cross' erected in memory of Lady Ellesmere. New road systems have not entirely ruined his work, though a wide mesh of motorways and bypass, 'the Spaghetti Junction', is now thrown across the land once his.

One can still hear above traffic noises that St. Mark's Church clock, incorporated in the new building strikes thirteen at one o'clock. Originally it told time for the Duke of Bridgewater's workmen at the canal basin. I doubt if the Duke was as simple as made out. When idle men told him they had not heard one o'clock strike the end of their dinner hour he showed his grasp of workmen's psychology. At once he had the mechanism altered for thirteen to follow twelve. And so it has been, since 1789.

Smithills Hall

Hultons, Radcliffes and Bartons of Smithills

On any warm afternoon in summer the old residents at Smithills Hall emerge from the Victorian south-west range to sun themselves on the terraces, whilst entering the medieval and Tudor north-east is a stream of curious visitors. It is a rewarding visit, if the changing history of seven centuries interests them.

Old tales say King Ella had a hall at The Smithills; that King Egbert, father of Alfred and ancestor of the English royal family, kept his court here; but I prefer to consider the beginning of the story the twelfth century when the Knights Hospitallers of St. John of Jerusalem held the land.

With the coming of Richard of Hulton in the days of Henry II and King John, history is better documented. His wife had a favourite great-nephew, and to young William Radcliffe The Smithills came. This must have pleased him mightily, his eldest brother being heir of Radcliffe, and another granted Ordsall in

34

Salford—three distinct branches thus continuing down the centuries.

Ralph was the name favoured for first-born sons, so several Ralphs succeeded, each knighted and called to represent Lancashire in the King's Council and Parliament, until Ralph IV (1485). There were no more Radcliffe sons: Ralph IV's daughter and heiress, Cicily, married her 'cousin' John Barton, so beginning long Barton ownership.

Imagine Smithills of early Tudor times: the great hall old then and like to outlast Bartons and others who came after, the same inside walls, the same splendid roof timbers, the same high arch and speres, with screens passage and arches leading to the servants' quarters, pantry and buttery. The kitchen has gone, the roof level has been lifted and outer timber walls rebuilt in stone, but returning Radcliffes and Bartons would feel at home. What a setting for the 'medieval banquet' junketings so popular now! Instead, Smithills Coach-House restaurant draws in the 'good eaters'.

Andrew Barton settled down in 1516 to make the hall bigger and better; times were settled too, so there was incentive to build for comfort. He began extensions beyond the solar at the east end of the great hall. A withdrawing room was built (where the Bartons withdrew from the noise and hurly burly of the communal great hall), its walls panelled in linenfold, and some panels with Barton portraits and emblems and devices, "on which the artist wrought out his seven years' apprenticeship". The windows of this room, and the bedchamber above, overlook the courtyard. These, both beautiful rooms, and the rebuilt family chapel at right angles to them, were work on which Andrew put his seal with justifiable pride.

In Queen Mary's reign his son Robert, a declared Papist at that time, examined the Protestant Vicar of Deane, George Marsh, and sent him off to his trial. Barton's questions all attempted to make Marsh himself prove his heresy, but he refused to recant or conform to Papistry. "Between me and them let God witness," he cried, and, looking to heaven, "If my cause be just, let

Andrew Barton's 'bar-tun'

this prayer of thine unworthy servant be heard!" He stamped his foot as he spoke, leaving an imprint "red as blood". This is subject for many a tale.

"In a passage near the dining-room door is a cavity in a flag bearing resemblance to a man's footprint—the supposed place where the holy martyr stamped to confirm his testimony," wrote Baines. "Curiosity led us to survey the print," wrote Dodd. "We saw an impression certainly—but if it is the Martyr's footprint the worthy man must have had a foot of no common length." "When a cup of cold water is thrown on the place, certainly a red mark does appear on the stone," reported one gossip, and others told of what happened when two boys lifted the footprint stone and threw it in the ravine behind the hall. Fiendish noises were heard, terrifying everyone until the lads confessed and the stone was replaced. In 1732 a ghostly figure, like a clergyman in white surplice and Geneva bands, was seen wandering sadly through the Green Room!

The true story of George Marsh highlights a sorry chapter in history. His death in the flames at Chester was but one of 300 during Marian persecutions; he was the only Protestant martyr in the North-west.

When Barton died his widow, Margery Legh of Lyme, married a Protestant, Sir Richard Shuttleworth. His wife's home proved better placed than his own in the Calder valley. As 'Mr. Sergeant' he made frequent and difficult journeys to the courts at Chester Castle; his brother Thomas looked after Smithills—the two Barton boys being too young to take over the estate—keeping detailed accounts of all expenses and revenue. These make fascinating reading, revealing the background to the history of an important Elizabethan household.

The steward's house and farm accounts for Smithills kept by Thomas Shuttleworth on his brother Sir Richard's behalf, begin in September 1582 and continue in his hand until his death in early 1594, when the Reverend Lawrence, the third brother, carries on with them. In the days when a family's income was entirely from its land, and the household was almost self-supporting, the records of the Barton/Shuttleworths are representative.

Incomings were from widely scattered properties—at Hoole, Horwich and Blackrod, Clitheroe and Padiham, Hurstwood, Westclose and Ightenhill, and farther afield from Austwick, Barbon and Lawkland. Revenues came from corn mills, gisting of other men's cattle, "besse (beasts), stirks, twinters (two-year-old animals) and colts"; sales of surplus tups, wethers and horses; of mutton; sheep and calf skins sent to Ormskirk glovers; pelts, skins and hides sent to local tanners.

Outgoings? Subsidies: for Her Majesty first part, 35s. 7d.; lent to Her Majesty for the year, £25; oxen for Her Majesty's provision. There were payments for furnishing soldiers and providing men to attend many musters and shows before the Lord Lieutenant, as in 1587's show of horses at Wigan and show of light horses and demi-lances at Manchester. They paid their share in training soldiers and many entries reveal imminent danger to the realm and preparations for war.

1583. Towe sheffes arrowesse and a bow. Smith shod oxen, towe sheffes arrowes, ½ a thousand horse shoe nelles—4s. 8d. I lb gunpowder—16d.

1584. John Horrabin from Bowlton dressed, scoured Howle armore, made armor buckels—a dozen hempen alters—mended lantorn and a lether saddle.

Later in 1584. Expenses on Hempen halters, bridles, brestplates and bittes, 7 yards garth webbe and long tagges of lether. Bridel bittes, canvas to be saddelcloths, forthe parte of a thousand of oxe neales.

Among other moneys spent, galds or taxes were payable frequently for "Papistes and rogges at Manchester. Papestes and other prisoners; for a galde for keping of the becone" on Rivington Pike, Armada year; "for houseling of 7 persons"; for sacrament when the household "took wine with the Vicar".

There were a number of household servants paid the usual wages, "Elisabethe Ainsworth her holle yere wyeges—XXXs". Many casual and seasonal helpers were 'on the books'. "One of Henry Wyaker's childeren for dryving the plowe six days—6d"; "6 maids that did help to wash shepe . . .".

There was always constant activity around the Hall, a flow of folk all with good reason for being here. We know their names, recorded by Thomas Shuttleworth in his accounts. Today I watched numerous visitors, occasional workmen, tradesmen, driving up to the old people's home and the 'Coach-House' kitchen door Among those reported in 1583 were workers with jobs to do: "John Hewode for the dresing, wyedinge and kypinge of the gardens at Smithels. Oumfraye March for pullynge the shoulder of a cowe that was out of joynte, and laying bates to kylle mysse. Adam Odom the dyer, who dyed 2 lb yard blewe. Adam Cantell for weaving 2 pieces of blankets, Peter Unsworth for fulling of them and John Cramton, for sherynge and frissing of them". The wool was from their own sheep, woven into fustian for breeches, grey frieze for jerkins—and the 'blewe' for something special. Weavers also wove flax and hempen cloth from the raw material brought from Hoole mosses after the many processes of breaking and swingling which took a month, drying, pulling and rippling, laying it in water, washing and tenting it, till it came to Smithills.

October work: An Tong of Rivington brought a net she had knitted 'for drawing the damme'. Another delivered cord for the fish net to draw the "damme"; she was paid 2s., for the cord 2s. 6d.

Many brought in supplies according to the season. Lent, 1583: "4 melles of muskelles and koccles fetched, at 2 sundry times XXIIIJ^d—24d. $\frac{1}{2}$ messe of herrings. 3 salt fishes. Salt and freshe salmonde. Salt eeles, red herrings and a hundredth of sprotes. A quart of vinegare and saffron". Lenten preparation was in quantities as for a siege. At other times large numbers and varieties of birds were consumed to eke out uninteresting winter salt meats: thrushes, blackbirds, ousels, teales, felfares, snipes, green and gray pluffe. In summer two dozen larks cost 2s. a dozen. Redshanks, heronshaes and yowlerings appeared at the table.

Gifts, from friends possessed of parks with game, were received regularly:

August 1587: James Leigh [Marjory's kinsman?]—venison.
Keepers from Hapton with a stagg.
My lorde Derby at Pilkington, $\frac{1}{2}$ buck. A fat stag.
Mr. Bold, a buck. Mr. Walsh, fat mutton and capons.
T. Marshe—fish. Robert Hesketh, turkey and 2 capons.

Thomas also sent gifts and gave to wandering players and the needy:

Sent a woodcock pie to London. A dozen woodcocke to London.
Given to a pore scoller of Oxforthe—4 shilling.
To 2 fellows of Clitherall which came with lime—12d.
To musicians of Sir Peter Leghe—12d. Waits from Halifax—12d.
Given to players of Downham 5s., at Christmas.
To 2 pipers—To one begging for prisoners in the Marshalsea— 2 shilling.
For a minstrel, and one with an ape—8d.

1592 was a sad year, for 'my Lady' died in April, bells were tolled at Smithills, Deane Church, Leigh and Winwick; to the last her coffin was borne on a litter draped in black, drawn by horses barbed with black. Five pounds of silver was distributed to "pore

Turton Tower, medieval and Tudor

foulks" *en route*, and ale given to gentlefolks at the funeral before leaving Smithills. Sir Richard, sorrowing, needed "phissik". The next year Thomas the secretary died. So many mourners were at the funeral at Bolton in the Moors that three of the town's innkeepers "dyned 9 score and 31 at 6d or 5d the meall".

Changes followed for now the Barton sons were more able to cope. Thomas' children Richard, Nicholas and Ughtred were sent to Burnley to be lodged and schooled. Sir Richard and the Reverend Lawrence prepared for the move to Gawthorpe, where the Shuttleworth history continues. The elder Barton boy took over Smithills; the younger, Barton-in-Amounderness.

Orrells and Chethams of Turton

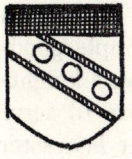

How many travellers on the Manchester to Blackburn railway have noticed that the bridge over the line near Turton Station is best Victorian Railway Gothic, battlements, look-out turrets and all? The reason: it was mock medieval to placate the landowners of adjoining Turton Tower. In winter, trees being leafless, the house can be seen too, a black and white Elizabethan half-timbered building with a dark stone pele above.

Not many towers of defence were built so far south; this could be early fourteenth century—a particularly disturbed period, with troubles rife among neighbours as well as from the Scots. The existing tower today has its original thick walls but no cattle housed in the vaults; no arrow slits but large mullioned transomed windows which once would have asked for trouble under assault. These 'improvements' came when the Orrells thought they were entitled to more comfort, and safe enough to make their semi-fortress more like a home. After the York-Lancaster conflict, perhaps? And in the 1590s low chambers in the tower were heightened by removing floors, raising the roof line, the original three floors making two; and one floor was added on top.

Most attractive, erected against the east tower wall, is an Elizabethan gabled two-storeyed porch and side chambers in half-timber construction. On the north side was a 'living quarters' wing, low in comparison with the tower itself. The whole, impressive then is as interesting now, though the last of the old family of Orrells, John the improvident and spendthrift, had to part with it in 1628. In the 1970s it is a splendid museum of by-gones and local history, and the meeting place of Turton U.D.C.

In Norman times Fitz Robert was manorial lord, then Henry of Lancaster whose daughter Blanche married John of Gaunt. Lathoms held it for nearly two centuries before William the first Orrell, fortunate in marrying the heiress, arrived on the scene in 1420. Both Lathom and Orrell lying 'Wigan way', these families were transplants from West Lancashire, but they put down very strong roots farther east in the far wilder moorlands merging in the Pennines.

In 1626 William Orrell realized it quite impossible to save what John his brother had swamped by debts. The only way, loans or mortgage out of the question, was to transfer the manor and lordship, the tower, demesne, cornmill etc, to their good friend Humphrey Chetham, gentleman, for £4,000. Here was a 'trades-man'—Chetham engaged in Manchester's fustian trade, where the money was—who made a fortune quite honestly, bought up property and entered the lists of landed gentry. A simple good-living man, he refused a summons to Charles I to receive a knight-hood (not the only absentee), but he could not refuse to serve as High Sheriff or to appear at the Shield Hanging at Lancaster Castle minus a shield. What he thought of it as he handed to the Constable of the Castle his bright new escutcheon, we can only guess—red griffons and red chevrons, nothing but vanity! You can see the Chetham Arms on the Turton inn, a picturesque building in the village street.

When I attended a shield hanging all the gentlemen present wore morning dress. Humphrey Chetham's friends and attendants all wore coats made from material from his own warehouses!

He proved an unwilling collector of the Ship Money demanded by Charles of the Salford Hundred—no one liked this tax—neither was he enthusiastic in collecting subsidies for Parliament, tasks high office forced on him. He lived at Clayton Hall when doing business in Manchester, whilst farm activities and corn-milling went on in parts of Turton Tower he had no need to occupy on his occasional visits. He kept an eye on local affairs, remembering Turton Church when disposing of his collection of theological books—some still 'chained' there—and sons of the village poor when making his will. He already maintained twenty-two poor boys in and around Manchester, but now he stipulated that eighteen more between the ages of six and ten should be elected "of honest, industrial and painfull parents and not of wandering or idle beggars—nor bastards nor such as are lame, infirm or diseased . . .", five to be from Turton.

He was a good man. "A masterpiece of beauty. God send us more such men," one wrote. Turtonians long discussed at village level a fitting memorial to him, and one was designed, "a tower 100 feet high to have either a golden eagle or Master Humphrey on top"; but nothing came of it. Chetham's School is his best monument—though the old Manchester Manor House, once residence for De La Warres' College of Priests, is much enlarged and many more than forty boys—and now girls too—benefit from his 1653 bequest. At the west end of the Manchester Cathedral nave is a statue of Humphrey with bluecoat boys gathered round him.

Humphrey's nephew succeeded him, Chethams owning Turton for another century, the Tower gradually deteriorating into a farmhouse. In 1885 James Kay the new owner changed all that; with his wealth as cotton spinner, he enthusiastically began restoration, sometimes with good, sometimes lamentable, results. I walked round one day 'with' Dodd, whose *Pictorial Lancashire* contains lively tit-bits. He approved of Kay's new work "with strict regard to the original style of architecture—and of good taste within", and provided with a haunted room.

PART TWO

Families of South-West Lancashire

Families of South-west Lancashire

There was a time when south-west Lancashire, between Mersey and Ribble, from the lonely shores of the Irish Sea to the wild moorlands of Rivington and Winter Hill where the Yarrow and Douglas rivers are born, was considered backward and uncivilized, a refuge for outlaws and desperate men. The miles of meres, mossland and swamps, breeding ground for ague and haunt of Will o' Wisp, Jack o' Lantern and weird mermen, made a dangerous barrier for strangers, and travellers needed local guides to lead them safely from Liverpool and Ormskirk to Preston. Such isolation prevented free trade, commerce and movement, preserving old ideas, traditions and loyalties. It was an old-fashioned part of the county, excepting the narrow belt along its fringe, where there were pockets of settled life on the coast and good lands possessed and developed by families like the Blundells, Molyneux, Lathoms, Fittons and Heskeths, Scarisbricks, Halsalls —and the Stanleys who became acknowledged top dogs, wielding almost feudal power for many centuries.

These families were of the lowlands, home of lost causes which they espoused wholeheartedly, many remaining Papists when south-east Lancashire had turned from Papal authority; supporting Charles and the monarchy when the south-east's up-and-coming merchant classes saw Parliament's cause suited them best; remaining Stuart loyalists and Jacobites. The marvel is that so many survived, carrying on through the eighteenth century as agriculturalists, reclaiming land and draining the swamps. Their names only faded away when they failed to produce sons.

Geographically the landowners by Yarrow and Douglas belong to this south-west region. They are Pilkingtons of Rivington, Andertons of Lostock and Euxton, Charnocks of Astley, Standishes of both Standish and Duxbury; with others of the 'Wigan Group', Bradshaws of Haigh, Dicconsons of Wrightington, Chisnalls, Rigbys of Harrock and, once all powerful, the Hollands of Upholland. They in the main were, with the Earls of Derby, faithful to old ideas and ideals. Land reclamation did not fill their coffers in the hill country—but coal mining did, and sometimes drove them out. A fascinating story, that of West Derby and Leyland Hundreds.

Stanleys, Earls of Derby

To which Lancashire family do these earls belong, by no means the oldest, but for centuries acknowledged as the foremost? Who was stepfather of the king, and entertained that king at his house, so grand Richmond Palace was built "like unto it"? Who were "esteemed with little less respect than kings in the north-west", and no sovereign could afford to leave them out of his counsel? Whose fifth earl, because of his royal blood—Tudor and Plantagenet, met a tragic death, maybe because he aspired to Elizabeth's throne? Whose fourteenth earl was 'offered the crown of Greece on a plate' but refused it, preferring his Lancashire home to the Acropolis? Whose eighteenth earl resigned from the almost hereditary office of Lord Lieutenant of Lancashire so that the muzzle of impartiality should be removed and he could speak up for Lancashire?

Answer—the Stanleys, Earls of Derby. Strange that in five books I have read on Tudor and Stuart England, not once does this name find a place. Sometimes we must think Lancashire's part in English history was negligible, or nil! Or has history been written with a southern bias?

Compared with Asshetons, Blundells, Molyneux, the Stanleys were late arrivals in Lancashire, their earlier 'attachment' being

Lathom in 1640

46

further south. Norman ancestors, father and six sons, came with the Conqueror. One son won a well-endowed Saxon bride, and took the name Stanleigh. Descendants worked their way north with a Audithley (Audley) heiress into Staffordshire; and later a Hooton heiress with lands in Cheshire brought Stanleys to the Mersey. Not till 1385, when young Sir John claimed his wealthy bride, Isabella heiress of Lathom, did they make a final and lasting leap into Lancashire.

The Lathoms were rich and important, and freely gave of their wealth. One founded Burscough Priory with a pious prayer—"for pardon and rest for the souls of Henry II, Prince John, himself and all his ancestors". He wished the Kingdom of Heaven on all who added gifts to the priory, but  for those who did not, "let the Devil and all his angels take them".

The eagle and child legend belongs here. Sir Thomas fathered many bastards, loving above all one son, young Oskatel, for whose sake he cunningly misled his wife. Together they found the babe beneath a tree where eagles were wont to nest. Lady Lathom pitied the foundling and suggested he shared her only child's nursery. Little Isabella had hardly a look-in when Oskatel was about. But Sir Thomas was not allowed to disinherit his daughter for the bastard's sake. She was betrothed to John Stanley; if she lost her inheritance his family would consider the contract broken. Sir Thomas facing Stanley opposition gave his blessing; gratefully John adopted the eagle and child for his shield. The boy Oskatel founded Stanleys of Alderley, a minor branch of the family in Cheshire.

John's was a success story from his early days at Richard II's court. Later he switched his allegiance to Henry of Bolingbroke by helping to overthrow the Percys of Northumberland. Henry IV made him Lord Justice of Ireland. In 1405 he became the virtual King of Man—for a cast of falcons at each coronation—and built Stanley Tower to protect Liverpool's waterfront and shipping.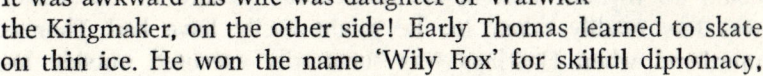

His son Sir Thomas was Henry VI's Chamberlain, trusted leader of the King's forces in Lancashire when the Wars of the Roses began. It was awkward his wife was daughter of Warwick the Kingmaker, on the other side! Early Thomas learned to skate on thin ice. He won the name 'Wily Fox' for skilful diplomacy,

The Eagle and Child pew end in Manchester Cathedral

sitting on fences. When Henry fell he became a Yorkist, temporarily serving Edward IV as Justice of Chester; until his father-in-law's plan to put Henry back on the throne looked like succeeding. He smiled his way in the royal procession, taking Henry to thanksgiving at St. Paul's. Then, when poor Henry was back in the Tower, he won Edward IV's trust once more. In fact, no king could do without him in his household. Richard of Gloucester was less readily taken in; he might easily have had Thomas murdered when Hastings was summarily executed outside his council chamber, but he could not be found, for he hid under the table when daggers were flashing. Richard could smile blandly, when his watchful eye was on Thomas.

Sir Thomas, back in favour, carried Richard's mace at the coronation whilst his lady-wife held Queen Anne Neville's train. The second countess was the learned Margaret Beaufort, the widowed Countess of Richmond, mother of Henry Tudor in whose veins ran blood of Welsh princes and heroes, as well as John of Gaunt and the Plantagenets. By marrying Stanley she was able to safeguard secret plans to put her son on Richard's throne.

Richard III was beset by enemies: friends of Edward IV's tragic widowed queen, who swore vengeance for the death of her two little sons, and others he had angered. This made Margaret Beaufort's plotting the easier. To ensure no suspicion fell on Thomas she made a vow of chastity and mortified herself, "wearing coarse shifts and girdles of hair". They lived well apart! Plan one failed, but her Stanley stepson withdrew his 10,000 troops intact from the abortive rising. When Buckingham, leader of the plot, was declared a traitor his forfeited lands were given to Thomas Stanley, "for the good and faithful service he hath done and intendeth to do." The King forbore also punishment of Margaret, Thomas promising to "keep her in a safe place at Lathom without servant or company", well knowing it was but for a short time. Henry Tudor was already on his way, invasion was imminent.

In August 1485, Thomas in London was stricken with a virulent fever for which he insisted the only cure was good Lathom air. His recovery was quite miraculous: he had 5,000 men at Lathom, 'ready for off' to a secret rendezvous with his stepson. Brother William at the same time had his men lined up, in opposition, with Richard's royal forces! Perhaps Thomas was no more unscrupulous than the next man. Then one had to be bloody-minded to survive. He was typical of his time.

Everyone knows how on Bosworth Field near Leicester Thomas Stanley "hung between the two armies", that Sir William's men switched sides at half-time by orders, winning the day for Henry Tudor; and that Stanley 'discovered' the crown in a bush and was there waiting to place it on his stepson's head. The follow-on needs no telling, how Thomas became first Earl of Derby, built Knowsley Hall to receive the royal guest and repaired—or rebuilt—Warrington bridge, "conferring a benefit on the two palatinate counties by his munificent act", to give Henry VII safe passage over the Mersey.

Henry's crown was worn uneasily for rival claimants now appeared, rising followed rising. From each Earl Thomas benefited, acquiring the forfeited estates of Lovells, Pilkingtons, Broughtons, Harringtons, and others who espoused the cause of false claimants. William Stanley, the unlucky brother, lost his head and his wealth filled the royal exchequer, after implication in the Perkin Warbeck rising. Men had heard him say, "If this youth is indeed a Plantagenet, how can I refuse him?"

Many young Stanleys were then of marriageable age and numerous heiresses were waiting to be snapped up. Henry VII had made Thomas guardian of two Harrington heiresses, excellent matches for fifth son Edward and a nephew. Edward's wife outlived her sister, so all the Lonsdale lands came to Sir Edward, Lord Monteagle the victor of Flodden, and Hornby Castle became his seat.

For one who lived so dangerously, 70 was a ripe age for Thomas to attain. George, the second Earl, had as wife the heiress of the Stranges, this bringing a title for Stanleys' eldest sons. Edward first Lord Strange, became third Earl when 11 years' old. Cardinal Wolsey was his tutor, preparing him well to play his part in stirring times ahead, through the Reformation, the Dissolution of the Monasteries—when Henry VIII, his step-cousin, authorized him to supervize its smooth running in Lancashire. The Pilgrimage of Grace he quelled as leader of the King's forces. As King's deputy he organized mustering and training of troops in each Hundred of Lancashire for defence of the realm against the Scots. He saw the first stages of the establishment of the Protestant Church. He preserved peace when the untimely death of young Edward VI led to his Papist sister's accession as queen, by wisely returning to the old faith so that he remained in her Council. Mary put implicit trust in Stanleys, honouring them at court, even offering her palace for the new Lord Strange's wedding festivities. Yet he kept the family motto, "Sans Changer"!

Ten years later, to Elizabeth's relief, Edward returned to his Protestantism, so she was able to call upon him to ensure the loyalty of Lancashire. At times his daughter-in-law's royal blood was cause for concern: as great-granddaughter of Henry VII, Margaret Clifford was a possible claimant for the English throne. But as Countess of Derby she very prudently forgot her royal lineage, avoiding politics and choosing the company of learned men, actors, playwrights and poets of London, honoured by all.

In those golden Elizabethan years the Stanleys were "esteemed with little less respect than kings in the north-west"—as were Countess Derby's family, the Cliffords, in their Yorkshire territory. Lathom, long considered as "a little town in itself", had pleased Henry VII so much he "decided to build his new palace at Richmond like unto it". That the third and fourth earls lived in almost regal splendour at Lathom, New Hall and Knowsley, their meticulously-kept household account books prove. The third earls household expenses were £4,000 a year. No wonder it was written: "With his death the glory of hospitality seemed to fall asleep". The "Checker rowle of My Lordes Household Servants" in 1587, headed by Mr. Steward, Mr. Comptroller and Mr. Recyver Generall, listed 140, two only—the laundresses—being female. The earl's table had eight gentlemen waiters of good family to attend him; nineteen Yeomen Officers were ushers in his great chamber; two "clerkes of the kitchen", and no other dressed his meat. Master cooks supervised ten kitchen staff, caterer, slaughterman, baker, maltmaker and 'hoppeman'. Also, besides garden and maintenance staff, there was a candleman, two trumpeters—and Henry "ye ffoole"!

All these stayed at Lathom. When the family made its frequent moves from hall to hall or to London; or the earl went to the Assize Courts of Lancaster or Chester, or to attend family estate business at Wigan, Manchester, Pilkington or Upholland, a large entourage accompanied him. Great pomp and circumstances followed him as ambassador to the Low Countries, and military might accompanied his travels north to defend the borders.

For hospitality the Earls of Derby were renowned. Family parties of married sons and daughters, with grandchildren and their nurses, arrived—Lord Strange's brood, Stanleys of Cross Hall from Liverpool, Sherburnes, Halsalls—and a constant flow of friends and neighbours paid courtesy calls or came to crave help and advice. If they had come far and a Sunday intervened, they attended preachings; clergy from Stanley livings provided a rota Sunday by Sunday. Often 'My Lord Bosshoppe' was present.

House parties needed great diplomacy, skilfully selected to cause least chance of friction or distress. Notable Papists—the Molyneux, Norrises, Talbots and Southworths, Cliftons and Middletons—were as frequent visitors as Protestant notables. But what was discussed, I wonder, when 'My Lord Bosshoppe' was entertained the same weekend as a mixed bunch—Sir Richard

Molyneux, John Southworth, a Sherburne, a de Hoghton and a Bradyll?

Matchmaking brought parents to Lathom or Knowsley. Four uncles arranged a betrothal between young Mr. Salisbury and the earl's bastard daughter Ursula, and later Thomas Hesketh arrived from Rufford when the affair had been settled—probably to offer his Rufford Hall players to act at the wedding festivities. Did he approach young Will Shakeshaft when he returned home, about a nuptial ode for the young couple? Was Shakespeare's "The Phoenix and the Turtle" written for this marriage? It seems a doleful subject.

Lord Strange was mixed up with the theatre of the time, as was his mother to whom Robert Greene dedicated a poem. Edmund Spenser claimed kinship with Ferdinando Stanley's bride, a Spenser of Althorpe, "the youngest daughter but highest in degree". John Nash in one poem called her "the sprightly Amaryllis", and Ferdinando was his Amyntas—"the matchless image of honor, Jove's eagle-borne Ganymede, thrice noble Amyntas".

Throughout his life the fourth earl endeavoured to keep the peace, see justice done, practice mercy, and, as the Queen's lieutenant administer her laws. His authority was needed to settle the matter of the killing of Thomas Hoghton by Baron Langton of Walton; his intercession saved the Baron's life. He was required to commit to Chester Castle Papists like the Blundells found harbouring priests, and Father Woodruffe was with them. In Mary's reign he had performed the same duty when the Protestant Vicar of Deane, George Marsh was condemned to death at Chester.

One brief entry in the records in 1590 states, "Came the Earl of Tyrone." Hugh O'Neale, Irish patriot, had earlier been granted his earldom by Elizabeth, but later he turned against English rule and, with help from Spain, hoped to win a 'holy war' against the Queen. Lord Mountjoy's taking of Kinsale put an end to his hopes. Tyrone fled to Ulster, thence to Lancashire. Was this when he came to the earl—before going to London to offer submission and obtain Elizabeth's free pardon? The next entry says four tailors set to work on "a tente for my Lorde", for some campaign.

Three years later the fourth earl died. Ferdinando was fifth earl for a tragically brief time. Had his mother inculcated too well his pride in his royal blood, his eventual ruin? There was an abortive plot to further his claim to the ageing Elizabeth's throne.

His death was sudden, the cause unknown. His friends were discovered and one, Sir Richard Hesketh of Rufford, was executed. "Mourne for the truly honorable Ferdinando's death, true object of everlasting mourning from the Sacred Muses who, languishing with late sorrow for the father's death want strength and leisure to weep for the son's eclipse", wrote another friend in 1595.

The old Lady Derby continued to hold her own for many years in court and literary circles. When she was 72 Milton wrote of her:

> Might she the wise Latona be, or the tower'd Cybele,
> Mother of a thousand gods; Juno dares not give her odds.
> Who had thought this clime had held
> A Diety so unparalleled.

Ferdinando's brother, William the sixth earl, inherited from his mother's side not pretentions to sovereignty but the wanderlust of his Clifford grandfather, the buccaneer who sailed the Spanish Main, fitting out ships at his own cost for the greater glory of Elizabeth. The verses in which he is remembered are not high-falutin' adulation as poured upon his brother by London poets, but simple ballads in which he plays the wandering hero, the long-absent son who turned his back on "lovely Lathom and Stanley Towre by Mersey shore" with a vow to be away for thrice seven long years.

There is no map of his travels to "gather Arctic ice and melt it in a hotter zone", nor showing how he crossed Europe to become prisoner of Turkish infidels. He had his moments. A rich Eastern lady gave £500 to rescue him from horrid death for refusing to renounce his Christian faith, and to enable him to return to the Arctic and Greenland shores once more, travels taking up the latter years of his three times seven. The twenty-one years' vow completed, back he came like wandering Ulysses to the gates of Lathom, where the porter thrust away the vagrant. His father recognized him and welcomed him home, then gave him serious responsibilities to settle him down; and off he went as Governor of the Isle of Man. When his brother's death so soon followed his father's, as sixth earl he dutifully continued the family traditions for the next fifty years, a long life of responsibilities.

The heir Lord Strange and his young French wife were friends of Prince Charles and Henrietta Maria, moving splendidly through ceremonial, court occasions, festivities and masquerades together, none with any apprehension of dark years ahead or the deaths they would die. They were so young and gay together and the Court

53

smiled on them. Masques were written, the Prince and Princess always playing chief roles, but the Stanleys were supporters, grouped in romantic tableaux nearest to them. In "Love's Triumph" they were at the foot of the King's throne; in "The Masque of Chlorinda" Charlotte was a nymph floating around the goddess, Henrietta Maria, though she was equal in blood, a Bourbon princess.

> She of the Princely Orange a branch,
> Impaled on the high Tremouillan stem of France.

Perhaps in those early years at Court Charles was subconsciously jealous of the handsome, popular Lord Strange, a weakness to have serious effects. When Charles became king, passed unpopular laws and levied even more unpopular taxes, Lord Strange did not question his royal prerogative nor did his allegiance falter. Southwest Lancashire, because of in-built respect for the Stanleys, paid the levies and taxes, though neither collector nor payers were enthusiastic. When there came an unbridgeable rift between King and Parliament, Lord Strange stood by Charles and southwest Lancashire and the more rural conservative areas of the county stood behind Stanley. The old Earl of Derby being old and soon to die, they naturally turned to Lord Strange as leader. Protestants firm in their trust of the monarchy, and Papists ready to take up arms if allowed them, thronged to his side. At once preparations were made to defend Manchester, Wigan, Preston and Lancaster for the royal cause.

On two notable occasions King Charles gave orders with disastrous effect; each curbed Lord Strange's movements and left Lancashire vulnerable to Parliamentary attack. In 1642 the King ordered young Lord Molyneux to divert his horse and foot to Nottingham, though Lord Strange was expecting these reinforcements outside Manchester. Manchester was lost by the weakened Royalists. In 1643, when the Queen landed on the Yorkshire coast, Charles ordered the entire Royalist forces to be taken from Lancashire and over the Pennines to join her; against his better judgement Stanley obeyed. A few days later the army of 2,000, led by Stanley—now Earl of Derby—and his captains, suffered an unexpected and humiliating setback just east of Whalley.

It was no battle that was fought in Read Lane where Sabden brook is bridged, but an ambush; "the stout churls of Calder and Pendle", Parliament men and Shuttleworth backers everyone of them, deciding to 'have a bash' at the enemy. In a narrow lane the small scouting party surprised by fire was unable to turn. There was chaos, a plunging retreat, and utter confusion among the men coming up behind. The effects were catastrophic. The next Sunday Parliament held a thanksgiving service at St. Paul's for the miraculous victory. The Lancashire Royalists were now scattered and the Earl's hopes of holding the North for the King shattered. Whilst he tried to recoup his losses the Cromwellians won back all he had gained and quickly strengthened the defences of hitherto Royalist-held towns.

In 1644 Prince Rupert of the Rhine arrived in a whirlwind campaign, relieving towns, capturing castles, raising sieges—as at Lathom, where Lady Derby, her children and a few young officers had for three months been surrounded by Parliamentary troops. The Prince brought renewed hope to the North; after his defeat by Cromwell's army at Marston Moor outside York the reversals were the harder to bear.

Lancashire was also attacked by "Almighty God the Plague". In its wake life came to a standstill, trading stopped, markets were not held, towns were silent. Victims of the pestilence cowered in cabins outside the towns. No barricades were needed then. Famine did more to reduce the population than the years of fighting. Parliament was now in control; the Presbytery, ousting Anglican clergy took over the churches. Malignants, whether Protestant or Papist, were fined unmercifully, their lands forfeit.

In August 1648 Cromwell and his well-trained army crossed the Pennines into Lancashire, to Longridge and Preston, there on Ribble banks to win the decisive battle against the Duke of Hamilton and his force and leave the river "with blood of Scots imbrued". Following his victory by 'mopping up' along the Chorley, Wigan and Winwick highway, his campaign ended successfully at Warrington Bridge. The war was virtually over.

In January 1649 the head of Charles I dropped from the execution block in Whitehall. The Earl of Derby was commanded to surrender the Isle of Man to Parliament; two little daughters were seized as hostages.

After the King's death the Cavalier Earl had bided his time at Castletown. When news came in August 1651 of Charles II's attempts to claim his crown, he left the island from Derbyhaven with 300 Manx tenants, landed at Rossall and, crossing fords of the Ribble from Fylde to Hesketh, reached Lathom. He met the young King in Chester prior to the royal forces moving into the

Midlands. Derby was ordered to intercept the oncoming Round-heads near Wigan. On the 24th, with 600 men, he came up with Lilburne's 3,000 near 'Hay', in Wigan Lane. "Dispute was hot and manly on both sides and a good space very doubtful how it would go", until Roundhead reinforcements arrived. The Earl had two horses shot from under him. He mounted the horse of Lord Withrington—slain. In the battle he received six shots on the breastplate, thirteen cuts on his beaver-covered steel cap—and this cap he lost in final flight with blows raining upon him.

With six companions he galloped into Wigan. He evaded arrest at the Old Dog Inn, where the housewife hid him until danger was passed. 'They say' a trail of blood led to the door. Soon he was out of Wigan to join other survivors, whilst his leaderless Manx soldiers "being poor naked snakes, were scattered up and down the country", and those caught put to work. "They proved very fals and treacherous to their masters," and stole away to the coast and back home to Man till "within noe time there were none of them to be seen". Who could blame them?

Many who joined Charles and fought at Worcester were killed, or scattered and finally captured. As James wrote to Lady Derby from Chester Castle, "I escaped from danger at Wigan, but worse at Worcester, being not so fortunate to meet with any who would kill me and put me out of reach of envy and malice. Lord Lauder-dale and I having escaped, hired horses, falling into enemy hands were not thought worth killing." They were given quarter by a Lancashire Roundhead called Edge, "one that was so civil to me, that I and all that love me are beholden to him". In a letter from Chester he wrote to his wife, "my dear heart", telling of a visit from two daughters who were hostages, and of his concern for her. "Take it not as from a prisoner for if I am never so close confined my heart is my own, free still as the best. . . . Have a care my dear soul of yourself and my dear Moll, Ned and Bill. . . ." He escaped by rope—but was soon recaptured—some suggest in the Wirral.

The earl had been court martialled after the Battle of Worcester. Now he was sentenced to death at Chester Castle, but believing vengeance on the 'Great Earl' would be sweeter if his execution was at Bolton, Parliament gave the order. At Bolton his Royalist troops—though he was not leading them—had once made the defenders pay for their opposition in fierce reprisals; Bolton would enjoy the spectacle on the block set up in Deansgate.

Bolton Library has numerous contemporary archives of the event. Like Charles in Whitehall, Lord Derby "nothing common did, or mean" on meeting his end. They kept him waiting at the Man and Scythe Inn, near the church and facing the scaffold. Tradition tells of difficulty in finding an executioner.

Many bystanders wept whilst Roundhead troops encouraged counter-demonstrations, shouts and kept up a great clamour so that few heard his last words.

"I die for God, the King and the laws", he cried.

"We have no king. And will have no lords", yelled the Roundheads.

The earl waited till all was ready. He felt the axe edge, kissed the blade, gave gold to the headsman. "This is all I have. Do thy work well", he said. Then asking for his friends' prayers, he knelt himself and prayed awhile. Asking that the block should face towards the parish church, he laid down his head. "Blessed be God's name for ever and ever. Let the earth be filled with His glory!" Thereupon he signalled the executioner. The axe fell, and a sighing sound like a sudden wind passed through the throng.

His remains were taken to be placed with his ancestors, in Ormskirk Church.

The axe turned up a century later, at Bird's Folly Edgworth, sold by the farmer in a sack of old iron. The Turton sexton recognized what he had bought. His nephew made a new haft from the old chapel altar rail, burnished the blade, and sold it! In 1851 the landlord of the Star Inn was showing it as a great curiosity. Since when, who knows what has happened to it?

Some time after the earl's death, William Christian in Castletown decided to accept Commander Dukinfield's surrender terms for the Isle of Man, on condition Parliament allowed the islanders "to enjoy lives and liberties as under the Stanleys". The Commander summoned Lady Derby to hear the terms. He referred bluntly to "the late earl". So did his family learn for the first time of his death.

How irksome the next ten years were for heirs like young Charles Stanley, deprived of all rank and possessions. He was with Sir George Booth's supporters when they made a gallant, ill-timed attempt to hasten Charles II's return in 1658. The youth was imprisoned and declared a traitor, but two years later came the joyful return of Charles II which would restore the Royalists to their pre-war status. Royalists believed that in slaying King Charles the Martyr of blessed memory, men had interfered with one of God's most holy laws. He had been placed on the throne by God and man had no voice in it. "Nothing will prosper till the rightful king returns. . . ." Now he was back on English soil so all would be well.

So they hoped. Charles Stanley received titles and honours, but no other reward. He carried the third sword in the Coronation, but his father's lost estates were not to be his. It was said, the eighth earl "was possessed of no estate in Lancashire, Cheshire, Westmorland or Cumberland, Yorkshire, Wales or Warwickshire, from which he could not see another of equal value lost in the Civil War". He stayed away from Court, in the country. Six sons died, and seven nephews. The family stock dwindled, two brothers succeeding as ninth and tenth earls.

The ninth earl felt deeply the family's decline. He bore the second sword at the coronation of James II, the sovereign who later deprived him of the lord lieutenancy handing the office to a Roman Catholic Molyneux. The sad state of dissension during James' short reign in addition to links with the House of Orange through his mother, as well as his wife—who was a descendant of Henry of Nassau, a Dutch prince—caused him to join the welcome to William of Orange.

His brother James succeeded as tenth earl in 1702. He had a reputation as a fine soldier, and in periods of peace when he followed the lead of country gentlemen improving or rebuilding ancestral halls he showed himself as a man of taste, a patron of the arts.

Knowsley Hall was brought up to date by him. For his noble apartments he needed works of art. An artist commissioned to bring him the best, returned from Holland with a fine collection of Flemish paintings. He walked his splendid rooms, surveyed with pride the palatial front with its classic portal and paired Ionic and Doric columns—about which critics had their doubts some preferring the first earl's Tudor. He was growing old now, still keenly regretting the ingratitude of kings. He could not allow Charles II's cold-shouldering to be forgotten. On the new façade was an inscription indelibly carved in stone. "James Earl of Derby Lord of Man and the Isles, grandson of James Earl of Derby by Charlotte daughter of Claude Duke of Tremouille, was beheaded at Bolton on the 13th of October 1651 for strenuously adhering to King Charles II, who refused a bill unanimously passed by both houses of Parliament for restoring to the family the estates which he lost by his loyalty to him."

He was last of his line, the inheritance now passing to a Cross Hall Stanley, descended also from the first earl and a namesake of the heroic Monteagle. His line had no feeling for the untrustworthy Stuarts; in politics they were Whig. The twelfth earl, Lord Lieutenant for fifty-eight years, preferred sport to Parliament or Court. He is remembered as the first sporting earl, breeder of fighting cocks, founder of the Derby in 1780. His first wife was daughter of the Duke of Hamilton of Ashton Hall near Lancaster, a great landowner of Fylde estates. His second wife, Mrs. Farren, a lovely Drury Lane actress, "filled her role as Countess with outstanding grace and dignity".

The son of the thirteenth earl, a wild lad at Oxford was in a riotous party which destroyed the statue of Mercury in Tom Quad—He had varied talents. His brilliant translations of Homer's *Iliad* in English blank verse sold five editions in seven months. Equally good were his Latin, French, German and Italian translations. A scholar and statesman, Edward the fourteenth earl was a Tory, Sir Robert Peel's colonial secretary in 1841, but broke away because of differences on 'protection' and joined Disraeli's supporters. He was Prime Minister but never with a big majority. Gladstone once said of him, "At the age of thirty Stanley was by far the cleverest young man of the day, and at sixty would be the same, still by far the cleverest young man of his day".

Some thought the fourteenth earl enjoyed sport more than politics. He played many parts, equally at ease in all, as much at home mingling with "black legs, betting men of the Turf, as with intellectuals and high society".

His son Edward, who served in his father's government, shared some of his father's attributes, a brilliant scholar who took his first-class degree in Classics at Cambridge and was elected to Parliament the same year—aged twenty-two.

I think these two Edwards would approve the eighteenth earl's project to make of Knowsley in the 1970s a wild-life safari park. The thirteenth earl had a well-stocked menagerie at Knowsley which he valued so much he called in an able 'animal artist' to make drawings. His young children were enchanted by the artist's company and conversation. He made funny pictures for their amusement, with nonsensical verses to match. Yes, Edward Lear's visit was an unqualified success as far as the future fourteenth earl was concerned. He was the first to hoot with laughter at those rhymes which sent a century of youngsters—and others—rocking with mirth.

The fourteenth earl filled many parts in Tory governments, in foreign, colonial and Indian affairs. He was three times Prime Minister. When Greece, having won her independence, looked around for a fitting occupant of the empty throne they offered it to Edward, then Lord Stanley.

Disraeli wrote of this: "So the Greeks really want to make my friend their King! This beats any novel, but he will not accept. It is a dazzling adventure for the House of Stanley, but they are not an imaginative race, and I fancy they will prefer Knowsley to the Parthenon, and Lancashire to the Attic plains". He was right. The earl devoted his life and talents to England. In 1865 he was staying at Windsor when news came of his first grandson's birth. This boy, one of ten children, followed his uncle the fifteenth, and his father the sixteenth earl, in 1893. He was the *Earl of Derby. The King of Lancashire*, of whom Randolph Churchill has written so fine and full a biography. He is the larger than life figure many of us remember at the centre of Lancashire life for nearly fifty years—until the Second World War when age and increasing disability forced him to retire from public life to Knowsley Hall. He lived there alone with Lady Derby and Priscilla, their granddaughter, a Wren in Liverpool who returned in her free time to help the old people.

In 1948 at the age of 83 the seventeenth earl died. As Randolph Churchill has written, "Since Tudor times no territorial magnate had exercised a wider influence than he—certainly not so benevolently. It is unlikely any will ever exercise such influence again. . . . The genial sunset of an age has departed".

Legends grow up around such a great and much respected character. One windy day a gust tore the hat from the head of the earl, on a visit to Bolton as Lord Lieutenant. He looked towards the monument down Deansgate. "Better my hat than my head!" he remarked as he replaced it.

John Stanley returned after the war—with his M.C. bestowed for gallantry on the Anzio beaches—to be very soon his grandfather's successor. In recent years he found the restrictions of his office as Lord Lieutenant did not allow him to speak up for Lancashire as freely as he wished. He wished to be a spokesman for the county when he believed it was not having its fair share and say in the nation's affairs.

Knowsley Hall is not what it was. The great earls of the postwar years had to be realists. The vast palatial mansion, though Victorian additions and other features architecturally less worthy had been removed, was too big even for a Stanley. So the earl and countess moved out to a smaller house in the park, passing the great hall to the Lancashire County Constabulary. This is a less bizarre fate than was shown in the national papers early in 1971 —the Earl of Derby riding Womba, one of Jimmy Chipperfield's elephants, across the lawns in front of the Hall.

I was about to write of Knowsley as an ancestral hall *not* to be seen by the public, but from summer 1971 it has been seen—from a reasonable distance—by the car-borne visitors to the newly opened safari park. It will be when all is complete the 'biggest in the world outside Africa', with families of baboons, scores of giraffes, elephants—Richard Chipperfield went off to Kenya to capture twenty for Knowsley—rhinos, hippos; and, roaming freely under south Lancashire skies, zebra, eland, cheetah and ostrich, with the King of Beasts free ranging! I like the plan to introduce breeding herds for their conservation. Knowsley Park covers 14,000 acres—and of this 360 acres is a good start.

A pity Edward Lear lived a century too soon!

Molyneux, Earls of Sefton

Molines (the name was changed to Molyneux in the thirteenth century) were at Hastings and after doing their stint for the Conqueror were in the first share-out of English land. This brought them Lancashire —to 'Sephton' on Alt banks centuries before the first Stanleys arrived. They left these ancestral acres 500 years later when Liverpool commitments made Croxteth a more convenient base. Sefton Hall is now very much 'site of', with a busy Liverpool-Southport highway cutting through it, just west of the ancient parish church.

When the owner of Sefton Old Hall Farm led us to a nearby pasture, under the wide sky across which sea winds blew great clouds from the Mersey, it needed all the imagination I possessed to picture what once was. This trampled grass was formerly the inner courtyard, four ranges around it—much as at Moreton Old Hall or Speke. The shallow surrounding ditch was a moat to prevent night entry by envious neighbours. A pile of masonry showed the stone causeway in collapse, and a hint of the gatehouse and drawbridge over which went Molyneux sons bound for the Crusades, for the Border and Scottish campaigns, for Crécy, Agincourt and that final fight when William Molyneux "wan the Erle of Huntley's armes at the Battell of Flodden Field". Warriors all; if no Molyneux was knighted on any battlefield it was because none were old enough at the time to bear arms.

Between campaigns at home or abroad, cavalcades moved from Sefton south to the Mersey. An early De Molines, follower of Roger de Poictou, received custody of a castle watching the river long before Liverpool town was envisaged. In 1207 King John made plans to coax the folk of Derby (West) from the old hundred 'chief town' to the Pool, granting them burgess privileges if they took sites offered. So were Liverpool town and new port founded. Constables of the new castle, commanding all, were Molyneux, for many generations resented by the burgesses and at odds with

Stanley tower and Molyneux castle, Liverpool, 1670

the Stanleys when a century later they became custodians of a waterfront castle closely concerned with shipping and royal vessels bound for Ireland. A Molyneux (the seventh Earl of Sefton) was Constable of H.M. Castle of Lancaster until his death in April 1972.

Whenever Molyneux supporters armed to the teeth sallied forth towards Liverpool when England was officially enjoying peace, then some private affray, like a Capulet and Montague brawl, with the Stanleys was imminent.

In 1424 Molyneux gathered 1,000 armed men. Stanleys had over 2,000 backers. The Sheriff came between them outside Liverpool demanding to know the cause—too often he had been called to quell street fights and family affrays before. Said an angry Stanley with blazing eyes, "Sir Richard Molyneux cometh with great multitude to slay me and my men". The Sheriff at once arrested him, then went on to intercept the rival faction at West Derby, "arrayed in manner as to battle", and seized Molyneux.

62

The one was banished to Kenilworth Castle, the other to Windsor, well away from northern support. Peace settled on Liverpool once more.

The two families were near and uncomfortable neighbours at Sefton and Lathom, at Croxteth and Knowsley, down the centuries. Their fortunes sometimes were allied, more often opposed. Stanleys and their numerous sons and nephews rose high in the favour of kings. When wealthy heiresses were waiting for husbands, the Stanleys could usually provide them. At such times the Molyneux produced minors, too young to seize the shining hour and make good of it. Before the Tudors under whom Stanleys became indisputable 'top dogs', Molyneux had equalled them in office and rank.

They held important posts with many 'perks': Stewards of West Derby Wapentake, Master Foresters of Salford, the Constableship of Liverpool Castle from father to son. They 'bought' the parish church—and put sons in Walton Rectory—and Liverpool's farm lease. No wonder with so many fingers in the Liverpool pie they chose to move to Croxteth, building there a fine Tudor hall.

The Stanleys, of the same mind, beat them to it leaving Lathom for their new Knowsley Hall of palatial proportions—and fit to receive the king who was a stepson.

Only war against a common foe made them sink family differences. William Molyneux being five years old when he inherited avoided the troubles of the York-Lancaster war and early Tudor conflicts, but was of age to ride forth side by side with the Stanleys to Flodden, and return with glory.

He lived forty years more, during which time the old Sefton church was demolished by James Molyneux Rector, all but tower, steeple and north aisle, and rebuilt most splendidly in Tudor Perpendicular, many Tudor rose motifs and cross moline displaying loyal and family sentiments. This was continued by another Molyneux rector, Anthony, who at Oxford erected Magdalen College garden walls. His work at Sefton—east end, sanctuary and vestry, was completed by the 1540s. This made St. Helen's one of the most perfect churches in the county. The Earl and Countess of Sefton were at the eighth centenary celebrations in September 1970, a great occasion with general thanksgiving.

Among the treasures here, the tombs of generations of the family, none is more interesting than Sir William's who was laid to rest in 1548. A splendid brass hidden under a carpet to preserve it from over-eager 'rubbers', covers his and his two wives'

Sir William Molyneux and his wives, Sefton Church brass

remains. The armour Sir William is wearing is of ancient pattern, as worn by ancestors two to three centuries earlier. One can imagine the great hall at Sefton hung with antique armour discarded by warriors in Edwardian campaigns. When command came to Sefton for Molyneux men to proceed with all haste to the Border, they had hastily to take down and don the heirloom suits, and so to Flodden. In later years Sir William came face to face with the Scots on three other occasions, but at Flodden was his greatest feat of arms, his finest hour, therefore he is depicted on the memorial brass as on that battlefield. It is no good searching for the actual standards he won from the Earl of Huntley. Age destroyed them, and the banners once floating over the Scot's earl's tent have long been dust.

By Tudor times Molyneux and Stanleys had intermarried; the old feuds were forgotten, but there was constant friction with other neighbours.

Blundells and Molyneux share burial space under Sefton Church; alive they long disputed possession of estates, waifs and strays and wreck of the sea, and rights in hunting and fishing. The Molyneux—Mistress Jane fighting like a tigress for her young son's rights, and Sir Edward, priest of Sefton who siezed a fat ox and goods from Crosby Hall and caused Blundell and his son, who objected, to be clapped in Lancaster prison for fourteen weeks—should have known better. So should all the others who sallied forth from Sefton Hall to make life uncomfortable for Blundells at Little Crosby. Molyneux, having to concede precedence to Stanleys, determined to be next in importance. Often, by being Protestants in public, Molyneux had advantage over Blundells, who never conformed. Sir Richard Molyneux, Sir William's heir in 1548, husband of two, and father of nineteen—for the family group see the brasses inset into the tomb between the Molyneux chapel and chancel at Sefton—attended the coronation of Mary, was High Sheriff of Lancashire and knighted in Elizabeth's reign. But on his deathbed, with his son John and three daughters present, he vowed the Pope was Supreme Head of the Church, and received the last rites.

John, his successor, made a clean break with Sefton, taking up residence at the New Hall, Croxteth. Younger sons lived on at Sefton, the 'manor place' for several generations. Richard lived at Melling, Alexander occupied the rectory at Walton as Anglican priest, whilst Anthony, for his recusancy as Papist, left England for the West Indies. These, and five unmarried daughters, are among the rows of children shown on Sir Richard's tomb:

> Dame Worshoppe was my guide in lyfe
> And did my doings guyde
> Dame Wertue left me not alone
> When soule from bodye hyed. . . .

So begins his epitaph. No mention of his heir who died before him, one year earlier, leaving a ten-year-old grandson to inherit.

Young William was placed by Elizabeth in a strict Protestant household, Gerrard's, and though many close friends were later 'Papists of evil note', he was in public for Church and State and could persecute Blundells with conscience clear. James I conferred upon him a baronetcy, and for Richard, his son, the Earldom of Sefton was to follow.

At a tender age little Richard Molyneux was led one day to Sefton Church to meet and hold hands with his betrothed, four-year-old Fleetwood Barton. Her grandfather, whose heiress she was, was anxious to cement family friendship. In 1607 the boy

E   65

refused to go on with the marriage. It was duly dissolved, the little girl marrying Richard Shuttleworth of Gawthorpe, Puritan, highminded and later a pillar of Parliamentarianism. Richard was now free to wed the daughter of his guardian, Lord Strange. She was named after Henrietta Mary, and this alliance placed him among the foremost Royalists, a kingsman in the Civil War from the word 'go'.

The outcome of the war, in Lancashire, might have been different had the King's jealousies not clouded his better judgement. He ordered Richard to put off helping Lord Strange to hold Manchester, and to bring his men to the royal army at Oxford; so was the town lost to Parliament. His brother Caryll led Lancashire Royalists in many places. He was in command of Liverpool town; his boyhood home the castle he knew blindfold so he was of great help to Prince Rupert and his besieging Royalists on the June night when they surprised the Roundhead garrison, burst through the defences and added this to the list of castles taken.

Both Molyneux brothers after exile returned with Charles II. Caryll as third Lord Molyneux settled in at Croxteth, there formulating ambitious plans for Liverpool's advance in the nation's trade and commerce. His town planning included the extending of Lord (Molyneux) Street to the Mersey pool where ships lay at anchor, and bridging of the stream flowing to the river. At every step the townsfolk thwarted him. Finally in 1672, with a 700-year lease still to run, he sold the manor to the town—the bargain price, £30 yearly plus the rent Molyneux had always paid the Crown.

Stormy years faced the family. The Test Act of 1673 shocked all non-Protestants. Caryll, heading the list of Papists debarred from all public office, was excluded from the House of Peers. He retired to the seclusion of Croxteth—until Roman Catholic James became king.

In 1685 there was a turning of tables, Papists, as the Molyneux now were, were thrust into prominence none had enjoyed for a century. The King took power from the Stanleys, the Molyneux being his obvious replacements. With himself as Lord Lieutenant of Lancashire and his friends as deputies, Croxteth, in Caryll's time was the new centre of public life, a golden time beginning. Differences were obvious. The Stanleys' long period of power had been balanced; they served all, at all times. Now the Molyneux circle consisted of Roman Catholics, and no others.

Molyneux were always closely linked with the Stuarts. Lady Sefton explained to me why portraits of two of King Charles II's 'ladies' hung in a gallery, one of Barbara Villiers, the other of Louise de Keronaille. A son of one family and the daughter of the other generations later married, their daughter becoming bride of a Molyneux, so introducing a strain of Stuart royal blood.

England saw that James II's throne was insecure, but not that it would topple so soon. Papists, now able to practise their faith openly, determined to support him at all costs, staked all—and inevitably lost all. The Glorious and Bloodless Revolution put James' daughter, Mary, and her husband William of Orange on the throne. And Protestants were back in office.

Caryll Molyneux was ringleader among the underground revolutionaries working for James' return. They were allowed to carry on their plottings unaware of the spy ring employed to discover them—and invent what they did not discover! Wealthy Papists were fair game. Evidence was found against them—from false witnesses if by so doing Parliament could get its hand on their property. Three prominent Whigs had great incentives to employ informers when the Lords of the Treasury offered each one-third share of the property of any found "practising idolatry". A tissue of lies round a little truth caught Molyneux, Blundells, Cliftons—and many more.

Lord Molyneux had a servant called Abbot, captured when embarking from Liverpool "to bring back my lord's daughter to Croxteth from Drogheda". For subservice activities they imprisoned him with short breaks on bail for two years, wearily waiting for his case to be heard. At Newgate in appalling conditions, threatened with leg irons because he could not pay for free movement, with fear of being thrown among the worst criminals, he begged to return to Lancaster for a fair hearing. He constantly denied high treason, that he had given money for murder of William III; and in the Lancaster Summer Assizes of 1691 was at last discharged, 'not guilty'. His journal of his years in prison makes interesting reading. So does an account attributed to him of the 1694 trials at Manchester, where he heard the evidence put up by paid government informers against his master and the Lancashire plotters.

He must have had uneasy moments, for many accused had taken part in collecting arms, furnishing men and planning for James' return. Fortunately the Grand Jury, men of integrity, refused to credit the lies of Lunt and his cronies, rank perjury, and set the prisoners free.

In 1700 Caryll Lord Molyneux Third Viscount was laid among his ancestors in the south-east chapel at Sefton. Only two years earlier William Blundell the Old Cavalier was carried to his burial in the north-east side. Both were staunch Papists, given resting places within the parish church.

The fourth viscount took over his responsibilities in easier times. For two generations no money had been available to improve the Tudor Hall at Croxteth, a pleasant enough gabled house of mellow brick. Now he could set architects at work on a mansion as grand as Knowsley—a gracious Queen Anne house encasing what was left of the old.

The June day when I visited Croxteth the house glowed in the warm sunshine, as only centuries'-old brick and sandstone can. For years I lived in West Derby near the park gates but this was the first time I had entered in. Lady Sefton met me by car near the church, the distance to the hall being quite as far as she had told me. Croxteth Hall, built by the Molyneux descendants of bold Sir Richard, made Chief Forester of the Royal Forest and Parks in West Derby for his valiant leadership at Agincourt, was a stately home well isolated from village life; and so was the even statelier mansion enlarged in the periods of William and Mary, in Queen Anne and in later times. There was no connection with the ordinary folk without the park pale. What long walks they had when they went to the village—but did they ever walk?

West Derby residents talked of Lord Sefton, mostly of his sporting activities warming up towards the Grand National. Some showed interest about guests at the National Night dinner, and there was speculation about winners of the Waterloo Cup. "Lieutenant Dashalong", the Second Earl of Sefton, was patron of the first Grand National and prime mover of greyhound racing on Alt banks, not so far from the ancestral hall of Sefton. In the County Record Office is a plan showing the first lay-out of the Aintree racecourse drawn in July 1829, ten years before the first Grand National was run. Since the course was owned by the Earls of Sefton, this was among the family archives.

I once received warm welcome into a group of greyhound-racing enthusiasts in Dublin by a mere mention of knowing farmers who raised the whelps of aristocratic lineage on the earl's farms near Abbeystead. The Mansion or Lodge at Abbeystead—

Lady Sefton's favourite place—was built in the 1880s when the earl gave up his Scottish grouse shoots and bought extensive moors here, above Over Wyresdale that highly romantic and wild country between the Trough Stone and High Cross Moor, on the way to Quernmore and Lancaster. At the same period he rebuilt some of the decayed farmhouses on the estate, and the cottages in Abbeystead—those picturesque groups which look solid enough to outlast another two or three centuries. Left-over masonry went to the building of The Mansion and the York and Lancaster lodge gates. From here royal guests like George V, as well as the noble and great, have taken part in sensational shoots. A record-breaking bag followed the outbreak of war, the 1915 guns on Tarnbrook Fell accounting for 2,929 birds.

The late Lord Sefton stayed around Croxteth near his stud farm, stables and estate offices. Liverpool begins outside the confines of the park, much closer than in his grandparents' days, building development coming nearer—and nearer!

The hall looks as though Time has laid a gentle hand upon it. A blow-lamp left against the front door by a careless decorator caused a devastating fire, grand apartments are scaffolded and may never again be used; but outside all looks untouched. And the rest of the hall remains worthy to stand among the most grand of the great houses of England—architecturally, and because of the interior work and the works of art contained therein.

Perhaps there are fewer family portraits than in similar halls, the Molyneux giving daughters pictures to take away to their new homes on marriage, leaving a few Knellers, a Gainsborough and Lelys. Two I thought most attractive showed the daughter who became Countess of Craven in green riding habit, and a family group of Lucys of Charlecote, a daughter of Sir Thomas marrying a Molyneux. Naturally the collection of sporting prints is a fine one; but there are no paintings of horses by Stubbs, though he was almost on the doorstep. As contrast, there are objects of most delicate beauty—the panels from a quilted Watteau screen now reset in the lace-like wrought-iron work of a balcony.

Only part of the south side with dormers, and an inner stone doorway with Tudor arched lintel and the original bolted hatch, four centuries old, remain from the earlier hall.

In April, 1972, came the sad end of the family, a line going back over nine centuries.

Blundells of Crosby

I have returned from that corner of Lancashire so flat that slim church spires rising above tree belts and potato fields are the only landmarks. One points the whereabouts of Little Crosby, a most inconspicuous village with a long history. A stranger may be excused for not guessing the existence of Crosby Hall, hidden behind the Park wall.

There I was welcomed by one in direct descent from Nicholas Blundell, the Diarist, and William, the Cavalier—who was half way back in time to Osbertus of Aynesdale the first known Blondell of the family of a Norman Blondell the Fairheaded, who with his sons did bravely at Hastings and was named on the battle roll.

Other families claim ancient lineage, but how many are still living on the same land granted so many centuries ago? The Blondells sat on their estate in West Derby Hundred; and still do, for Mrs. Whitlock-Blundell after the death of two brothers, the last male Blundells, took the family name; and there are seven children to carry it on.

In their heyday, before the dark shadows of persecution fell, they were possessed of Little Crosby Manor, Moorhouses and Ditton in Cheshire. "Many houses, cottages and tofts, dovehouse, windmill, 200 gardens, 100 orchards, 1,000 acres of land, 200 acres meadowland, 1,000 of pastures and vast acreage of woodland, heath and lenz, marsh, turbary and mossett", scattered throughout Little and Great Crosby, and adjacent manors were recorded in 1591. Fifty years later their losses, through fines, sequestrations and arrears of payment backdated to great-grandparents' days, had swallowed up revenues from land so that William the Cavalier reckoned he was "worth less than nothing by £81 18s." Another fifty years, another Blundell had to buy back milk from his own mortgaged farms—a landless man!

All this we know, the whys and wherefores, because William's diaries and notebooks record eighty years of the seventeenth century; and Nicholas the diarist recorded day-to-day affairs from 1702–28. The family is rich in having so many recording ancestors, in addition to a mighty tome called the Great Hodge Podge, containing scores of letters, accounts, jottings from the 1590s to the nineteenth century which Colonel Nicholas wisely decided were worth preserving within the same covers. What fascinating reading! I considered myself fortunate to be able to turn the pages and feel history coming to life.

We sat by a crackling fire in the library, surrounded by old books—and there was no sign of the 'secret' door which is entrance to it. Here I handled also a small pocket Bible, the 'Dowy' version, in translation unfamiliar, but as distributed among Papists from the presses of Douai when it was powerhouse of Roman Catholicism. The yellowed pages had faint underlinings and comments in faded ink, made by the Cavalier, or his father, during long captivity. They were good men in prison or free, with the strength of their convictions never wavering.

Crosby Hall, 1870

On the landings and stairs are portraits of long-dead ancestors —the kindly Old Cavalier, the pious Emelia who in widowhood entered her daughter's convent in France, young hopefuls, sons and their brides. But now there is rich young life filling the old hall, a happy house. Much of the building is unchanged. A Tudor wing was removed and rebuilt in 1609, the opposite wing remodelled in 1770, but the central block, the heart of Crosby Hall, is 'as of yore'. Not far away are William's stables (dated 1637), and that capacious granary so often mentioned in Nicholas Blundell's journals—scene of so many merry nights and festivals long ago, and now good for centuries more, renovated for twentieth-century junkettings, dances, parties and plays. The masonry, of great age, glows in the mellow sunshine.

Was this peace really shattered by the stormier passages of Lancashire history, and were the Blundells, home-loving squires caring for little but their farms and fields, their family and tenantry, and hunting shooting and fishing in their own preserves, truly dragged off forcibly to prison as a dangerous threat to the community? They were—not once, but time and time again.

Too often the Molyneux, as most uneasy neighbours, were to blame. Blundells as part of feudal military service had to pay them a 4d. rent and a red rose at midsummer for certain lands. But Molyneux demanded more, especially when the menfolk were away in the wars. Dame Molyneux and a Sefton priest of early Tudor times seized stray Blundell animals, laid claim to wrecks of the sea that the Blundells believed to be theirs, and frightened off Blundells out for a day's shooting on their own land. Old Nicholas asserted his rights so forcibly the Molyneux dragged him, and one of his twelve children, to Lancaster Castle, where they were confined twelve weeks before Cardinal Wolsey worked their release. A nice old man, Nicholas once said of his wife, "Neither could find faut with either." Hunting was "his great tresur and plesur". He enjoyed a good scrap too, if thwarted.

A time came when the local families, all caught up by other troubles, had no time for such feuds. In 1590 only two names in a list of local Protestant gentry were underlined as completely trustworthy, the Earl of Derby and Legh of Lyme. Some were Protestant in public, through prudence; some wavered; some recanted on death beds if not before. But Blundells were firm then and 'for always'. In 1598 Molyneux and the parson of Sefton wrote of them as "evil persons who do greatly hinder the race of the Gospel especially in these maritime parts and daily threaten dangerous events". They were appealing for the release of Emelia Blundell, weak and ill after imprisonment at Chester, but of William her husband's company they wished "to be freed if by lawful means he might be removed from us".

William had shared prison with his father for recusancy, after being apprehended with Robert Woodruff 'the Seminary'. Killing prison fever took the father in 1591. Now the son was again to be thrust in prison for five years. They set him free at last, but he was on the run, in hiding, for two more years. Emelia knew prison too well, one of her sons "suckled if not born in jail".

Elizabeth, the old queen, died. Surely James' reign augured better? He started well in granting pardons—for money. William bought his, "free and large, for 40 or 50 shillings". The Protes-

72

tants were apprehensive at the honours now given to Papists: knighthoods, invitations to court—and liberty of conscience "as long as they kept themselves upright in all civil and true carriage to the King". James saw this rising antagonism. So he stopped "stroaking the Papists", abandoned leniency, and signed new laws penalizing them. All hurt the Blundells.

For two generations Blundell sons and daughters had been passed out of the country for education in France. James' new law levied £100 fine on any who sent his child abroad to receive Romish schooling. If the child on returning refused to conform he could not inherit or enjoy his paternal estates. Any ship owner taking as passenger anyone under twenty-one, without licence, was to suffer loss of his ship, forfeiture of his goods and twelve months' imprisonment. Yet the flow continued. To the young Blundells it meant many years' exile, no returning home until schooldays were over. Daughters did not return from their convents.

The next rigorously enforced law for recusancy was a £20 fine for each lunar month's non-attendance at church. "to take wine with the vicar". From those who could not pay, cattle, furniture and clothes were taken 'in lieu', to be sold. Also two-thirds of land was forfeit. All clergy were bound to denounce cases of non-attendance of Papists over thirteen years old. In 1590, 941 persons were prosecuted as recusants before the official list was produced, and 800 afterwards. In 1604 there were 6,426 Papists in the overcrowded jails. James "had hitherto stroaked the Papists but nowe he did strike".

Then an impossible £2,000 fine was demanded of William, for breaking the law in enclosing a private burial ground for his family, refused interment at Sefton. They clapped him in "Ye Fleete prison", and levelled his graveyard. When he died in 1638 his heir, a young grandson, had all these debts on his shoulders, and cares beyond his years.

We know all about the happenings of William Blundell the Cavalier's long life; he recorded them. He had time and leisure to do so. Two years after he became head of his family the Civil War began. He gladly accepted his captain's commission, raised 100 dragoons and rode proudly out of Crosby to fight for King Charles. At his first taste of battle, attacking the Lancaster defences, a musket ball shattered his thigh. Friends carried him over the hills to Dinckley Hall on the Ribble where Mistress Talbot nursed him back to health. But never again was he to take up

73

arms. Lamed for life, 'Halt Will' was a prisoner on parole, and his every movement was reported to the Liverpool Parliamentary governor as long as the war lasted.

No dark omens had shadowed the departure of young William, "a dashing young sprig of fifteen in scarlet", when he left Crosby Hall in 1635, his adoring family waving him godspeed on his way to meet his bride in Northumberland. Neither did the future trouble the young couple in their first two years of married life. "I was father of a child and my own master, God knows, before I was 18", he wrote. He tackled the inherited debts. He raised £30 annual payment to farm his own estate—forfeit because of the family refusal to conform. He recovered from the sorrows of the year which carried off his mother, his little daughter and his sister from the same malady, and with patience faced the outcome of the Civil War—all at an age when young men of his standing were still sowing wild oats. Such character one must admire.

Blundell women were loyal and uncomplaining. When he was away and the enemy soldiers came to carry off all their stock, but one horse and two oxen, they went on valiantly coping with the farm work as best they could. When marauding troops carried off stores of food and quartered themselves with the unprotected women and children, they hid food from meal to meal against starvation. The few old servants left at Crosby were equally staunch. Standing in the same stable yard I imagined what took place one day when Roundheads stole away without paying for their quarters. As they hurried to mount their horses Blundell retainers appeared brandishing sticks, and some with swords drawn blocked the stable door. "Pay what you owe", said they, "or else!" The Roundheads produced 17s. 6d. most reluctantly.

Not long after he had been injured at Lancaster, friends came to William at Crosby with offer of help. They had found a good surgeon in Cheshire who would cure his wounds, and a boat was ready to carry him over the water from Speke to the Wirral. He would not go with them, fearing this would bring danger to the family. In fact this would have been so—Moore's spies had information and already had captured the boat.

Later, to leave Crosby was the wiser course. A wife was allowed one-fifth of her absent husband's estate, for her own and the children's support, with the condition "that the children should not refuse to be educated at Protestants". The eldest was six, the youngest an infant; how could they accept or refuse? So they held on, whilst father William hid in many places: sometimes in Wales—relatives lived near Wrexham; sometimes with the Stanleys at Castletown. And for a while he was imprisoned in a Lancaster Castle cell. His sisters, whose fortunes had not been forfeit, rallied when a ransom was demanded for his release.

After the Battle of Naseby, with Parliament in control estates of Royalists were confiscated and sold "for good of Parliament and nation". That was when William valued himself "worth nothing by £81 18s., my lands all being lost". At Crosby with all his children around him he decided, in spite of heavy fines if caught, to have a priest under his roof to teach them. No tenant told of this, though a sum equal to that for informing against a highwayman would have been paid as a reward. There was always "a gentleman at the top of the house", a priest in the Crosby Hall attic.

At last the war was over, Charles beheaded, his son in exile, the Earl of Derby executed. William sought distractions from his sorrows. He must buy back his Crosby estates. Friends, Protestants among them, rallied round, his in-laws and his sisters together raising £1,109, half the sum needed. A document twenty feet long lists in minutest detail every sum borrowed in getting back Crosby from the Parliament. Then came a mighty blow which would have floored a lesser man.

Wily lawyers, on behalf of the Commonwealth, had been unearthing old documents dealing with fines for recusancy, and discovered large arrears dating back to the 1590s. He was presented with fines owed by his grandfather and father, now totalling £1,167. William paid the fines, and all debts owing to his friends. He arranged a secret passage to France for his eldest son—who did not return for twenty-eight years—and despatched his young daughters two by two, to nunneries. Years later when the Commonwealth was failing and restrictions less stringent, William Blundell himself accompanied his last two daughters to France. When he had seen them settled in their convent he turned to the court of the exiled king. So it was that in 1660 he returned to England with Charles II and witnessed the first chapter of rejoicing at the Restoration.

Surely a better time was ahead? He found a Derbyshire bride, Mary Eyre of Hassop, for his son and the son of Lord Mountgarret of Kilkenny, young Richard Butler, as match for Emelia. He waited for signs of gratitude from Charles; they did not come. Instead Charles was over-ruled by Parliament in plans to ease the burden on Papists, many of whom had sacrificed so much for his father. Under pressure in 1673 he sanctioned the Test Act; all who bore office in the realm must take the Anglican sacrament and deny transubstantiation. That, of course, debarred Blundells from public office. Wrote William: "All in dreadful high suspence here considering the late rigorous proclamation against our lives and fortunes. We have not known the like with so many circumstances of terror for twenty years past". Suggestions were made concerning emigration to Maryland. But William was too loyal an Englishman to quit.

Five years later a new hate campaign against Roman Catholics was sparked off by Titus Oates who 'discovered' a plot to murder the King and with French help to bring back the old religion. Amongst the first victims of the plot was William's eldest son, Nicholas, now a priest newly returned from France. He was arrested and thrown in prison accused of bearing on his person plans for burning down London. The saddened Cavalier wrote: "None but madmen can execute these cruel things threatened against his Majesty's Catholic subjects. There is no defence against madmen by paper walls. If we must therefore beg or hang, I pray God bless the King, and God's will be done".

He was always loyal to Charles even when most sorely tried. The King forgave many Parliamentary leaders and restored to office old enemies, Cromwellians. One day the Cavalier was forced to give up his "trusty old sword, my companion when I lost my limbs, lands, my liberty acting against the rebels, taken by an officer who had been a captain against the King in the War". From old enemies he had jeers for his loyalty to the monarchy when Charles himself ordered that Blundell lands should once more suffer sequestration.

In 1678 William Blundell was pronounced "an enemy to his country"! Lord Caryll Molyneux and the Blundells, William and his son, headed a list of those worthy of banishment. During that year he was in prison for the fourth time, a spell which might have proved more arduous had not his eight month's confinement been "rendered extremely pleasant by having Mr. Towneley of Towneley to share it. His cheerful society would make life pleasant anywhere", he wrote.

Back at Crosby, a sad state of things. William and Mary were now on the throne, but no relief was possible for families like his. Soldiers without authority roamed round the house and stables, looting, carrying off arms and horses, terrorizing the household. Roman Catholics were forbidden to own good horses so soldiers robbed a servant attempting to hide a gelding. Protestant friends had provided William with two more mounts, but one was seized.

Among his papers was an unposted letter to the King James II, pleading for aid. "I have lost estates and land sequestered, I bought my land off the rebels, I was 4 times prisoner and paid my ransom twice, all for loyalty to my King." His loyalty to the sovereign whatever his religion was never in doubt. "I believe all Catholic subjects of a Protestant king are obliged to adherr to that king in all invasions whatsoever though made by Catholic princes, even by the Pope himself." And the following year, 1691, he wrote, "We have reason to pray for the King for without his favour we had all been prey to the Law or the rabble."

Three years later the rabble was roused. Law might have become a travesty at the Manchester trials had not a fair-minded Lancashire jury prevailed against false evidence and evil informers. After the verdict, and his son's release—he had taken the place of the old Cavalier now too old to face a trial or prison, William took up his quill again. Doubtless as he wrote the happy voices of his son's thirteen jubilant children filled the house in welcome. "We have now every reason to pray for the King and may sit very securely under our own vines."

Quietly he continued among his family, wandering round the estate, talking with the countryfolk, discussing farming and fruit growing, writing down useful recipes, cures for ills and helpful hints.

On apple growing: "Make a hole in the principal root of the tree and put in a pretty quantity of that you wish your apples to taste of; as of cloves, mace, nutmeg and the like."

On cure-alls: "A balsam of rare virtue. Yellow wax, Venice turpentine, sallet oyle, oyle of St. John's wort, sack and red rose water. Pleasant cuar for wounds, broken bones, bruises, cuts, headache."

'Cuar' for colic: "Lie with the belly on a cold marble stone, one which the sun has never shined upon." A drastic remedy—kill or cure!

A recipe which should emotionally involve all gardeners who go a-slugging: "Burn southernwood to ashes and mix with sallet oyle or what is better, the oyle or fat of black snails. Sprinkle the snails with salt and hang in a net. They will work themselves into a fat. Let the fat drop into a dish. A cuar for baldness."

William Blundell, the man of his times: "It were good to have steps or seats—as in a cockpit—for better sight of public executions and trials as at Westminster Hall, Tyburn."

In 1698 the aged Cavalier died. A great body of Blundell kith and kin conveyed his body for burial in the family chapel beneath the floor of Sefton Church—in the north-east aisle. Eighty-seven of them were Roman Catholic priests.

Nicholas Blundell the Diarist

Chief mourner, his son William, died suddenly two years later on a visit to Lord Molyneux at New Stand. Nicholas, the eldest son, inherited a mass of debts and the care of his mother and eight younger brothers and sisters; also the loyal and generous great aunt Frances who had stayed with the family through thick and thin. The day William died Nicholas opened the first page of his "Diurnal and Daly journal"; he did not miss an entry for the next thirty-five years. His diary not quite so revealing as his grandfather's, and very cautious about his political views, but it is very 'quotable'.

To marry a wealthy bride was urgent and essential. Arrangements began, through go-betweens, for the hand of Lord Marmaduke Langdale's daughter Frances. Settlements were duly drawn up, but, times being dangerous, the young couple were not told 'the day' until the previous evening. Secrecy was essential. An informer's reward was £100, the celebrant of a nuptial mass faced a lifetime's imprisonment. The celebrations in this case must have been obvious, musicians playing, bells ringing, and a tip of 10s. to the collector who came for the Queen's due, a bridegroom tax of £5 2s. 6d. A team of fine horses drew the bridal couple's coach (the Blundell chariot) north to Crosby where "musitians were at my hombringing and many neighbours to give me joy". Where the secrecy?

Seventeen-year-old Frances came with a £2,000 dowry, enough to cover debt re-payments and ensure a fairly stable future. Nicholas was 'careful'. His 'bride's gift' of coffee spoons (gilt) and a "fals diamond necklace and a fals diamond ring" did not cost him the earth. He gave her no allowance for fifteen years. Her 'bottom drawer' and ample wardrobe as a bride sufficed and no replacements were needed for years.

The honeymoon over—the visiting and being visited by all and sundry, taking the waters at Lathom Spaw and the more fashionable Wigan springs, visiting St. Winifred's at Holywell and there praying for an heir—it is back to normality. Frances took over housekeeping with little success, nor would she take advice. Mother-in-law and aunt were in constant disagreement with her and servants threatened to leave. Nicholas in his journal called her "she" at such times.

After fourteen months the first child was expected, Frances frantic with toothache and Nicholas with not a word of commiseration! He bought muslins, holland and flannels for "babby cloaths", a linen basket and cradle, and quilt priced 5s.

That September Great Aunt Frances, after sixty years, left Crosby. The midwife moved in. On the 20th. "My wife began to feel ye paines of labor. I brake flax"; on the 21st, "Discoursed with tenants on watercourses"; on the 22nd, "My wife delivered of her first Chylde called Mary". On the next day many invitations were sent out and food ordered for a grand christening; so many came to thanksgiving that the small family oratory was overfull, so "we prayed on ye Stares". Little Mary had another sister Frances, eventually the sole heiress and wife to Henry Peppard of Drogheda—but this was years ahead.

Crosby soon saw many changes. Old Mistress Blundell decided to join her daughters in France in the convent over which one was Mother Superior. The plans were, perforce, secret. Other secrets were equally well kept—the outlawed Butler cousin, Lord Mountgarret, returning to England, was hidden at Crosby in a secret chamber. Danger surrounded them, but Nicholas said a firm "No" when Frances suggested they should sell all to live in Ireland. He was as staunch an Englishman as his grandfather, and attached to his ancestral acres.

Anyone interested in the daily activities of a 'working' squire in Queen Anne's reign could do no better than read what Nicholas did with his time. He was an indefatigable 'improver'. West winds blowing drifting sand inland have long menaced south-west Lancashire coasts. Nicholas planted thousands of 'heps and haws' creating a wild rose tangle and thorn break, and tall windbreaks and broom banks were his doing. The same sea-winds at times blew in ships and wreckage was scattered on the shore. Smuggling was approved but rarely mentioned. Once he wrote: "Cargo of 16 large ones [barrels] brought to White Hall in a cart covered very well with straw."

Then marl was used freely to improve light soils. Blundell fields were marled in rotation every twenty years. To get marl took many weeks with much labour involved—from a morning in spring at the 'setting out' of the selected pit, to a day in late summer when all who had hewed, filled carts or spread marl dined and drank with the squire at the hall. He himself tunned the marlers' drink weeks earlier, expecting enormous thirsts. July 22nd: "Abundance of neighbours eat and drunk with me. They brought sugar, chickens, butter. All my marlers, spreaders, water balys and carters dined here. We fetched home ye Maypowle from the Pit, had sword dancing [the eight men trained by the expert Nicholas] and had a Merry-night in ye Hall and ye Barne. Richard Tatlock played to them".

In the same barn I can imagine it all, and the children laughing at the gaiety; and the tinsel garlands and caps their father had shaped—the Crosby lasses helping.

So many fields now have ponds which were old marl pits. When all marl was taken away the hole was allowed to fill with water, but not before it had served as a bullbaiting ring. Nicholas offered a prize collar for the winning dog—that one which survived three baits during which eight or nine lesser bulldogs had been eliminated. There were no protests about bloodsports then!

Marlings were often marred by tragedy, like the sad end of one at Ribchester, remembered on a grave-stone at the church door:

> His transient life was with hard labour filled
> And falling in a marlpit he was killed.

Other work was with hemp and flax, when Nicholas organized forty labourers in the many processes of breaking, rippling, scutching and swingling. After which, as was expected, Squire put on a grand supper, "Tatlock played the fiddle", four "disguisers" or mummers added to the revelry, the Great Crosby Garland was put on. "And all made very merry."

Nicholas had jolly names for horses, gender not matching. His "Bonny Buttocks fowled a filly". Patient Grissel, a gelding, was a pacer. The coach horses doubled as farm horses, hauling the carts to Sir Richard Bradshaw's pits at Haigh for loads of clean burning house coals, cannel. Turf from his own mosses provided tenants' hearths and the mill and kiln with fuel with some left over for sale.

All work and no play? Indeed not, for Nicholas enjoyed fox-hunting, shooting kites and crows—cunningly using a dead mare's carcase as decoy—and the excitement of exterminating adders. One summer 112 of these were killed in hall and barn, and twenty-two turned up by pitchfork under dung and old straw in the stables.

In 1714 the Sefton parish meeting surprised him by electing him churchwarden. A Roman Catholic! How could he accept? Friends and his priest prevailed upon him to take office. He did so with great sense of duty and thoroughness. When the church roof was repaired, pulpit stairs mended, a new corpse cart (parish hearse), needed, then Nicholas supervised every step, working with bishop and parson for the good of the parish, exercising his outstanding capabilities as organizer.

This tranquil state was ended on Queen Anne's death. Nicholas, ever cautious, reveals little in his diary. In August 1714 he avoided making the Oath of Allegiance to Protestant George I, by a payment of 1s. sent by express letter! In September 1715 came rumours of the Jacobite rebels. He made his fourth will, gave notice to four servants and made visits to lawyers. In October constables came to his door "for aid to arm the militia against the rebels", the same day he "perused papers, bottled ale and trained a greyhound, laid up apples, attended Crosby Goose Fair". Reading, one might think his chief worry was news of a "great distemper of milch cows". In fact he was a very anxious man.

At the month's end, he "came not in till dark"—hiding from whom? The Langdales his in-laws, were kinsfolk of important Jacobites, Widderingtons and the Earl of Derwentwater, which brought suspicion on the Blundells. On 12th November the rebels were at Preston and Nicholas drank a health in punch—to James III? Blundells always turned to punch when rejoicing, but the next days held none. On the 16th he "sat in a strait place for a fat man", huddled in a secret hide for several days, whilst Frances offered unwelcome guests outdoor sport to allay sus·picion. On the 20th he had "a bedfellow" in his hide. A week later he began a nine days journey ending in London. The rising was over and he witnessed the London mob insulting the rebel prisoners then arriving, "yet all showed sympathy for ye Earl of Derwentwater". He was still in London, suffering greatly and planning to take his family into exile, the following February— and attended High Mass at the French envoy's after the execution of Lords Derwentwater and Kenmure.

Now Papists were having to pay the bill for the rising. Frances "hid church and mass things in a fals roof" at Crosby; discovery would have meant loss of all they possessed, one-fourth to the informer, the rest to the Crown.

In spring 1716 there were no Blundells left at Crosby, all being safely lodged with friends in Flanders, Nicholas leaving first with a pass, his wife and two daughters following later. He lodged near his sisters, of the Benedictine Dames at Ghent and the Poor Clares in Dunkirk, giving help in the convent garden, "trimming espalier trees, sowing seed, pruning and nailing vines, trimming apricocks" and making "mous traps". He learnt French, and met a Monsieur Blondel—a Frenchman of the same stem?

They eventually left the little girls in a convent—farewell for six years—and returned in 1717 on the "Betty Yot" to begin life again at Crosby on £482 a year. This sum, oddly enough, placed him fourth in wealth—after Molyneux, Shireburne and Gerrard of Garswood—among Lancashire gentry.

All this in the diaries, and the two volumes compiled from them by Margaret Blundell, the latest family historian, in 1952. Nicholas was the last Blundell until his daughter's son, Henry Peppard, assumed the name and arms. Henry's son lived through better days when Roman Catholics could share in public life. He and Colonel Nicholas, the collector of the family documents in the Great Hodge Podge, were both J.Ps. A son was named after Osbert the first Aynesdale ancestor.

So much has been left out, for so much was written of the Blundells by the Blundells. To read, then to be welcomed at the hall where each lived, moved and had his being, was a rare experience for me and most memorable. So much sorrow and so much fortitude—and yet the stock survives. It is so very English.

"There is nothing like a large family to bring an old house like this to life", as Mrs. Whitlock-Blundell said.

Blundells of Ince Blundell

The Blundells granted mossland east of Crosby, at Blundell's Island or Ince Blundell, in the twelfth century were not related to Osbert of Aynesdale's family. His shield bore ten white billets on a black ground, theirs a squirrel. Often they were at loggerheads but when religious troubles tore Lancashire apart they too were recusants, and Royalists and Jacobites. In the eighteenth century their hall was a Jesuit headquarters with the Reverend A. Babthorpe as superior over thirty priests. They had much in common, Nicholas the diarist and Robert of Ince, and were close friends. When Frances was 'awkward' Nicholas moved over to stay

with Robert and was doubtless interested in his plans for rebuilding on the grand scale.

Ince Blundell Hall within its spacious park—the Southport to
Liverpool road passing through the dark plantations—reminds
me of a smaller chateau by the Loire, the same brick walls, stone
quoins and elegant charm. Robert's forbears had been forced
into exile in Ireland but he saw brighter days ahead, greater
security for his descendants. A pity his son Henry seemed dis-
inclined to marry but indulged a lifelong passion for antiquities,
sharing his interests with Charles Towneley, the Jacobite exile
who searched for the treasures of Greece and Rome. His collection
of marbles grew, and a garden temple, with Tuscan columns and
a frieze in relief, was built to hold them. When this proved too
small nothing would suffice but a 'purpose-built Pantheon', an
extension of the Georgian garden frontage. Over the outside door
he set figures of men and horses battling in some long forgotten
war, and lions and mounted warriors in gladiatorial combat.

All this we admired one October afternoon. Unlike the private
house at Crosby, Ince Blundell Hall now a convalescent home of
the Augustinian Sisters, allows visitors to look around in the afternoon. The reverend mother showed us the notable rooms, architecturally famous: the beautifully proportioned drawing-room of
1750, its ceiling most elaborate stucco; the library where shell
embrasures once held statues or busts. But the Pantheon she left
us alone to enjoy saying, "Full of rubbish." The Sisters are very
practical!

To see some of Blundell's antique treasures, go to Liverpool Art

Ince Blundell, 1970

83

Gallery; here The Pantheon is nothing but a 'do' room, a 'rumpus' room for parties and the like, with dangling paper streamers, paper flowers, and coloured light bulbs at the centre of each rose motif in the panels of the great dome. We trod the smooth paved floor, stroked the cold marble of the tall pillars. The niches were all empty, but some cameos on the blue frieze were as Henry Blundell designed them. Maybe his returning ghost rings its hands and, lamenting changing times, haunts the unchanging park, by the pines about the temple, along the shores of the dreaming lake.

No mansion more fine, in a setting so fitting, is there in Lancashire. Nor a place more tranquil to get well in, the outside world and its stresses and strains, far away. Golden leaves rained down in the courtyard from an aged oak; there magnificent beeches standing singly, low branched chestnuts dropping conkers, avenues of limes, made lovely our way to the long lake. White gulls were reflected therein, and small waterhens fussing between the lily pads. A robin trilled and a small wren's voice was loud and clear, all else being so still.

Blundells must have been sorry to part with all this. Henry Blundell's niece, wife of Weld of Lulworth, inherited. In 1837 a younger son became Thomas Weld-Blundell of Ince, and his family continued here till the 1950s.

Butlers of Bewsey

Some artistic license was drawn into eighteenth- and nineteenth-century pictures of Bewsey Hall on the Mersey at Burtonwood near Warrington. It was very charming, a 'beausite', with fronting lawns, backed by tall trees, and swans preening themselves on the river banks. Less remains now to fire the imagination.

In the twelfth century the 'botellers' of the Earls of Chester came here as Lords of Warrington, and generations rode out as barons and knights of the shire to sit in the council of kings. With retainers wearing their badge, three covered cups, many Butlers went forth to war.

In 1579 after serving both Queen Mary and Elizabeth in turn, the accommodating Thomas Butler died. A few years later his son Edward, "last in the long line of Lords of Warrington", died too. The Bolds of Prescot thereafter replaced them in south-east Lancashire. Another side-branch of the Butler's tree, descended from a younger son of a thirteenth-century Lord of Warrington, was of Rawcliffe, Kirkland and other estates in the Fylde until the eighteenth century. Of these Butlers, see the Fylde family histories.

In old books tradition takes up more space than history and fact. A Bodleian M.S., "to be relied on with regard to main facts, corroborated by tradition and the horrible event retained in north country annals", perpetuates one legend.

Bewsey Hall in 1840

About the beginning of Henry Tudor's reign, imagine Lord Stanley, Sir Piers Leigh and Master Savage meeting one dark night on the south bank of the Mersey, and at a signal from a hall window rowing silently over the moat in leather boats, and so breaking into the sleeping chamber of Sir John Butler and his lady wife. The same false porter who brandished the signal light, a "grim false-hearted knave", led the three "foemen fierce" to his master's bedside. First they made a "ghastly corpse of the faithful chamberlain", then Sir John

> With wicked hands and weapons keen
> Him piteously they slew.

This was not the end of the Butlers. A little page carried off, unseen, the infant heir in a basket. When the evil porter stopped him, he said, " 'Tis Sir John's head I bear." He then ran from Bewsey to hand the babe to the friendly Austin Friars in War-rington. So says the ballad.

In truth Sir John died thirty years before Henry VII became king, so could not have refused 'Lord Stanley's' request to be one in the cavalcade of gentry accompanying the King to Knowsley —the reason in the ballad for Stanley's vengeance!

So, leave the Bodleian story to the ballad singers, and keep to fact. There was some cause for Butlers to dislike the Stanleys, Thomas especially for he rebuilt Warrington Bridge before his stepson's visit, depriving the Butlers of pontage (tolls for goods brought over the river), which they had levied from 1285. However, the children of John living at the time of the royal visit should have regarded Stanleys with some gratitude, for when he inherited as a one-year-old, and his three little sisters all 'infants', his mother Isabel Harrington was victim of a most cruel abduction. She, an unprotected widow, was violated, forcibly married at Bidston by a man called Poole and carried off to a lonely corner of Wales. She must have later escaped, or been abandoned, for Sir Thomas Stanley of Hooton found her at Birkenhead, and appealed on her behalf to Parliament for redress. Her ravisher was never brought to justice.

Many earlier Butlers were characters from chivalry and romance. William the Butler fought valiantly in Edward's Scottish campaigns. His grandson, William of Bewsey, joined Thomas of Lancaster and was in at the murder of Piers Gaveston, for which he was pardoned, and switched sides. He was Keeper of the Peace in Lancashire in 1323, which required him to raise men for defence against the Scots, and to join the King for service in France where he became 'Le Chivaler'. His son Richard took part in a daring rescue of a noble prisoner from Charles de Blois' camp in 1342, and for his heroic part was extolled in Froissart's chronicles.

Sir John, his successor, took his twenty local archers to fight with their king in Acquitaine, and to serve behind Richard Assheton, commanding in the Irish wars, with ten men at arms and thirty archers bold. In 1389 he fell into the hands of Barbary pirates and was ransomed.

What tales were told round the fire in Bewsey's hall in those days when Butlers were great, brave, and respected by kings. Sir William was renowned as a fearless fighter; he died of pestilence at the siege of Harfleur. His infant son became Sir John when Edward IV was king. His life story is most complicated—and his love life mixed up. His first wife Margaret Gerrard of Bryn died in 1452, after which he made an unfortunate match with Isabel, Lord Dacre's daughter, who kept her earlier marriage to Thomas Lord Clifford a dark secret. When this marriage was dissolved John wed Margaret Stanley, a widow. Their son, ten-year-old Thomas, was to have been knighted when the little King Edward V came to his coronation. The coronation was not to be, and the knighthood was deferred until peace was cemented and the white Plantagenet rose grafted onto the Tudor stock. When Henry VII and his wife Elizabeth were crowned he received his long-awaited knighthood. In 1513 he lived on to talk of Flodden, where many of his tenants and retainers were killed.

The family seems to have waited for coronations to acquire honours. Thomas received the accolade from Henry VIII at Anne Boleyn's crowning. He was content with two wives, the first marriage, to Peter Legh's daughter being dissolved. His successor, another Thomas, also married twice, firstly Elizabeth Huddleston, secondly Anne Norris of Speke. His heir Edward was a sore disappointment and source of anxiety, so unreliable, profligate and spendthrift that Thomas decided to lease Bewsey to his daughter Elizabeth. The youth was mixed up with the more extravagant at Elizabeth's court. He was guest of the Earl of Leicester during the royal visit to Kenilworth in 1575, after which —maybe because of money losses—he tried to mortgage on expectation his estates to William Booth of Dunham Massey. He was a bad lot by all accounts. He refused to consummate his marriage with Jane Brooke. Therefore, seeing no future for the Butlers if Edward the heir had a hand in it, his father debarred him from all claims after his death. A few years later the Boteler estate had a new owner, Robert Dudley Earl of Leicester. Bewsey Hall then was "environed with a fayre moat, over which is a strong drawbridge. The manner house is large but one half of it is decayed—the other half is a new building and not decayed".

There were no more Butlers here, never no more! The Irelands, yes. They entertained James I. Rectors of Warrington pulled down old parts, and altered the hall—so that only a Tudor south wing is left, together with the depression once a moat.

The Norris Family of Speke

 When Butlers lorded it over Warrington and the Asshetons at Ashton upriver, downriver near Liverpool lived the Norrises from King John's reign to George I's—through five centuries. Norrises produced soldiers and statesmen, like Sir Nicholas who was thrice M.P. for Lancashire in Edward III's Parliaments.

Then at Speke the clear Mersey water flowed shallow over a

nearby ford at low tide, at high water they ferried a boat to Cheshire; both methods meant important links with the outside world. For their shield they bore a fess azure, a blue wave, the bright river at their garden gate. They were not completely at ease with neighbours, so a moat gave a feeling of security, with drawbridge and high outer walls.

Like Molyneux and Blundells, the Norrises saw no reason to change their faith permanently in Tudor times. In spite of great pressures, they remained Papists and received royal favours under Queen Mary and James II during periods of temporary preferment. They were behind Charles I in the Civil War, and no doubt would have been Stuart Loyalists and Jacobites in plots and risings in '15 and '45 had they been around at the time.

But the last male Norris had died and Mary his heiress was a Beauclerk; her husband was as much of a gay lad, gaming, drinking and 'womanizing' as his grandfather, the Merry Monarch. Topham Beauclerk was friend of Samuel Johnson, being something of a literary gent, and, with associates like Reynolds a great patron of the arts. He was hardly a steady husband, however, and drove his poor Mary to end her life, and her child's too. She threw herself in excess of grief into the moat, and both were drowned—a tragedy which gave Speke Hall a haunted room, a pale ghost and an empty cradle rocked by invisible hands.

The Tudor Norrises were great at demolition and rebuilding, and the old hall replaced by the new in Henry VII and VIII's reigns. In the high panelled hall, with its south windows framing the wide Mersey and the green hills of the Wirral, they banqueted, and entertained guests, and for background music minstrels played

Norris' Tudor Hall, Speke

in the gallery. So little is changed that I can imagine all this today.

Sir William was required to attend military musters with local men, and to go off at the sovereign's bidding to wars—usually against the Scots. Norrises were with the Stanley forces at the Battle of Flodden, with Molyneux and Blundells and their tenants too. Speke was represented in the Scottish invasion of 1544, and Norris followers were among victorious English soldiers who overran Edinburgh and looted Holyrood Palace. Edward Norris received £5 6s. 8d. yearly from the Crown for himself and his heirs forever. Was this for valuable books looted from Holyrood and handed to the Crown? His father wrote: "Edys Borow wasse wone ye VIIIth daye of Maye ano dni Mcccccc XLIII and yt ys boke was gotty and broght away by me, Willm Norres of ye Speike". It was said Sir William's share in the pickings was a supply of rich panelling stripped from the palace walls and that his son used it for the great hall. Both completed interior works at Speke in the 1550s and 60s—when a west wing was added.

At this time Norrises realized Speke with its ford and boat was going to serve as an active reception and departure post. The red danger light was burning warning that Papists were in for a bad period. They called in skilful contrivers of hides and secret rooms, all to be well used in Elizabethan times. Ornate carved fireplaces and overmantels, the intricately designed plaster ceilings, panelled walls, and a garden gate dated 1605, all concealed some hidden chamber, peephole, listening place or cunning entry to a veritable rabbit warren of escape passages, running all round the hall.

Very closely guarded secrets, these hides were known only to the head of the family and his elder sons. Of Sir William's nineteen offspring and Edward's nine, of the Romanist families into which they married—Molyneux and Blundells included—many came to know the confining walls of these places of concealment. Many came and went, helped over Mersey's dark flood by night and away to safety in the Wirral or Wales; priests, some.

Norrises had constantly before their eyes their favourite texts, lettered in gold. One over the Great Chamber door reads, as a tip for the night: "Slepe not till you have well considered how thou hast spent the day past. If thou have well don, thank God. If otherwise, repent ye." Also: "The straightest way to Heaven is God to love and serve above all thing."

As a family, Norrises, because of wealth and importance, had immunity from arrests and imprisonment not enjoyed by their in-laws. Their hides were so effective all raids were foiled, or only half-hearted.

When James I came to the throne they sat in Parliament and were mayors of Liverpool. One refused to pay the King's demand for Liverpool to have its charters, freedoms and liberties renewed. "Nothing doing," cried Norris, leading a protest. "It is not lawful."

By the 1620s Norris sons were entering trade or commerce. Large families were proving a liability and younger sons were expected to fend for themselves when Norris finances were strained.

Young Henry, Sir William's seventh son was bound apprentice in 1622 to a London merchant, who received £100 to teach the youth his trade. But he was taught nothing, was used as a mere servant, "sent with a basket four or five times a day to market", and treated so badly he pleaded to have his indentures cancelled. "Begone," cried the master, and thrust him out of doors. Henry was the eighth apprentice he had ill-used. Henry later joined the navy and as Captain Norris fought well in Flanders.

The Civil War left them almost destitute. The men empowered by the Commonwealth to seize Royalist property bled the Norrises to the point of exhaustion. In 1659 Norris accused the sequestrators of "taking from Speke goods, chattels valued at £500", and demanding payment of £200 a year for ten years as valuation of revenues from rent, lands and corn mill. Other large sums were exacted from these Papists and Royalists, and payment was rigorously enforced.

Later Norrises fared well when James II put Roman Catholics in posts held formerly by Protestants, but Thomas adopted the wiser course when William and Mary reigned, for he conformed: he became High Sheriff—and he 'married money'. The Aston heiress brought a useful and necessary £2,500 dowry. Their eldest son gained preferment by becoming a Whig politician.

It is not surprising that, like many Liverpool burgesses of 1700, the Norrises also had the urge to see far-away places. Mersey ships were about to sail to the Seven Seas, and Norrises in them, lusting for high adventure and rich reward.

In 1699 William Norris set out to India with the King's commission as ambassador and a new baronetcy on his shoulders. The King's ships reached the East Indies safely but once there Sir William was beset with ambassadorial troubles. However, he sent home rich cargo ahead of his own ship, including hoards of rupees and his Sword of State carried before him on his visits to the Great Mogul. This sword was in 1702 presented to Liverpool Corporation as a memorial of respect—for Sir William had not returned. He died near St. Helena. The wealth which reached Liverpool caused endless litigation among his many relations, his seven brothers all squabbling in the share-out.

One brother, Edward, a doctor of medicine, was with William in the Indies. John was a seaman in the merchant service; he did no good and intemperance left him a very poor man. Richard became mayor of Liverpool, was an M.P. and Sheriff of Lancashire. Thomas, as eldest, was kept busy caring for Speke.

It was unfortunate he had but one child Mary, who married the son of the Duchess of St. Albans, the mistress of Charles II. She was Lady Sidney Beauclerk, her son the 'rake' Topham Beauclerk, and in the next generation the last son of the once-proud line. In 1797 Speke Hall was sold to a West India merchant, Mr. Richard Watt, and his descendants remained there till the 1920s. By 1942 Speke was at last safe and secure in the care of the National Trust, its ancient atmosphere protected, intact.

Speke Hall, praise be, after Watt's restoration had never suffered a neglect which was the unhappy fate of the ancestral halls of many of their contemporaries in Lancashire.

I have stood alone in the cobbled courtyard under Adam and Eve the venerable yews, on a still autumn evening, owls flapping in the dark branches, and time has effortlessly rolled back four centuries to the days when the yews were planted—and the Norris (Norres or Noreys) family were set on building a far finer house. I have spent summer afternoons idling in the surrounding gardens looking at the magpie design of the walls and timbered gables; and winter afternoons—only a rare visitor about—enjoying the magnificent panelling and fantastic Italian stucco ceilings, the Tudor work of the great hall. Norris heritage is now ours!

Hollands and the Lords of Upholland

Upholland has character in striding steeply from hill foot to church, historic buildings between humbler cottages of the village street including the Owl Inn and the courthouse wherein Stanleys once conducted manorial business, as the badges of the Eagle and Child and Three Legs of Man tell the well-informed.

The Stanleys feathered their family nest when, being close to

Henry VII, they acquired what the unfortunate Lovells lost through being loyal to the House of York. The Lovells in their earlier turn had arrived at Upholland in 1372 after Sir John married the sole heiress of still earlier Lords, the Hollands.

Lovells are almost forgotten, though they were here for two centuries. Theirs is a tangled history; more tradition than truth has survived. One Lovell, a Lancastrian, wandered 'they say' as a penniless suppliant in Flanders, fugitive from a Lancastrian defeat, the Battle of Barnet. Another sharing a similar sad fate, being on the wrong side at the Battle of Bosworth Field, fled the land as a traitor, returned to fight again on the wrong side at Stoke and again was forced into exile in Flanders. His corpse 'they say' was washed ashore at Dover. Somewhere these stories, the details hazy, could concern the same Lovell. All that is certain is that a Lovell did forfeit Upholland for High Treason; and in came Stanleys.

Of the Hollands, pre-1372, little survives, for the meagre relics of Robert's fine priory are merged with the parish church, and nothing remains of the great hall where he—Edward I's noble follower to Scots wars and Welsh campaigns; a baron; Chief Justice of Chester, Rhuddlan and Flint; Guardian of the Northern Marches and Governor of Beeston Castle—feasted with his equals and dispensed hospitality and largesse to the poor.

"God's blessing on good Sir Robert", the poor folk cried, leaving his table with 250 more every St. Thomas à Becket's Day replete with good food, or recipients of the daily dole of trencher bread at his gates.

Neighbours nearer to him in the social scale were less vocal in their appreciation. Jealousy of a great man showered with honours by Thomas Earl of Lancaster, whose right-hand man and military aide and organizer he was, soured their judgement. Being so close to the great earl he became acknowledged leader of the faction opposed to his cousin Edward II. Thomas attempted to overthrow Edward's favourites, and Hollands were wholeheartedly behind him, especially after the humiliation of Bannockburn when all looked to the earl for new leadership. When he delegated more power to Holland, neighbours in south-west Lancashire, numbering those who wished to gain favour by siding with the King, decided their chance had come to curb his power. In 1314 Banastres, kinsmen of Samlesbury, Bickerstaffes, Bradshaw of Haigh, Sir Henry of Lea and disgruntled tenants of the earl gathered, stormed the arsenals at Liverpool, Halton and Clitheroe castles and, well armed, attempted to battle with the earl's supporters, Nevill, Pilkingtons and the Holland forces at Preston. A semi-private war, it was soon ended and the Banastre party crushed. A reconciliation of the royal cousins was short lived. The north was in turmoil, Scots raided and devastated the country as far as Samlesbury and Chorley, and worse came about after the cousins fell into worse disagreement, a rift this time impossible to breach. Earl Thomas in open rebellion was defeated at "Borobrigg, sad Borobrigg", refused trial by his peers and hurried to a traitor's death.

Holland, it was said, had deserted his prince before battle, but he lost estates, was thrown into prison—and the Banastres, rejoicing, began to overrun lands once his and to poach the earl's former domains, joining the King's friends in raiding and plunder. At the same time the earl's supporters, now dispossessed, as openly took from lands once theirs as by right. Holland men took from Bradshaws, Leybourne's party "took weapons, farm gear, harvested and garnered wheat etc." from Holland's Hall at Samlesbury, carting all away in stolen wains. Never was Lancashire so sorely distressed. The King himself arrived at Upholland, and from old Sir Robert's priory dispensed justice. Four years later he was dead, and young Edward III at once released Holland from his cell at Dover Castle and restored his lands to him.

No one ever solved the mystery of Holland's death within a year. Murder, poison? His 16-year-old heir showed wisdom beyond his years, wise counsellor and brave warrior like early Hollands. His two younger brothers moved in royal circles, one finding a royal bride, Princess Joan of Kent, who on Thomas' early death married England's darling, the Black Prince. Her Holland sons became half brothers of princes and of the boy king Richard II who conferred dukedoms on both. Four Hollands were founder-members of the Order of the Garter. The higher the climb the greater the fall. Inevitably the Hollands fell when Henry of Lancaster contested their young half-brother's throne. Henry IV exacted punishment, and a Holland head fell.

The next heir stood for the House of Lancaster. Soon—the end of the name, in come the Lovells. Out go the Lovells—in come the Stanleys. Such is Upholland's story—and little enough to show for it today.

Bradshaws of Haigh

A Wigan bus conductor who thought I was a stranger said confidentially as we passed near the canal wharf, "We're passing Wigan Pier." The old music-hall joke! The man sitting behind me spoke. "There *was* a Wigan peer—Earl of Balcarres. That's what it means."

Whether the joke began there I am not prepared to argue. The twenty-fourth Earl of Crawford was created Baron Wigan of Haigh Hall. How come? His mother, last of the Bradshaws of Haigh, married Alexander Lindsay, sixth Earl of Balcarres, in the 1780s. A change of name after almost five centuries.

The Bradshaws entered into Haigh when Sir William's wife, Mabel Norris (related to the Speke family), handed to him her great inheritance—Haigh, Blackrod and neighbouring lands—in Edward I's time. These two were the chief characters in Wigan's sad tale of Mab's Cross, which has a number of variants.

The likeliest story is this. Sir William joined local discontents in the Banastre Rising—a purely Lancashire affair directed against the Earl of Lancaster and the powerful Holland family. As this was the losing side he became an exile for some years, delaying his return overlong.

A woman of property with no man at her side in those disturbed lawless days had a most unenviable position. At last, believing Sir William was dead, Lady Mab married a "Welch knight". An unfortunate alliance for he took all control into his own hands and misused her. Or so it appeared to the absent husband, returned after ten years to Haigh, disguised as a pilgrim or a beggar, as he watched at the hall door. The Welsh knight's behaviour was cause of great distress to Lady Mab. Had she been happy, his intention was to go away—and disappear. Now he declared himself. The Welsh knight took flight, but not until he reached Newton Park—in Makerfield—did Sir William catch up. They fought, and the Welsh knight was killed.

The two were happily re-united. Lady Mab for her bigamy had to do penance "by going onest every week bare-foute and bare-legged to a cross nere Wigan called Mabb Cross".

The Bradshaw tomb in Wigan Parish Church is splendid, in recent years restored, possibly for the second or third time. The effigies had a chequered history. In 1829 they had become unrecognizable, battered and covered with many coats of whitewash. Wiganners called them Adam and Eve! Then, in the 1850s Lord

Haigh Hall today

Crawford set an artist to touch up poor Lady Mab. She looks so meek, hands piously folded; but Sir William was past redemption, a new effigy was made to replace the old, copying the original posture with hand on sword hilt.

In her will, Lady Mab made provision for there being no "issue of her body" nor a son of Sir William's to inherit. In this case the "Manor of Haw" was to go to Alan Norris her cousin; and all her other estates "for the gentleness she found in him" to Sir William's brother John, he being "full of children". The lands did all come to this John Bradshaw, passing in the male line until the eighteenth century.

By this time Haigh had brought them wealth because of the rich minerals underlying—coal, and a special coal called cannel. Leland in Tudor times told how Mr. Bradshaw had found "moche se cole in his ground very profitable to him". Every travel writer

95

made his way to Haigh to see the mines in Bradshaw's Lordship and to marvel at the properties of cannel cole. It was so called because "a piece when lit was both candle and candlestick, its light so bright folk could work by it. It was so clean it would not soil a white cambric handkerchief." It was soft, easily workable and could be turned with a lathe. Skilful craftsmen produced objects like stand dishes, trinkets, ornaments and portrait medallions from it. In their gardens a summer house was built entirely of blocks of cannel "by Lady Bradshaw's direction". Polished, the coal looked like jet. The pity was "Sir Roger had no way of sending his coles to London, a ready market, for want of water carriage to the sea."

The first Sir Roger, baronet, was created by Charles II—and three succeeded him in turn, each developing the mines. One engineered The Great Sough to take the surplus underground waters from the pits to the Douglas river a mile away—"17 years of labor, charge and patience" for seventeenth-century labourers. They were increasingly interested in the canalizing of the Douglas and cutting waterways to take coal barges down to the Ribble estuary and the sea. Better, cheap water transport and their fortunes were made. In 1792 folk could buy cannel cole at the pit mouth for 5d. a hundredweight; at the canal quay it cost 7d.

The Bradshaw's coal mines made their wealth but severely undermined their ancestral hall. It was so shaken at its foundations that the twenty-fourth Earl of Crawford in 1832 decided to rebuild, the new site levelled to bedrock. He was his own architect. He wanted a fitting background for his pictures and books —like Stanleys, Blundells and Towneleys, he was an art collector and bibliophile. He designed a stone-cutting machine to be used at the Parbold quarries whence the building material came; it was carried along the canal to Haigh. He also decided on the iron work to be used, directing the making of it. The french window fastenings are special, simple burglar-proof latches of his own invention.

Nothing of the ancient house remained except for an eighteenth-century staircase, three wood arches and linenfold pillasters of an arcaded screen. Not even an authentic gallery for Lady Mab's ghost to walk!

There must have been good labour relations between the miners and the Haigh pit owners. In 1842 came a period of great unrest in the Wigan area, with many mines closed and the men on strike. The Wigan men planned to attack Haigh Hall. Haigh miners, officially on strike too, made a cordon round the Hall.

They were not going to allow outsiders to upset the Old Lord. "We'll see he has his port in peace," said they, and remained on guard until the danger of attack was over.

Earls of Crawford and Balcarres no longer live at Haigh. With Wigan Corporation as owners, the Hall has a new role, for use of the public. Corporation gardeners have taken over from the earls' and fine shows they make in the hot houses, the long herbaceous borders, and in what is my favourite place—the quiet, sheltered walled-in rose garden.

Heskeths of Rufford

Down the Douglas where it slows down to the lowlands is Rufford, and the ancient hall of the Heskeths on its banks. The family history is equally involved with that of Martholme, and I have dealt with it in the Calder section.

It is a National Trust property on the main Preston-Ormskirk highway, as good a place as Speke or Samlesbury for recreating the background against which Lancashire landed gentry of Tudor and Stuart times lived. The great hall is splendid, its fine roof timbers supported by large angel corbels, and at the Speres end stands a rare example of a moveable screen. Every room is fascinating, and there is always an added fascination in knowing William Shakeshaft was one of Hesketh's household, a member of his band of players in the 1580s.

Rufford Hall

Standishes of Standish and Duxbury

 In New England, U.S.A., is a town called Duxbury wherein stands a statue to Miles Standish, a man of Duxbury near Chorley, Lancashire, who left England in the *Mayflower* in 1620 "for conscience sake".

Miles had a military record, he "had fought in the Low Countries where he joined the Church of Leyden. He came with the first planters to New Plymouth and bore a deep shair of their first difficulties", his training of them in defence of the new colony showing his skill as a soldier.

New Englanders think highly of him. So did Longfellow, who wrote a very long poem about his 'Courtship'. Local chronicles after his death in 1656 told how this brave man "expired his mortal life, grown ancient, and sick of the stone"; he had, after "suffering much dolorous pain fallen asleep in the Lord". His great-grandfather was a second (or younger) son of Standish of Standish, and "real heir of estates surreptitiously detained from him".

Miles it was understood could trace his pedigree back to Hugh Standish of Duxbury Hall, son of Ralph and grandson of Thurstan of Standish. "He was deprived of his rightful inheritance", and a Chorley Church register which one may examine has a peculiar omission relating to the entry of his baptism; an erasure —or merely a damp mark?

In Chorley Parish Church is a most imposing Standish family pew, with canopied throne-like seats and the armorial bearings of the family crowning the structure. The mayor and civic dignitaries occupy this pew on important occasions. A new American flag hangs over it, a gift from New England.

Another relic of earlier Standishes is in a wall cavity in the chancel. In 1442 Sir James of Dukesbury presented a "relic of St. Lawrence's head brought by his brother Sir Rowland and Dame Jane his wife out of Normandy". Twenty years later this 'sacred object' decided the patron saint in the church's dedication. Modern experts have cast doubts on its authenticity. Maybe Sir Rowland bought in good faith the bones of some quadruped!

The Duxbury Standishes outlasted the senior line of Standish, not dying out until the 1820s. They dwelt in a most "elegant mansion" on Yarrow banks—now, alas, no more. They had gone their own way, conforming whilst their Standish kin remained Papists, fought as Roundheads and not for the Stuarts; so they survived the difficult and dangerous Tudor and Stuart times. But within the Duxbury family were divided loyalties.

In 1640 the father, a Puritan, was Preston M.P. He opted for Parliament in the Civil War, had a son killed at the Manchester barricades fighting for the King's cause. Another brother was a colonel in the Parliamentary Army, yet his son fought as a Royalist and received a baronetcy from Charles II. They obviously decided for themselves, as did Miles when he realized there was little prospect left for him in England.

The ancestral hall is no more—carried off to be rebuilt on New England soil. Standish Church contains the family chapel at the east end of the south aisle, where a storied window shows how the heroic Ralph Standish saved the young king Richard II's life when confronted by the peasant mob at Smithfield. Anticipating that Wat Tyler was about to strike, he slew him—and for reward became Governor of Scarborough Castle. A new east window contains the figure of Miles Standish in his role of Military Governor of New England.

The Civil War brought constant action to Standish, being so near Wigan the Royalist H.Q. The Cavalier Standish had many hair's-breadth escapes from death when hiding in or near the Hall. A probing sword blade came within a fraction of an inch as he crouched in a chest. Only the sleek cat dozing on a sunny window ledge of a farm where he had raced for refuge, once saved him from discovery. Cromwell's men stamped to a halt at the door. "No need to waste time here," said their captain, "No stranger lurks within. See—the cat sleeping undisturbed—!" To keep the story alive, a house in Pepper Lane, 'Cat in't Window', is plentifully embellished with black cats.

Standishes of Standish opted for the losing side throughout Stuart times, and were closely watched during periods of Jacobite conspiracies, real or imagined, by the Whig informers. Standish Hall was on the 'black list'. The chief informer, Lunt, in 1691 swore he had visited the Hall with secret messages from James II. Another Whig witness described at the Manchester Trial his de-livering a pack of arms in his carrier's cart, and depositing them in the inner courtyard there. The prisoners at the trial, swore this John Womball, had divided the weapons and drunk the health of King James. Another informer had seen Stanley of Hooton distribute money on King James's behalf and had helped in discovering bridles, saddles etc, hidden at Standish, obviously for use in a Jacobite rising.

So much evidence piled up against the Standishes it was lucky for them the false witnesses were finally discredited and, with most of the Lancashire plotters, set free. There was probably real cause for suspicion. In 1757 secret letters were discovered, written by Standish to James II in invisible ink.

The family stood firm, despite earlier misfortunes, fines and losses for their loyalty to the Stuarts. Standish, without weighing the possible consequences, made his way to Preston to meet the Jacobite rebels of the '15. His friends—the Dicconsons, Towneleys, Butlers and Daltons—were there too and all were caught, imprisoned and tried for treason. The death sentence was passed on him. In June 1716 a reprieve came.

Standish Hall, 1900

There was not one of the family left to take part in the '45 rebellion, for the male line had come to an end at Standish—and the Duxbury branch, never having had a romantic attachment for any Stuart, were for King George and Protestant succession. They, and Duxbury Hall, outlasted the Standish branch for only a century.

Dicconsons of Wrightington

Other active members of the Standish/Wigan group in the seventeenth century were the Chisnalls and Dicconsons, as loyal to the Stuarts and the Jacobite cause.

The Dicconsons were of Wrightington, where their Hall is now a well-known hospital within a park alongside the Parbold road. In June the fish ponds are extremely beautiful in their spectacular frame of rhododenrons and azaleas. In Tudor times they had a town house in Wigan's Standishgate and, being Papists and friends of the recusant John Gerrard, they were able to hide wanted men; it is probable that Nicholas Owen, kept busy devising secret rooms, worked for Dicconsons here. The house was used for mass whenever priests were in the district. Later it became the 'Dicconsons Arms'.

According to a brass memorial plate in Eccleston Church William Dicconson was "sometime Steward over that Most Honorable Household of that Most High and Mightye Princess Anne Duchess of Somerset" in 1604. A century later a namesake in exile with James II at the Court of St. Germain was both Treasurer to the Queen and Governor to Prince James Edward—hence the Jacobite 'badge' pinned on those in England.

Dicconsons were listed among the Lancashire Plotters and outstanding in the subsequent Manchester Trials. In August 1691 the spy Womball after "delivering"—so he said—at Standish Hall took another load of arms to Wrightington, "but half way there the mare stumbled in a pit and pistols were scattered over the road". Later, when a search for hidden arms was made at Standish, Dicconson was present and vocal in his protests. "It is no new thing to hear of sham plots", he cried, "forged by persons with interest and design". Stanley of Hooton cried out also against the 'bloody conspiracy'.

Mistress Dicconson helped to expose and discredit the false informers. Friends of Grays Inn had heard from a man called Taafe anxious to help the 'plotters'. Taafe agreed to meet the chief informer and provide him with masses of new invented evidence sure to 'discover' so many Jacobite suspects "no prisons could hold them". The Whitehall bloodhounds were willing to believe any story against a known Stuart loyalist, especially if he were wealthy. Taafe's fake list was shown to the Chief Justice who bade him keep it till the trial.

A Dicconson tradition tells how young Roger, disguised as a carter, entered a lawyer's office in Preston and offered information to a gathering of Government spies. What details he gave, all bogus, to willing ears! Names, detailed descriptions and, above all, their movements on certain days. The informers took copious notes of Roger's 'suspects'. "Remember to tell the Court these men were seen by you at their homes on the days I have given you." They were all days of obligation—Corpus Christi, Church festivals, saints days and the like—so well marked each would recall exactly where he was on that special day.

When Lunt the arch informer stood up in Court at Manchester the detailed evidence confused him, as was intended. He knew not one man on his list, had never visited any at his home. Faced by the prisoners he did not know which piece of evidence applied to which. All had perfect alibis for the days on which they were supposed to have committed some act of treachery against the state.

Roger Dicconson was present in a vagabond role. "Throw out that rogue", shouted the attorney when he presented himself as witness for the prisoners, "That fellow is a branded felon". Roger bared his back. Sensation in court!

At the acquittal there was great rejoicing in Jacobite houses around Wigan. However, all did not escape fines or forfeiture. William of Wrightington was forced to leave England, his estates confiscated and handed to the Bishop of London, except a portion settled on Roger his younger brother. Staying on at Wigan Roger watched the troubles from the sidelines, helping friends in prison, exposing faked charges.

In 1707 occurred an abortive French invasion on behalf of the king 'over the water', which brought suspicion on Roger; again he was able to wriggle out skilfully and avoid arrest. In 1715 he was not so fortunate in explaining why he was with the Jacobites. Outlawed as a rebel, he joined the large emigré set in Flanders. He was at the Spaw in Liège in 1717 when Nicholas Blundell the Diarist made a visit. The association of Lancastrians was strong in banishment in those years between the two risings.

Chisnalls of Chisnall Hall

 Chisnalls of Chisnall Hall espoused the Stuart cause so wholeheartedly they too suffered. The Hall had a sad fate, for it was sitting on rich coal seams; when the old family disappeared subsequent owners exploited the mineral wealth. Now what remains is the N.C.B. office, and the estate lies beneath mountains of accumulation, black peaks which were only partially removed when M6 was made through them. Mineral shale came in useful for motorway hard core.

Chisnalls were not on the 1639 list of Papist recusants, but in the 1650s, as Royalist malignants, they had to pay £800, compounding for annual rental of lands confiscated.

Andertons crop up in many places and on scattered pages of history. The old name of Rivington on the Yarrow was Andertonford, and their Hall was nearby. They were of Lostock too, near Bolton, coming into this estate, formerly belonging to Irelands of Lydiate, when the last squire, as a Jesuit, had to relinquish in 1644 his ancestral lands. Sir Charles Anderton, who married Margaret Ireland, became the second baronet of Lostock. Like the Euxton Hall Andertons, long considered 'stubborn' Papists, and kinsfolk of the Gerrards and Tyldesleys, equally 'stubborn', they were dogged by troubles, religious and political. In Thurstan Anderton's time—he built the hall at Euxton in 1594, a very useful reception centre it was for priests making their secret ways across Lancashire—they were constantly watched as potential lawbreakers.

With such ancestry the Andertons were inevitably loyal to the Stuarts. Christopher Anderton commanded the beleaguered garrison holding Greenhalgh Castle for King Charles in 1644.

Sir Francis Anderton was caught with the Jacobite rebels at Preston in 1715. He was just able to avoid the death sentence, but his property was forfeited. This property had become his when his elder brother Lawrence made his religious vows; as a Papist priest he was debarred from inheriting. Lostock was seized by the Crown, but not Lydiate, which was claimed as hers by right by his widowed mother, Margaret Ireland, who determined to hold it intact for her son until better times returned. To ensure this she 'willed' it to a Protestant lawyer, knowing he would keep

Lostock in 1770

103

his trust. He died too soon, and his son, discovering the deed, claimed Lydiate as his: he won his case.

Sir Francis lived quietly as a tenant at his country home, Lydiate being good for hunting and shooting in the eighteenth century. Brother Lawrence, hoping to preserve his rights in Lydiate, decided to renounce his vows and so he conformed in 1726. He died the same year. No Andertons allowed themselves to be involved in the '45 rebellion.

It was left to a Blundell nephew to buy back the Lydiate inheritance from the lawyer's son, after Sir Francis's death in 1780. In the nineteenth century the husbands of two heiresses shared Anderton's properties. To Mr. Stoner passed Anderton Hall, to Sir Charles Tempest went Heaton. To Charles Blundell of Ince Blundell, and to Thomas Weld Blundell in 1834, went Lydiate. The Euxton Hall family outlived the other Anderton branch lines.

Charnocks of Astley Hall

Charnock is a 'good old Lancashire name', with long associations with Heath Charnock, Charnock Richard and Astley, where early tenants of the Knights Hospitallers of St. John belonged to the same family.

Impetus to build for posterity came in Tudor times, with ownership of the land they stood on. This older part is now at the back of Astley Hall, originally half-timbered on four sides of a courtyard. In the next century Richard Charnock rebuilt the south side, in a far more flamboyant style, typically early Jacobean.

The present frontage rises to three storeys, more window than wall, the central door opening into a magnificent great hall with a most splendid plaster ceiling—richly adorned compartments with flying cherubs complete with bows and arrows, festoons and flowers—the great achievement of a later generation with high-flown ideas. And we should be glad they did 'think big'.

The last Charnock at Astley Hall, 'one-eyed Charnock', dying during the Commonwealth, had an only daughter as heiress, her husband being son of Sir Peter Brooke. They 'thought big' too, pulling down part of the old Charnock house, raising this *coup d'oeil*, which surprises and delights all who come suddenly upon it, reality and reflection in the still waters of a lakelet.

On the walls are numerous portraits of Brookes' wives, daughters and Cheshire ancestors. I look at them, then imagine them here, as living people. They must have looked well in these beauti-

Astley Hall, Chorley

ful rooms, promenading in the long gallery which runs along the upper storey of the hall, stepping with dignity or grace down the handsome dark-oak staircases, with background music of Arne or Purcell.

Astley Hall is Chorley's precious and well-cared-for possession which we are now free to enjoy. Brookes, who took such pleasure in creating a fine home for their heirs and successors, in turn failed to produce sons. Parkers—kin of the Calder Valley Parkers —carried on when Susanna Brooke married Thomas Towneley Parker. On the walls is a goodly array of portraits of parents and their children in late-Georgian finery. They sat at dinner in the great hall round the long oak refectory table which was brought here by Robert Towneley Parker from Extwistle Hall.

The Parkers survived here until 1906—a long innings. A nephew, R. A. Tatton, inherited, but eventually made his splendid gift to the town in 1922.

In history the owners of Astley had their share of troubles. 'One-eyed Robert' was an interested party when it was agreed by Chorley's town fathers that the decayed schoolhouse should be rebuilt by public subscription and the old grammar school given a second start. Robert generously offered bricks for the building and £6 in money. In August 1648, when Robert as a

Royalist had to compound for his Astley lands—this cost him £260—and life was hazardous, his park and Hall were commandeered and overrun by Roundhead troops. There could be truth in a tradition that Cromwell slept at the Hall in the so-called Cromwell Room—in the old part of the Hall, a fine oak-panelled Tudor room—but not in the so-called Cromwell bed—of the right period, but 'imported'.

The Roundhead officers were so pleased with Chorley's hospitality they actually decided unexpected arrears of pay should be handed over for use of the grammar school "in the Church yard". Major Assheton's brigade presented £86 3s. 3d.

Many of the Charnock's friends and neighbours were less enthusiastic about the presence of the victorious Roundheads. These were the Royalist Ffaringtons of Worden, Leyland, the Andertons of Lostock and Euxton, and Molyneux relations.

In 1715 the Chorleys of nearby Chorley Hall also chose the doomed-to-disaster cause of the 'Chevalier de St. George', being taken with the rebels at Preston, as were the Gillibrands of Astley and the Andertons. Later their confiscated estates when sold by auction put £5,000 into Parliament's exchequer; these were bought back by the eldest son of Susanna Brooke, who lived at Cuerden Hall, whilst his mother with her first husband Towneley Parker, and later as Lady Hoghton, wife of Sir Henry, dwelt at Astley Hall. The joint estates made R. J. Parker owner of extensive acres—the green park of Astley and well beyond, almost to the domains of the Andertons of Euxton. Chorley's share of this gives the town a precious green belt.

Pilkingtons from Stand to Rivington

The Pilkingtons had more than their share of ups and downs, from Norman times when the first known and named Pilkington was given a land grant near Bury. Being a 'trusty' of the great De Grelley (Greslet), as a man of sound judgment and integrity he was called to the baronial courts at Manchester. This first Pilkington had an outlying hunting lodge at Stand. All his family were land-greedy in those days. Alexander Pilkington acquired much around Rivington Moors and on the Pennine slopes at Worsthorne above Burnley. His grandson did even better when his Chetham bride brought with her Whitefield, Unsworth, Crompton, Sholver and Wolstenholme manors—scattered holdings useful to provide for numerous sons, and give rise to many family feuds.

Adam Pilkington in a bitter quarrel killed the brother-in-law of the Chetham heiress. Men then were quick as Westerners on the draw: out came swords and daggers at the least provocation. Only with wars to fight were energies directed into legitimate channels. Roger fought so bravely in foreign fields, in France with Edward I, that he was given £100 from the royal exchequer in payment for military aid. He lost twice this amount in Edward II's time when, in siding with Earl Thomas of Lancaster against the young king's

Great Hall Barn, Rivington

minion Gaveston, he was taken prisoner. This time he was pardoned, but not so in 1322 when he was with Earl Thomas at the tragic defeat at Boroughbridge, taken and again clapped in prison. Two hundred pounds was collected for his release, but he died soon afterwards. Few long survived when freed.

A number of Rogers carry on the family history. The next Roger won Alice of Bury's hand and more lands with her. There was a Roger, a staunch Lancastrian who fought behind John of Gaunt, now 'Old Lancaster'. His son fought bravely with Henry IV in Scotland and was knighted at Agincourt by Henry V. Their wives hardly saw their menfolk and children forgot fathers in those warring days. The Margery Pilkington abducted in 1431 by

107

a gang of men from Blackburn way—De Clayton of Great Harwood and thirteen Liveseys—and carried off together with "£40 of goods" was probably a lonely unprotected wife with an absent husband. She did not seem over-anxious to return to him. Nor were her abductors punished.

In 1483 Sir Christopher Pilkington died without male heir. After four centuries an heiress took Pilkington land around Worsthorne to Sir John Towneley. Other less-known junior branches came to the fore.

About this time Pilkington's Lancastrian loyalties were transferred: Thomas Pilkington the next head of the family became a great fighter for the Yorkist cause, which proved in the long run an unfortunate change-over. Edward IV favoured and trusted him. He was twice High Sheriff and created Knight of the Bath. But for the Pilkingtons Nemesis was near. Their choosing Richard III's side was their undoing, for after the Battle of Bosworth Field all was lost; all they possessed was handed over by the victorious Henry Tudor to his stepfather, Thomas Stanley. This is why the Earls of Derby still own most of the South Lancashire manors once held by Pilkingtons.

The Stanleys were particularly fond of Stand and often went there on hunting sprees. It is now an elevated, built over region.

These heavy losses were not enough to destroy the Pilkingtons. They threw in their lot with Lambert Simnel, with those who hated Henry VII so much they believed, or preferred to believe, the young claimant was genuine. Many northern gentry fell at Stoke in 1487, Pilkingtons with them.

Was this when a Pilkington in hiding, his life in jeopardy, acted as the man with the scythe, the family crest? Or was he an ancestor in Edward II's time? Or some unnamed Pilkington far back in history? "Now this, now thus," is their motto—once well endowed with riches and lands, now in poverty—pictured, a country yokel in parti-coloured tunic, scything.

One bought back from the Stanleys their old Rivington lands, and there the late Tudor Pilkingtons won honour and credit. They dwelt in their ancestral hall above 'Andertonford' over the Yarrow (the Andertons their near neighbours) and sheltered by moors rising steeply to the beacon on The Pike and wild heights called Winterheld, Winter Hill.

One rebuilt the old church at Rivington about 1540. Educating his many sons was a costly business. James, the second son of Richard, was an outstanding scholar of St. John's College Cambridge, a Protestant by conviction, who did not change his religion when persecutions began with Mary's accession. An exile, he lived among the Protestants of Flanders, like Alexander Nowell of Read and Edward Sandys of Graythwaite. They returned soon after Elizabeth's accession and each rose high in the church, Nowell as Dean of St. Paul's, Sandys to be Archbishop of York, and James Pilkington as Bishop of Durham. His predecessors, clerics often compelled to become soldiers in periods of border strife, had not always found their cathedral close a pool of tranquillity; neither did he. James was there with his wife and family when the northern lords, Papists sworn to free Mary Queen of Scots, broke into Durham Cathedral precincts intending to pull down the Protestant clergy. All were compelled to flee for their lives—the Bishop, they say, in beggar's disguise. When this Rising of the North was quelled the Bishop returned with his wife and some of his twelve children.

In Rivington Parish Church is a copy of a painting on wood. The original, scorched by fire, is at the Rivington and Blackrod Grammar School; the copy, painted in 1833, was placed on the north wall. There portrayed are James, with ranks of solemn-faced sons kneeling behind him, and his wife, with rows of prim, doll-faced daughters kneeling in like manner. The background shows Durham, and dark hills which could be those of Rivington.

Having so many children in need of schooling, James Pilkington knew what was involved. In 1568 he founded a new grammar school near Rivington Church. He drew up a detailed list of rules to guide the early governors and masters. Stress was on training good Protestants, yet several sons of 'lapsed Papist' families were on the roll. There were periods when Norrises and Sherburnes were "Protestants through Prudence", and Standishes too, the Duxbury branch producing Miles Standish, a Puritan soldier among the Pilgrim Fathers.

The rules?

Those that can speak nothing but Latin,
At meat they shall not be full of talk, but rather hear what their elders and betters say,
Those that are too sturdy to obey and take correction from the master, to be banished from school.
No weapons may be carried, except a penknife.
No wagers are to be made when playing archery.
Dicing and gaming forbidden.
The Governor's duty is to search, spy and learn how every scholar behaveth himself.

No brawling or haunting alehouses.
Boys to be encouraged to read the Scriptures to the family in their lodgings each night.

Pilkington boys were so many their parents had to dig deep into family coffers to send them on to university. In the next generation poor Robert Pilkington could no longer continue at Rivington Hall. Two local buyers were ready, the Levers and Mr. Breres. Levers' daughter, Jane, married an Andrews; they bought the Breres' portion. In 1774 an elegant 'modern' house arose adjoining the venerable great hall barn, replacing a 1694 rebuilding of the ancient Hall. Some original masonry and mullioned windows remain at the rear, where not so obvious; the new façade was splendid by local standards.

Mr. Andrews also erected the square stone tower on the hump of the Pike to be a shelter and picnic place for his guests. In Elizabeth's time night and day watch was kept by guardians of the beacon, waiting for signals of the Spanish Armada; and Napoleonic invasion threats brought watchers to the Pike also.

PART THREE

*Families by Ribble, Darwen
and Hodder*

Hoghtons of Hoghton Tower

For years Hoghton Tower Hill and the sky above were my weather glass, foretelling with accuracy the rain from the west. That hill, heel-shaped, rising sheer above the Darwen gorge, gave Hoctonam its name and the pre-Norman family, of the blood of Earls of Mercia and Northumbria, their title. They survived the Conquest ensuring their future by marrying daughters to Ivo de Tailbois and Hervey Walter, powerful barons, and a son Adam to the daughter of Warin Bussel Lord of Penwortham.

De Hoghtons were respected in kings' councils and did kings' business as sheriffs and M.Ps. They successfully avoided wars and rebellions, though it was touch and go when Richard de Hoghton's bride, heiress of Lea, was closely related to the fighting Banastres who started a rising, lost and brought many others down with them. They issued intact from the Wars of the Roses.

They distinguished themselves on home ground. Sir Henry's many bastards were children of Helen Mossop, eighteen years his mistress before he made an honest woman of her, Papal Bull conferring legitimacy on their offspring. Two of these sons showed outstanding valour in Richard of Gloucester's forces and were both made knights banneret by Edward IV. Hoghtons did well by their 'natural' children, who frequently outnumbered those born in holy wedlock—which of course was usually a business arrangement, romantic love being found outside matrimony. Each took his father's name. One Henry became the King's officer in the royal park and chase at Leagram, his son founding the Hoghton line of Pendleton Hall.

In Henry VII's time Sir Richard wed one of the Assheton co-heiresses, Alice, seven years his senior. She died young, which led to much family bickering over her inheritance. The second wife's lot was as unhappy for her spouse, the King's trusty officer, who smoothly organized the dissolution of Whalley Abbey and dispersal of the brethren, an excellent and highly thought of High Sheriff, at home was a bully "and seducer of other men's wives and daughters". He shut his door in the face of the visiting herald in 1533, so he received an unsatisfactory write-up—well deserved and no one but himself to blame: "Sir Richard putteth away his lady wife and keepeth a concubine and hath divers children by her." A lively place, with three broods running around at the same time!

Richard and Alice Assheton's son Thomas, on succeeding in 1559 read the temperature wrongly. He thought the time opportune for leaving the damp bottoms by the Darwen for a high-level site where the old hilltop watchtower had stood, there to build a fine hall, full of light and space but within courtyards and enclosing walls. As a Papist he thought the future looked rosy. When Protestant Elizabeth soon followed Mary he did not think fit to abandon building plans. Work went on apace until a housewarming gathering in 1568, when a guest was Doctor William Allen, a dangerous Papist highly suspect, a watched and wanted man.

De Hoghtons were singled out and suspect too. They left the Tower without rousing suspicion, took ship down the Ribble from their Hall at Lea; and so to Flanders and long exile. They escaped the troubles of the following year when, with assurance of success

The outer gateway, Hoghton Tower

114

from Allen and the Pope's blessing, all Papists were ordered to rise against Elizabeth and her Church and with promise of Spanish aid put Mary Queen of Scots on her throne. Mary's letters expressing the belief that "in three months I will be queen and mass said over the kingdom" were intercepted. The Rising of the North was quelled, the rich rebels allowed to pay heavily for release, those with lands forfeited them in return for pardon; the poor, 800 humble northerners, were hanged.

In 1570 the Pope excommunicated Elizabeth "the pretended queen and those heretics adherring to her", and freed from oaths of duty and fidelity to her, all Papists. Those who disobeyed were bound under the same curse. The Hoghtons were well out of it, and when the Queen sent half-brother Richard of Park Hall to Flanders to offer Thomas a free pardon if he returned and submitted himself to her laws, he refused.

Richard was also a Papist, friend of the Jesuit Campion who organized printing and distribution of Popish leaflets printed on secret presses. He had been seen at Park Hall, it was reported, for which Richard was imprisoned for 'harbouring'. Not long afterwards Thomas' son, now a priest, was arrested and flung into Manchester prison, hardly having done more than set foot on Lancashire soil. He died in jail. His father died soon afterwards and was buried in Flanders in 1581.

Brother Alexander inherited Hoghton. At Lea Hall he had singing boys in his household, one a teenager, William Shakeshaft—and this during the 1580s, the poet's 'lost years'. Alexander soon succeeded by his half-brother, a second Thomas, a Protestant also who would have lived peacefully at Hoghton— but Fate stepped in. He was killed in a fray with a neighbour Baron Langton of Walton—of which more is written in the pages on the Banastre-Langton family—and his son, a minor, was placed with a guardian, Gerrard of Bryn, till old enough to return—with his Gerrard bride—to Hoghton. As atonement for his father's killing the heir had received Langton's Manor of Walton, thereby almost doubling his lands.

Richard and his growing family started to make the silent hall hum with life. His heir Gilbert went off to Court and became a favourite of King James, by whom he was knighted, a matter of Hoghton precedence among English baronets. He became a great friend of Prince Charles who had his loyalty years later when the Civil War tore Lancashire apart.

How different from the days of their youth! Then young Gilbert

115

was adept in music and dancing, a most lively lad; in the war he was advanced in years yet there was not a single skirmish, fight or far-riding campaign in the North-west in which the old Cavalier did not take active part, the leader of the King's men in Leyland and Amounderness.

Because of his 'malignancy' Sir Gilbert stood to lose everything to Parliament. His eldest son, opposed to the father in all things, was a Presbyterian, a Cromwellian and had almost brought the old man "with grey hairs to the grave" so sorely was he distressed by the 'traitor' in the family. Through him, however, Hoghton was saved for those who came after, the inheritance intact. This did not prevent Sir Richard giving allegiance to Charles II, nor future Hoghtons standing firm in full support of the Protestant Church and the Protestant succession.

During the war years I had the freedom of the Tower and the gardens. Sir Cuthbert was interested in my newspaper articles dealing with the local scene and invited me to his home. His, and the first Lady de Hoghton's, hospitality was heart warming. Under their roof was an evacuated convent from the South Coast and a gentle old Belgian evacuee priest from Louvain; and at lunch one day were a famous air ace test pilot from Samlesbury and commanding officers from regiments stationed locally. I thought of three centuries earlier when in the same hall Royalist military movements and campaigns were planned—and how one similar snowy February day in 1643 (this was the third centenary) the one and only tower went up in smoke!

Young Captain Starkie and Roundhead troops were that morning massed at the gate demanding surrender. The garrison realizing no resistance was possible accepted Starkie's honourable terms, which meant they could ride forth, heads held high, swords in hand, drums and pipes playing. After which the troops poured in, eager for loot, overrunning the courtyards, the silent rooms, and down to the cellars, a great attraction! To talk of Hoghton 'Towers' is an exaggeration. There was never more than one, placed centrally, and that was soon to disappear in a cloud of smoke and falling masonry. A tremendous explosion rocked the buildings. Later sixty mangled bodies of men from Calder and Pendle, young Starkie among them, were found. And how the disaster occurred no one knows, for sure. The Royalists denied leaving a timed device ready to fire the gunpowder stored in the cellars. One writer put the blame on the soldiers, "being burdened of their swearing, drunkenness, plundering, and wilful waste at

116

Preston, by the help of powder—laid a train fired by their neglected matches, or by that great Soldier's Idol, Tobacco, caused the explosion". The pious Puritan who penned this saw it as a sign of divine displeasure. "Oh that this thundering alarm might ever sound in the ears of our Swearing, Cursing, Drunken, Tobacco abusing Commanders and Soldiers unto Unfeigned Repentance."

One day Lady de Hoghton, daughter of Macdonald of Glencoe, showed me the few treasures which have survived the years. A disastrous fire destroyed most in the pantechnicon carrying them back to the Tower a century ago. Thomas the Exile's portrait, being small, was always held by the family, and two charming pastel drawings of small sons, by Gainsborough—"Like my two boys don't you think?"—were also preserved. As for the other ancestors we must imagine what they looked like.

Sir Henry Hoghton of Jacobite times supported the forces of law and order. "Rather German Geordie and his Protestants than James and his Popish priests" was his line in the '15 rebellion. Letter writing and reading despatches kept him busy.

Sept. 29. Fear no militia can be raised before Parlt. meets, in time to stop rebels.
Sept. 30. From Ld Derby. Secure all powder we can. Any danger of being insulted by the Papists at present unlikely.
Oct. 9. Rumours of 4000 fresh Highlanders.
Oct. 18. 6000 Danes expected to join rebels.
Nov. 6. Regiment to rendezvous at Preston. Not to face rebels but secure arms from falling into their hands.
Letter from General Wade to Mayor of Lancaster—sent on. Do not attempt to repel rebels but in small bands to fire over hedges to keep them from pillage and plunder will best embarass them.
Nov. 9. All Protestant householders aged 20–30 in England to be put under discipline.
Rumour rife and accurate information hard to come by.

When the Jacobites entered Preston he was far away with his family, whereabouts in Yorkshire unknown, and the militia also absent!

Sir Henry chose to live at Walton Hall, whereupon Hoghton Tower, empty and neglected for generations, became a sorry sight. In 1820 poor families tenanted one wing, weavers worked at their looms in another, farm animals roamed around at will. Courtyards were overgrown; in noble apartments where Hoghtons entertained King James and his retinue in 1617 there was "loathsome, rotting upholstery on the chairs in the King's Rooms, paintings fallen to pieces on the wall of the lovely Green Room, oak panelling hanging drearily".

Charles Dickens looked around, his quick eye noting William III's statue "like a guardian ghost in the courtyard", and gazing at blocked and broken windows, fallen beams, rickety floors under which rats scuttered, guessed this was a derelict farmhouse. From the minstrels' gallery he gazed down on the 'farm kitchen'—alas for days of past glory!—"fearing to see I knew not what dead alive creatures come and sit themselves at the old tables and look up with what dreadful eyes, or lack of eyes, at me".

"If only the Hoghtons would return, reviving the days of yore", sighed local antiquariens. And, of course, they did. Two brothers came a century ago, rebuilding, modernizing Hall and farms. Since when another century of change, and a backward swing of the pendulum.

For some years after the war Hoghton Tower was a much visited stately home, opened by Sir Cuthbert to raise necessary revenue for upkeep. Through the gateway arch folk passed from outer to inner courtyard, wandered into the banqueting hall to read with amazement the menu old De Hoghtons thought adequate for "the king's being ther". (The king was James I, who in 1617 in merry mood gave the accolade to a prime loin of Lancashire-bred beef—"And Sir Loin it has been ever since". In fact, sirloin was the name for this joint in Tudor times!) They saw the King's Table, the King's Room, and passed through linked bedchambers, each with fine panelling and four posters, into the gaming room painted with golden guineas. A splendid Tudor great house, one of the best afternoon's out in the county. But the thirteenth baronet, Sir Henry Philip Anthony Mary, has closed the gates once more.

Banastres and Langtons of Walton

 Early in the twelfth century the Hoghtons, quietly settled on their manor by Darwen banks, had new neighbours downriver: Banastres who said they were with William at Hastings and did so well in the Conquest they were given lands in North Wales, just beyond Offa's Dyke. They kept the Welsh so firmly on the right side of the border defending the English/Norman settlement that the King offered them as reward rank

of baron and the Fee of Makerfield. In 1130 Robert Banastre, very well-in with De Lacy, the great baron and landowner in these parts, received Walton from his hands and built his hall there. His land stretched far up the Darwen towards the moors.

To give them credit they gave away acres too, oak woods at Walton where the Stanlaw abbey porkers grew fat; and, as thanks to the good prior of nearby Penwortham, young Robert, who had been brought up by him as a child, gave more property in 1280.

Robert later found a suitable match for his granddaughter with John Langton, the son of good neighbours, the Barons of Newton, next to their Fee of Makerfield. Young John's brother was Bishop of Chichester and as Edward I's Chancellor had the King's ear. When the king was in merry mood after the birth of the first Prince of Wales, he readily granted to his Chancellor, for his brother John, fair charters for Newton and Walton.

Eight generations of Langtons lived at Walton, and their Banastre kinsmen south at Bank on the Douglas river, dangerously close when this truculent branch were up to the neck in rebellion, bringing half the families of south-west Lancashire into strife and bloodshed with them. The Walton cousins trod warily, and survived.

Each generation was extremely well connected by marriage. In 1500 the infant heir was handed into Henry VII's protection and he duly chose his stepbrother Edward Stanley as the little Langton's guardian—which provided him with an infant bride, a 'natural' Stanley daughter. Were parents philosophical and resigned when their little ones died like flies? Six sons of this marriage died, five daughters survived; and a grandson at eight years of  age inherited his grandfather's lands and title. He held them only twenty years, losing the Manor of Walton and bringing dishonour on an ancient name. He was lucky, thanks to the Earl of Derby's intercession, to save his life.

Neighbour feuds connected with straying cattle were the only reason for the tragedy. In November 1589 Widow Thomazine Singleton discovered a greedy brother-in-law had driven off her kine and oxen. A kinsman, Anderton of Forde, obligingly found them, then drove them to Lea, Hoghton's pastureland. Hoghton's servants found them and impounded them at Lea. So, as the next move, Anderton asked Thomas Langton to help him recover them, which he did with great vigour. He at once armed himself, tenants and friends, other gentlemen and yeomen of the Fylde with "long pikes, guns, Welsh hooks on long staves, swords, daggers, bows, arrow, bills"—the complete armoury from his hall?

Thomas Hoghton was not caught napping. Also with friends and servants, "with staves, one pike, one gunn charged with hail shot, 2 pistols, bows, arrows, swords and daggers", they waited from 9 p.m. at his 'mansion house'. The Langton party arrived from Preston Marsh one hour after midnight when with war cries of, "The crow is white," from his side, and, "Black, black," from Hoghton's, battle commenced.

"Richard Baldwin of Langton's company and Thomas Hoghton were there and then slain but by whom it does not appear." So wrote the distracted Hoghton widow next day to the Earl of Derby at Lathom and to friends, Sherburnes of Stonyhurst.

Thomas Langton had disappeared. Later he was apprehended at his hiding place, John Singleton's house, Broughton Tower, "where sore wounded he lay in a bed of sickness". It was the earl's responsibility as Lord Lieutenant to see justice done. He was engrossed with Baron Walton's business for some time; at the first trial it proved well nigh impossible to swear in sufficient impartial jurors. Eventually Langton was tried by the Star Chamber and, though he had merited the death penalty, 'frumgeld' was substituted. The Manor of Walton was given to the heir of the man he had slain.

That was not the end of the 29-year-old Langton. He found favour with James I, as a baron attending him at his coronation. When he died in 1605 he was buried with the royal and great at Westminster Abbey, but Wigan Church has his memorial. "To Oblivion and ye true bones of Sir Thomas Langton of ye honorable Order of ye Bath, Baron of Newton Makerfield ye last of his name descended from a most ancient famous and far renowned family in this county. A Gentleman yt many times tugged with extremities and made warre with the worst of misfortunes."

Today Walton Hall farm stands near the Darwen, all that remains of the place where Hoghtons lived in the eighteenth and nineteenth centuries, where Prince Charles Edward had his H.Q. in 1745, and the Duke of Hamilton and the Royalists in 1648. I doubt if anything is left of the hall the Banastres or Langtons knew.

Fleetwoods and Heskeths

The ill-starred Baron's possessions came to his cousin Joanna Langton, and through marriage to the Fleetwoods, to her son

120

Sir John. The Fleetwoods bought the Priory of the Blessed Virgin at Penwortham, building on its site their hall, much admired by seventeenth-century travellers. This hall has been demolished. But in the parish church steel helmets and a leathern jerkin painted with martlets, the family emblems, said to have been "left by Oliver Cromwell" in fact belonged to a Fleetwood. One son married Cromwell's daughter.

Fleetwoods produced eminent sons. In Elizabeth's time William Fleetwood was Recorder of London; in James I's reign, Sir Robert, his brother, was Attorney General to Prince Henry (who died young) whilst others stayed in the north and made good alliances. They were twice coupled with Bartons, Sir Thomas with Ann Barton of Smithills, and her brother with Ann Fleetwood her sister-in-law. Fleetwood was bestowed as Christian name on the little Barton heiress, her grandfather's successor, whose infant marriage to young Molyneux was dissolved—she but four at the time and he little older—so allowing her to marry Richard Shuttleworth, heir to Gawthorpe.

The two were married at Woodplumpton and eventually took possession of the newly-built Gawthorpe Hall; all their twelve children were born in the family bed now in the long gallery.

One Fleetwood was of Heskin. Another bought land formerly Cardinal Allen's at Rossall, not far from the sandy 'star hills' destined to be site for the new town and port of Fleetwood; this came after a Fleetwood heiress of Rossall and Penwortham had become wife of a Hesketh. Fleetwood-Heskeths made an excellent combination, both interested in their estates and with a passion for land reclamation.

As early as the seventeenth century when Mr. Fleetwood leased old Banastre's and Langton's Bank Hall—rebuilding as in the style of Elizabeth—he planned reclamation of its mosses and swamps; at first in 1692 with no success, but in 1714 the first canalizing was improved and higher floodgate thresholds kept back the high tides. This time it was not 'money down the drain'.

The present-day landscape of west Lancashire owes much to Fleetwoods and Heskeths, from Southport's coastline to Wyre mouth. The present-day head of the Fleetwood-Heskeths lives at a charming old house, Meols Hall—the name derived from sand hills rather than from the Celtic 'moel'—not far from the Ribble estuary, an old site owned in King John's day by De Coudrays, way back in the family tree. When Rufford Hall and Martholme were main seats this became the inheritance of a younger son.

Here the family also remained of the old faith, and, being well placed on lonely shores to welcome and shelter men in danger, their Hall was provided with priest's hide. Tradition claims Edward Campion was here, and that a ghostly apparition, a priestly figure in brown, began to walk after his time. Rebuilding was done from Commonwealth days, but within fifty years or so it was reduced in size and occupied as a farm—until one of the Heskeths decided, after his ambitious plans to build and develop the new Fleetwood had weighed him down by heavy debts, to sell Rossall Hall to a body anxious to establish a boys' school there. Family treasures were carried to Meols, the new home by the same tidal waters of the Irish Sea. What valiant work they wrought on their unproductive marshes, winning a belt one and a half miles deep from sea and swamp, carrying on the good work of generations.

Old Families of Livesey Hall and Pleasington

Receiving letters from readers in foreign parts is one of the pleasures of being a writer. I had a long correspondence with a Livesey whose ancestor was in the ship arriving on American shores after the *Mayflower*, a son of the James Livesey who as final flourish to his fine new hall above Darwen banks carved "To God The Glory. 1608". When news reached Rhode Island that Livesey Hall was to be demolished a letter came, "Can't we have the date stones; we would treasure them." I think had it been possible the English community would have bought the masonry, transhipped it and rebuilt on alien soil "for posterity's sake".

Liveseys contemplated building their new hall about the time the Hoghtons had completed theirs downriver. James's handsome dining hall, his nephew Ralph's north-east wing with huge chimney stacks, and a grandson's south wing of 1689 made a very fine house.

They were a prolific family—scores of their name inhabit the Commonwealth—but down the generations of stay-at-homes numbers dwindled till there were no sons. Nephews followed childless uncles, and in 1760 the last heir left Lancashire to live on Uncle Ralph Livesey's estates in Yorkshire. Two Blackburn brothers, land buyers with money gained from the industrial prosperity now reaching Blackburn, bought Livesey Hall in 1805. William Feilden let his half to a tenant farmer, but Henry allowed his share, the handsome central hall block and north wing, to

Livesey Old Hall before demolition

remain empty. Decay was rapid, and in the 1960s the end came, housing development taking over.

Neighbours across the valley at Pleasington Old Hall fared better. A young and wealthy heiress, Dorothy Winckley, in Elizabethan times was snapped up by three husbands in turn: her first, John Southworth of Samlesbury; her second, Thomas Hoghton, another Papist who took necessary precautions by contriving secret hides for the harbouring of travelling priests; and her third spouse, Lawyer Ainsworth, who had seen the wisdom of conforming. He brought safety and security and opportunity to improve the old house. The secret rooms were walled up, but he left work completed by Thomas Hoghton. He did not touch the oldest part, kitchen, buttery and dairy of the north wing, nor the chambers above which still had their timber uprights and walls of lath and plaster infilling. The façade, completed in 1587, had a fine double porch with the arms of his wife and three husbands carved on its door lintels. It was an intriguing porch, with its old tethering rings for horses and door panels of riven wood—bolted together, so they say and I believe—by 365 nails, their flattened heads protruding.

From the chamber above are wide views over gardens and duck-pond to the Pleasington Fields and the ridge where Livesey Hall once was.

About the time Puritan Liveseys were emigrating, Henry Ainsworth, an old boy of Blackburn Grammar School and a student

123

with advanced nonconformist ideas, was forced to exile in Flanders. Amsterdam gave his kind of religious refugee warm welcome, especially as in his case a reputation as a scholar had come ahead of him. Jewish scriptures being his special study, he was ready to seize the chance of learning more. He found a rare diamond, advertised the fact and eagerly opened his door to the Jew who claimed it as his. Henry would accept no monetary reward. "All I ask is that you arrange for me to talk with your rabbis on the Messianic prophecies". The Jew departed, neither he nor the diamond being seen again. Ainsworth's body was found, poisoned. Students of Hebrew acknowledging their debt, "to him we are

Pleasington Hall

obliged for his skill in Jewish antiquities, and our candles are lit from his", mourned his untimely death.

In 1777 sale notices were put up and "Pleasington Manor and its fine desmesne" auctioned at the 'Black Bull', Blackburn, and knocked down to Richard Butler of Preston for £11,000. Butlers, who built a Pleasington New Hall from their own quarries of Butlers Delph, were for some time to be neighbours of the Feildens when their respective wives induced them to leave their homes in King Street next to their offices and factories and to build mansions in keeping with their present affluence, at Witton Park and Feniscowles. This was happening all over Lancashire as the Industrial Revolution gained impetus.

Joseph Feilden who bought a share in the Manor of Blackburn for £2,880 had a town house at the church gates, went to Bath when his health required it, and married off two daughters to two young Asshetons of Downham. He called himself 'Gentleman'. Son William wed a Jamaican heiress and in 1808 set up house in the romantic hollows, beyond rocky heights on Darwen banks at Feniscowles, fancying himself as a country gentleman with 1,000 acres of game preserve and deer park nearby, as well as grouse moors in Scotland. He welcomed guests in full Highland chieftain's dress, Lochaber axe at his side. Henry his brother lived in a grander mansion overlooking wider parkland at Witton, his walls covered with valuable works of art.

Genealogists rooted back into the past and brought out a family pedigree with the Earls of Denbigh and the illustrious House of Hapsburg on the branches of the Feilden tree.

Why are they no longer part of the local scene, their halls gone? Both were driven away, victims of environmental pollution, the once clear rivers Blakewater and Darwen darkened, the sweet rural air tainted. Industry had made them; it also took away.

Earl Peel's Ancestors

One of the most prominent Lancashire families in modern times did not cross over from Yorkshire until the Industrial Revolution was dawning, settling near Blackburn in the mid-seventeenth century.

On the byroad from Sawley Bridge to Bolton by Bowland stands a very pleasant late Tudor farmhouse with a stone cross at its garden gate—Bolton Peel, looking across green Ribble pastures to the wooded heights of Bolton Hall. It seems likely that when Pudsays erected their fortified hall there in Edwardian times there was a pele a little distance away, an extra look-out for any approaching danger. The men who dwelt on the spot called themselves Del Peles. When living quarters grew too cramped they built the more commodious Elizabethan house and farm buildings not far away, and continued farming.

About 1640 Peels decided to move. Blackburn came to know them. One Robert of Hole House set his houshold to spin and weave wool and linen into cloth, and when they could not spin quickly enough to keep up with the weavers he employed local spinsters. Another Robert Peel in 1731 bought a larger farm then called Oldhams Cross on the ridge of Stanhill; he was a widower with four sons and seven daughters. William Peel carried on the house—now renamed Peel Fold—with the help of Jane his wife

125

and some of his eight children. Cousins were still at Hole House near Oswaldtwistle until Robert II thought prospects were brighter down in the market town of Blackburn.

They proved much better. 'Buttermilk Bob' who once sold milk in the little town found a place in the history of Lancashire textiles as 'Parsley Peel'.

Robert Peel, who began farming at Fish Lane in Blackburn in 1750, was no ordinary part-time farmer, part-time weaver. Soon he joined his wife's brother, an early calico printer, and his partner Yates, the landlord of the 'Black Bull' and put his capital into the printing venture. All had high hopes they would make the fortunes of 'Haworth, Yates and Peel'. Friendship was further cemented when Peel's third son, Robert II, married Yates's daughter.

There is a good tale with some truth behind it. War had cut off supplies of patterned materials and women were tired of plain. A flash of inspiration, and Robert searched his garden plot for a simple shape. He picked up a parsley leaf, rushed indoors where a maid was ironing, smeared a dye over the leaf pattern he scratched on a pewter plate, and told her to iron it off on a piece of cloth. A cotton print!

Parsley Peel! Intelligence, foresight, hard work, ambition—he and his brothers had them all and were carried far above their beginnings, destined to outdistance all competitors in the field of Lancashire commerce. He worked on new printing methods—and succeeded. He employed the local genius James Hargreaves inventor of the Spinning Jenny, in his Brookside printshop, installing a carding cylinder.

Oldhams Cross, Peel Fold

The partnership ended, but not the friendship, when with Yates he set up new print works at Ramsbottom—and out of the county at Tamworth. These and his own large mills at Bury reaped a fortune during the wars with France. During 1800 they were the only mills working full out, and for the duration of the war they produced 100,000 pieces yearly with a clear profit of one guinea on each. Twenty years later the tide turned. "New machines have speeded up all processes, 20 times as much produced—and Peel's profits cut to one twentieth", reported one newspaper.

The brothers Peel by this time had each amassed considerable wealth, and were all halfway to being millionaires by modern standards. Sir Robert rewarded with a baronetcy for his readiness to raise his Bury workmen and train them to repel any French invasion which materialized, had also in a burst of patriotism given £10,000 to "promotion of the war against France". His reputation assured, he could retire from commerce.

His methods of using mordaunts to fix colours of great brilliance, "no one in England excelling him in beauty of effect, extreme precision of outline in the patterns used", had brought wide demand for Lancashire prints.

"He placed his many sons in situations where they might be useful to each other, the cotton trade best calculated to secure this. He imparted to them intimate knowledge of all branches of the manufacture", and all without exception became opulent and happy.

Opulent and happy in a totally different way, his third son Robert, born at Bury, educated at Harrow—where he is named with Lord Byron in the school song—and with the Peel virtues of intelligence, love of hard work and Lancashire grit, rose to the office of Prime Minister. Men praised or reviled him according to their politics. He stuck to his guns over Catholic Emancipation, help for distressed famine-stricken Ireland and the Repeal of the Corn Laws—the last-named being commemorated by Peel Tower on Holcombe Hill.

A young Robert Peel interrogated by the Law about a motoring misdemeanour gave his true name, whereat the constable thought he was 'taking the mickey'.

"Better come to the station," said he heavily.

"I *am* Robert Peel," said the lad, "and if it had not been for my father's great-great-great-grandfather you might not have been here."

Sir Robert Peel was patron of Thomas Lawrence, whose por-

Robert Peel's farm, Fish Lane

traits are in the possession of the present earl; friend of Arthur Wellesley before and after he became Duke of Wellington; man of many parts and father of many sons. The eldest son, Sir Robert, M.P. and Secretary for Ireland, was third baronet. The sixth and last of his line and name was a young midshipman when killed on H.M.S. *Hermes* in 1942.

Descended from the fifth son of the Prime Minister named after his godfather, Arthur Wellesley, the present young Earl Peel of Hyning is of the sixth generation; he is also the eighth baronet.

The late earl who died in 1969 was a great and staunch Lancastrian, preferring to live at Hyning near Carnforth, a nineteenth-century house in a girdle of woods, a quiet haven to retreat to after work involving his many business interests. His father, William Robert Wellesley, second Viscount Clanfield and first Earl Peel, in 1899 married the Hon. Eleanor Williamson, daughter of Lord Ashton, inheritor of the famous Lancaster works founded in the 1840s by James Williamson for the manufacture of oilcloth, American cloth and table baize, and now developed far beyond all dreams of the founder.

At the Hyning I looked through a thick press-cuttings book, the pages, yellowed with age, reporting the day-to-day movements, speeches, successes of the great man of his time. Sir Robert the Prime Minister. A source book of future history? Weeks of reading in it.

A Frenchman called Sir Robert "the most liberal of Conservatives, the most conservative of Liberals and the most capable man of all in both parties". Prince Albert, after Peel had been reviled by corn growers and merchants, wrote: "he is abused like the most disgraceful criminal but shows boundless courage . . . he is at this moment playing one of the most important parts in the history of his country". Of himself Sir Robert spoke in his farewell speech as Prime Minister, hoping his name would be "remembered with expressions of goodwill by those who earn their daily bread by the sweat of their brow when they shall recruit their strength with abundant and untaxed food, the sweeter because it is no longer leavened by a sense of injustice."

Upstairs in the guest bedrooms were copies of my Lancashire books; one day I autographed them. And I promised to do sketches of the Earl's ancestral homes. This took me to Bolton Peel and to Peel Fold—still much as early Peels knew them; but for the house in Fish Lane I had to use an early photo taken before demolition a century ago.

Southworths of Samlesbury

Because of a certain large brewery gaining permission to build on a large patch of its green acres, and local residents' fight to prevent it, Samlesbury during 1970 hit the headlines and had a fair look-in on the small screen. Some said it was sacrilege to allow industry to take over so green and pleasant a landscape; others said it was not so beautiful as all that and was partly spoilt already. No one stressed Samlesbury's importance in Lancashire history.

Traffic on M6 speeds by at a high level across the river. The Ribble, as I see it now, flows swiftly, bank-high after floods and heavy rains in its cradle in the Craven mountains. Children's shrill voices from the school ring across the pastures; silence wraps round the old church, and churchyard.

Not long after the Conquest Gospatrick—probably Irish/Norse with such a name—dwelt in the hall of his ancestors by Ribble banks. In 1100 he and all his kin were assembled for a great occasion, the consecration of this plot of earth by Irish bishops. A son-in-law, the Dean of Whalley, and the Vicar of Blackburn had both given their blessing for the new chapel and graveyard.

To find the site of Gospatrick's first hall by the river follow the lane and track to New Hall Farm. The male line ended three generations later, two heiresses marrying, one a D'Ewyas, the other a Holland. The Samlesbury inheritance eventually came to the D'Ewyas grand-daughter, wife of Gilbert de Southworth, who took the lordship and with it a host of attendant anxieties and troubles.

Gilbert's hall occupied a strategic position near an important Ribble crossing much used by north-south traffic—English going to the borders, and Scots in reverse, and more often than not neither of them up to any good.

Gilbert fortified the hall, its stone pele and surrounding barm-kyn wall—probably like many nearer Scotland—to safeguard his dependants when danger was upon them. The church also was

Samlesbury Hall, 1970

additional refuge—as in 1322 when Scots came in force and roaring mad from a successful raid, flaming brands held high ready to hurl. Preston was already in flames, and Samlesbury Hall was to follow.

The timber hall blazed fiercely but the stone pele, into which family valuables had been gathered, remained, smoke-blackened but intact. All moveable goods the Scots carried off, killing a brave steward, William de Holden, who tried to hold them off. Then they made for the church, overcame the men who guarded it, burst into the nave full of terrified tenants, caught up chalice, missal and psalter and the priest's vestments, threw their loot on two wains—and away. They went slowly, for eighteen stolen oxen required herding over the ford and along the Roman way to Ribchester, which they fired and looted also.

When the smoke had cleared Gilbert surveyed the damage. This spot was too vulnerable. He decided to rebuild, but two miles away, in the oak woods eastwards. And there today stands Samlesbury Hall, the fourteenth-century 'halle' with nearby timber from the woods for its construction, and additions made by descendants of the sixteenth century; a fine black and white hall on the Blackburn-Preston new road and open to the public.

As Lords of Samlesbury, Southworths held land from the de Lacys of Clitheroe and from the kings under whom their sons fought in every war and campaign, paying their military service by so doing. They did well in choosing brides well endowed with lands so that in time they were landlords from Samlesbury to Over Darwen, Hoghton and Mellor, to Middleton and Southworth in south-east Lancashire, taking their name from the last.

Each generation added something to the 1340 hall, one a domestic chapel, and Thomas (a young hero of sixteen at Flodden) thirty years later added a parlour in Tudor style to link 'Halle' with chapel. In his time new ideas were taking shape. Louvres to carry away smoke from open hearths in mid-hall had been good enough for ancestors who shook away the hailstones and snow and shrugged off discomfort. Thomas installed the modern wall fireplace in spite of warnings from Spartans. The minstrel gallery and the oriel window, which gives a good view of all going on in the courtyard, were more to everyone's liking, especially the womenfolk.

Those were good days, the last these Southworths enjoyed. Neither they nor their in-laws would have anything to do with the new religion. Sir John, High Sheriff, seeing portents of danger employed skilful designers of secret rooms and hides to contrive several at Samlesbury. He could not have foreseen what great risks his family were to take for generations ahead or that one John the priest would be canonized in Rome in 1970, or that he himself, for his "obstinate recusancy", would endure great sufferings.

In Mary's reign the Earl of Shrewsbury welcomed his services as "a tall and toward gentleman—a trusted soldier, valiant for England" when with 100 men, and 100 more ready, he shared service on the Scottish border with the Warden of the Marches in 1557. How different was the situation in 1587—the year Elizabeth's Council put the pressure on known Papists, searched for non-conforming clergy, and listed those doubtful in their public worship.

The next year a copy of a 'letter of submission' was delivered to the 'doubtful' to read and sign. They were asked to confess to disobeying the church laws, to harbouring priests, to non-attendance at church and refusing to take communion; and each had to promise "to behave as becometh good, humble, obedient subjects —and not to assist or comfort any person living out of the

Tudor chimneys, Samlesbury Hall

Realm". Many would not sign, including John Southworth, his wife Mary Assheton, Thomas his heir, Ann and sister Dorothy Rishton. They were declared 'obstinate'. John was named as 'obnoxious' on the official black list, and Samlesbury Hall marked with a cross on a map of Papist houses.

This was, as far as the Southworth's were concerned, the seal on twenty years of recusancy. They were watched when conspiracy was afoot to dethrone Elizabeth and place the imprisoned Mary Stuart in her stead. When a Spanish invasion was rumoured pursuivants paid many surprise visits to the Hall when searching for Jesuit suspects or Cardinal Allen's spies in Lancashire.

In 1581, when priest hunts were at their height and notable Jesuits like Edmund Campion and Simpson were passed in secret from hall to hall, arrests came thick and fast. Prison accommodation at Chester was so overtaxed the overflows were sent to Manchester's New Fleet, "Diet there being easier for their keepers."

John Southworth was the only one who could pay for his 'diet', but after long detention his state was so pitiable he humbly begged leave to return home on bond. The next year he was in prison in London, foremost among harbourers of wanted priests. They said he was too dangerous to be freed to return to Samlesbury. He refused Lord Derby's offer of liberty if he conformed. Later, back in Manchester, he was allowed to walk in the Collegiate gardens—now Chetham's Hospital and then owned by the Stanleys—but he had no other liberties and was forbidden to speak to anyone. Another year wasted away, his money grew short. Unscrupulous keepers overcharged him until Mr. Worsley saw to it that 13s. 4d. was all he must pay. At long last, because of age and "former service to the nation", they let him enjoy the air in Aldport Park also. He could now talk with others of private matters, Mr. Worsley being present. One command he would not obey—he refused to listen to Bible readings before and after meals. Also he threatened to disinherit his son John, who was less firm a Papist and tried to have his father's imprisonment eased. When he, and old almost-blind John Towneley who had suffered imprisonment at the same time, were offered release on £500 bonds to be paid in London, they journeyed south to do so. But on second thoughts the authorities decided to hold them there. Young John pleaded so assiduously for his father's release he finally succeeded.

Back home all seemed at peace. Daily masses were said in the hall or at nearby houses, though servants swore to searchers no priests had entered the Hall for many years!

Sir Richard Brereton (his tomb is in Eccles Church) came to Samlesbury one November with a large body of armed searchers, clattering over the moat and hammering at the door. They thrust aside frightened servants and began their task. They ripped hangings, tore away panelling and ripped up floorboards, slashed bedding, uncovering a hidden altar canopy, two brass candlesticks, in a vault fourteen "superstitious images", and eleven Papist books. Were the books found in the priest's chamber over the oriel, and was the blood that caused the so-called stain shed that day? With forty people lined up before him Sir Richard could not believe all were of the Southworths' household. Not with so much damning evidence piled around, and a searcher holding the crucifix just discovered behind a sliding door!

When Sir John died the estates were much smaller, and debts were not paid off for seven years. The family lived with much diminished resources, like the Blundells, Towneleys and other Lancastrians. One son distinguished himself as a lawyer. Christopher, a priest as fiercely opposed to Protestantism as his father, brought about the arrest of the widow of John, the one who conformed, by rehearsing an epileptic teenager, Grace Sowerbutts, in false evidence about local witches for her to give at Lancaster court. The falsity was exposed at the famous Lancashire Witch Trials. Jane Southworth, "a widow, no mendicant or aged beldame with gobber tooth and stooping gait nor the wrinkles of an old hag", was accused of terrible things. Sir John, it was said, had never liked her, and never passed her doorway—because he refused to have anything to do with Protestants.

Sir John was the only Southworth who could have refused a daughter consent to marry a Protestant—that being the origin of the White Lady story, the truth of which is unlikely. The Lady Dorothy who walks on dark nights is on no Southworth family tree. They said she died or disappeared after her attempt to elope had been foiled by her brothers, and after the death of her lover in a fight with them. Bodies of two young men were indeed found when the new road was being made over the old moat in the 1820s. If dark and secret deeds were being enacted in your home and you wished to allay the curiosity and suspicions of the household quite the best deterrent was to invent a ghost—a white lady, a grey man, a black monk. Fear prevented investigation of night creakings, dark figures flitting along passages, moving lights.

Naturally Samlesbury had to be provided with the White Lady, as a cover.

After the 1612 witch trials a reporter pinned the blame for them squarely on the shoulders of "a seminarie priest, a Jesuit whereof Lancaster hath a good store", but, said he, the women escaped death by the intervention of "Almighty God who made frustrate the practice of the bloodie butcher, Christopher Southworth".

When James I made his northern progress in 1616 the head of the family, a declared Protestant, was there to welcome him, and receive a knighthood. Honours like this did not lift financial burdens, however, for sale of the Pleasington and Samlesbury estates was soon necessary. His grandson following him was so heavily encumbered by debts that he offered the ancestral hall on the Ribble banks to a likely buyer, son of the wealthy Judge Walmesley, a very downcast young man compelled to rob his infant son of another slice of the Southworth inheritance. He was cut off at 24, his heir a short time afterwards and the second son lived only six years. Two daughters lost their inheritance to an uncle under a strict entail. This uncle gained a hollow victory over his nieces, for knowing nothing of family planning he had to rear six sons and seven daughters with revenues woefully inadequate. In 1675 Edward his heir found it impossible to support his children on the estate, so willingly accepted his aunt's husband's offer to take over manor and land, promising annual repayments for its recovery. These he found he could not honour. His cousin, son of the dispossessed co-heiress Mistress Walmesley, arranged the sale of manor, Hall, demesne lands, cornmill and kiln to John Bradyll of Portfield, a lucky speculator, for £9,150.

Bradylls were important now, and John's son married to a wealthy heiress with a palatial home, Conishead Priory. The young couple preferred to live there. So Samlesbury Hall came upon sad times, used as a tavern, wayside inn, handloom weavers' tenement and workshop, a select girls' school; and eventually up for sale on its timber valuation. Rescue came. Now it is open to the public when not in use for some banquet, business conference or wedding breakfast.

Osbaldestons of Osbaldeston

The half-mile horseshoe bends of the Ribble valley were rich plums dealt out by Norman lords to their retainers, manorial lords like the Osbaldestons who lived two loops upriver from the early Southworths. The early lords of Samel's burh and Baldhere's and Osbald's tuns were roughly contemporary.

Earliest Osbaldestons were probably Angles. It is on record that Aelsius, holder of rich acres, "eyries of hawks, hives of bees and fisheries of great value", in the thirteenth century, gave to Hugh, his son, Osbaldeston, and to William he gave Balderstone. Each built a hall thereon.

Osbaldeston Hall, 1970

Hugo's son was lucky when, in marrying Katharine Molyneux, he gained Cuerdale six loops downriver, and also her grandmother's gift of Over Darwen. Their son fell in love with his 'cousin', Margaret of Balderstone, so both manors came into Osbaldeston hands.

A great pity they had so much friction with neighbours laying claim to the same pieces of land. The husband of a Walton heiress said part of Over Darwen was his. It was poor moorish ground not worth the fighting over; but this did not stop them. This claim Osbaldestons hotly disputed. Some feuds continued for generations, trouble flaring up with Southworths, or Hoghtons, or Talbots, neighbours and as hot tempered. Only when sons followed barons or kings to war did the quarrelling cease—unless the women carried on the family feuds. Might was right in the sixteenth century, in the Ribble valley as much as in south-west Lancashire where Blundells and Molyneux, Molyneux and Stanleys took the law into their own hands to settle land disputes.

136

In 1556 Sir John Osbaldeston thought he had a water-tight case against Sir John Southworth. He said Darwynd Moor was his and he had deeds to prove it. Osbaldeston declared that he also had deeds and took his case to the Duchy Court. Southworths had "let beasts and cattle eat up his growing grass, had digged up 1,000 lodes of turf and by force carried it away", and he, Sir John Osbaldeston, was lawfully seized of the manor and moor etc and all his Darwen tenants would back his claim! Osbaldeston derived moral moral courage from the Earl of Derby's support. This time he won—a foregone conclusion!

This was the Osbaldestons' heydey, the Manors of Osbaldeston, Cuerdale, Over Darwen and Balderstone theirs, as well as hundreds of acres of pasture, woodland, moor, rushland and heath in twenty-six different Lancashire townships—good arable land was not plentiful in the county in Tudor times—plus a Ribble fishery and a family chapel in Blackburn Parish Church. In addition, John's heir, Edward, claimed Darwynd Hall, a manor mill at Over Darwen, and pasture rights with a shepherd to watch his moorland flocks. This, in Mary's reign.

Osbaldestons' papist convictions were not so strong as those of their neighbours, Southworths and Talbots. They temporised like Thomas Walmesley, the Queen's chief justice in these parts; were loyal to Elizabeth and provided her courts with an esteemed lawyer. It was good to have a younger son in Law. This one was Justice of Common Pleas and earned a knighthood.

The Osbaldestons were entrusted to hold the highest office, levy troops, attend military musters, provide captains and lieutenants for defending the realm—and practised their old faith in private. Many of the best families did the same, sending sons to be educated in Flanders or France—and risking dire consequences as lawbreakers thereby. Such families were Englishmen foremost, deeply grieved at the Pope's edict which made it a passport to heavenly bliss for any who put down the excommunicated Elizabeth. The Pope did not realize the inborn loyalty of Englishmen for their sovereign.

The family endured many sorrows. Young Edward, educated at the school in Rheims, returned like young Thomas Hoghton, as a missioner, was discovered and died for his faith at York Castle in 1594. Thomas, in 1590 when he became head of the family, decided to patch up differences with the Southworths by marrying son Thomas to their daughter Margaret. He was known as 'the homicide' after a tragic killing—in a duel?—of his own sister's husband at the Hall. There is an 'indelible bloodstain' on floorboards and a wandering ghost moaning and exposing the gaping wound in his chest. I have seen the 'stain', but I do not see ghosts!

His eldest son Sir Edward was a credit to his name, knighted by James I, "a noble example of chivalry, high breeding, and scholarship"; with nobility from his mother a Stanley, and scholarship from education in France with sons of the noblest Roman Catholics. He was no bigot, nor dabbler in conspiracy. He lived quietly down by the river, trying out scientific experiments (did he exchange ideas with a Towneley also interested in science and mathematics?). None could better him in fencing and manly sports. Men said, "Sir Edward rides better than any man in the country." His Hall stood fair on the Ribble edge, sloping pastures and woodlands above and tall trees around. Ancient yews flanked the main gate, by drawbridge and moat. At the back door, steps went down to a tethered boat, always ready to ferry the family over to the Ribchester bank of the Ribble. Their travels were as often northward as south. Boathouse Field, where the ferry man's cottage once stood, is a very pleasant place to look over the river to the Hall, the nearest one can approach nowadays, a pleasant walk from Ribchester Church.

It was said that Sir Edward was "a most charitable, virtuous and gallant knight in whom was seen the full flowering of a long and honourable line". They buried him, mourned by all, in the family chapel in Blackburn's old parish church in 1637.

The end of the line was not far ahead. During the Civil War, the heir being but a child, the family avoided the worst losses. He was only 14 when he died, uncle Alexander, husband of Sir John Talbot the Cavalier's daughter, being his heir. The future seemed secure for they produced ten children. A kinsman Lawrence Osbaldeston was busy building a handsome house in a lovely setting at Oxendale, obviously not over-anxious about the future. Yet within two generations both families relinquished their ancestral acres.

In 1689 Edward Osbaldeston, dying intestate, left his wife Grace Bradyll of Portfield to administer what was left for her eldest son. He chose to live in Preston, and as Osbaldeston was mortgaged to the hilt when he died it was lost for ever. When the grandson of Lawrence and Rosamund who built Oxendale Hall, sold to William Fox of Goosnargh in 1714, this marked the last of one of Lancashire's oldest families—seven centuries from

Norman times, 1,000 years since Osbald and Baldhere settled here.

Many humble Osbaldestons survived, and at times claimants to the family inheritance cropped up—but with no success. *Finis* had been written for the family. But the halls of Osbaldeston and Oxendale still stand.

Talbots of Salesbury

'The De Tabley Arms' on Ribble banks near Ribchester changed its name from Bridge Inn when Lord de Tabley became heir of the Talbot estates. He inherited through the Fleming Leycesters and his grandmother Harriet the heiress of Sir George Warren, K.B., son of Dorothy Talbot, "heiress of John Talbot last male heir of the once potent family of Talbots of Salesbury, Dinckley, Lower Darwen, of Bashall, Holt and Carrs". These lands were possessed by three branches of the parent Bashall stock, descended from Geoffrey son of a Norman de Tabley in the eleventh century. The brother Hugh founded the Talbot line who became Earls of Shrewsbury.

The Southworths at Samlesbury, Osbaldestons, and then the Talbots, among them owned the best acres of the lower Ribble valley. Their story followed the same lines. Their ancient hall stood on a rich horseshoe of land below the dramatic gorge and Sale Wheel. The Roman road crossed a park where they had grants for free warren and free chase, and a boat was at hand to carry them over the water to visit kinsfolk, the Cliderowes of Bailey, the Bashall Talbots.

Nothing is left of the half-timbered homestead. The last part, a black and white barn rare in these parts, survived until a few years ago, but is now replaced by a functional one in steel and concrete. Here in the fourteenth century lived de Cliderowes, great landowners in the valley. About 1420 the Lady of the Manor of Salesbury wed young John Talbot, his older brother being Lord of Bashall. To marry Rosalia he had to divorce his first wife, pleading consanguinity, but it was worth it; he now became a landowner to reckon with.

Many John Talbots take up the history. 'Little John' married Joan Radcliffe of Ordsall. He and his son Sir John, who was knighted for gallantry on the battlefield of Hutton in 1483, were both active in that "ensanguined and vindictive civil conflict", the Wars of the Roses. Very much involved was their in-law, Sir

James Harrington of Hornby, a foremost Yorkist; their kin at
Bashall Hall were caught up too. The three men are named as
leaders in an act of treachery, one well remembered from the
stormy period which sent

> Between the red rose and the white
> A thousand souls to death and endless night.

They sent a king to imprisonment in the Tower: "King Henry
was taken in a wode called Cletherwode beside Bungerley hipping
stones by Thomas Talbot and Bashall, and John Talbot his cosyne
of Colbry with other moo. . . ."

Barn at Salesbury Hall before demolition

In 1464, after tragic defeat, poor Henry VI fled south from
Hexham for refuge among loyal Lancastrians, with Sir Ralph Pudsay at Bolton-by-Bowland, then on to Waddington Hall when his
whereabouts became known. The daughter of Tempest had recently married young Talbot, and through her his family were let
into the closely guarded secret. James Harrington assured them
that reward for the King's capture would be high. They were
tempted. At Bashall, always ready for action, their own retainers
were a private army ready for local feuds or chances like this. Off
they went. The bird had flown from Waddington over Waddow
Park, only to fall into the Talbot ambush by the Ribble ford at
Brungerley. They pounced upon him, sat him on a "sorry nag

140

with an hempen halter" and, heaping indignities upon him, carried him to London and the Tower.

We do not admire the Talbots for this. Folk said no good would come of their treachery; Henry's curse would follow them for the next nine generations. Being on the Yorkist king's pay-roll, Talbots laughed at the prophets of doom. With evidence of royal favour, a letter from Richard III thanking them for "Good and faithful service in capture of our great adversary, Henry late in fact but not of right King of England", and annual payments, who cared?

Several Johns made up the total of Talbots still to come before they died out—after nine generations! 'Long John' was well spoken of by the visiting Herald of 1533. "A very gentil esquire and worthy to be taken paynes for", he loved music and played on the virginals and regales. Having a weakness for the ladies, he had thirteen children, only two being his wife's offspring. His son was just plain John, but the grandson, 'John the Papist', with a Sherburne mother and an Osbaldeston wife, was to endure many disturbed years. Salesbury was frequently and thoroughly searched for priests in hiding. Suspecting John of harbouring, they haled him to prison in Chester Castle then to Manchester New Fleet, where he died. 'Limping Tom', his brother, avoided persecution by wrapping himself in his studies as antiquary, one of the family's scholars; he was Keeper of Her Majesty's Rolls in the Tower of London. He knew the history of the arms hanging on the walls of Salesbury, who had donned them and when the ancient corselets, coats of plate, calivers and morions had been in use, also which tenants had as billmen and bowmen carried the pikes and bows to fight the wars against the Scots.

As Papists they had to provide for defence of the realm, under Protestant Elizabeth as under Papist Mary, providing demi-lances as their share against Philip of Spain's forces—"Anti-Christ and his minions" according to 'heretic' neighbours.

A little grandson inherited the Talbot possessions when John the Papist died. He was young, anxious to welcome James I; and the King, ready to woo the Papists—at first—gave him a knighthood. Sir John had no doubts about joining the King's side in 1642, but he thought himself very astute in inviting leading Parliamentarians to his house "promising them kind usage and some other curtesies" if they came for amicable discussion. Unfortunately for him they doubted his intentions, being "a great Papist but one that hath long stood as a neuter". They smelt a rat! They arrived at Sales-

George Talbot's New Hall, now ruinous

bury, but armed and ahead of time, thereby catching the Talbot men making warlike preparations, saddling and harnessing horses —one hundred mounts ready in the stables and their riders party to a treacherous plot. Sir John and his men waited for no explanations; the first were away over the river before the advance party of Roundheads could bring reinforcements of three hundred men. When they reached the Ribble the followers plunged in, "pursued and killed divers of them, and drove others into the water where many riders were drowned and their horses taken". After which successes the Roundhead soldiers "found good pillage".

The Talbots were absent for some time. George the Cavalier, a son, was captured at Preston's barricades in February 1643. When peace returned he built the New Hall near Ribchester bridge, a tall grey stone house and a pleasant feature in a lovely land-

142

scape—until left vacant in the 1950s and filled with battery hens! Now the walls collapse in final decay!

Sir John was fined £444 in 1644, and later was pardoned and allowed to return to Salesbury, buying back the forfeited lands for a £600 fine—a shortlived pleasure for he died before Charles II came into his own again. Those who followed kept out of trouble. They lived quietly, caring for their acres; John and George, and Uncle Thomas the Antiquary always searching for and digging up Roman relics. The end was near, all John's sons dying—an only daughter Dorothy now sole heiress.

Talbots of Dinckley

Dinckley Hall which Dorothy Talbot chose as her home has fared better than Salesbury's. The other day I looked down on it with a feeling of great content. Early October, the sun turning white rime to diamonds on the lush fogg grass, a tawny autumn touch on the trees; but the day so still not a brown leaf fell. Small wonder early manorial lords chose this sheltered and tranquil spot for their Hall; it is a veritable sun trap, when I visited it summer flowers still bloomed in the garden.

The farmhouse has a smiling face. Unlike surviving local halls this still has its half-timbered gable, mullioned and transomed windows, and its Tudor chimneys. Only two wings remain of the courtyard house, the courtyard now replaced by a very pleasant flower-filled garden. Of course, during the tenancies of many farmers alterations have been made, but today rooms still have their exposed oak rafters and crucks, there is good oak panelling in the passage and the original doors of riven timber.

In the five centuries since De Cliderowes were here, and Morleys and Talbots, the setting can have changed hardly at all, except for the passing of the ancient Trows ferry. This was an important Ribble crossing which made the early owners settle on this spot, just as families downriver dwelt where old routes crossed the water near their front gates. Not one is near a highway now; but centuries ago they were very much on the beaten track. Folk come by in large numbers today, to cross the swinging footbridge (which replaced the boat in 1951). Some of the party of Nelson Ramblers I met must have remembered the boat, but not the 'Trows' of a century ago, two hollow troughs joined together and drawn backwards and forwards from bank to bank by ropes, handled by Old Charon, alias Thomas Hardiker.

Dinckley Hall Farm in 1970

A rambler of 1870 described Dinckley Hall with gusto. There were Mrs. Knowles' famous Yorkshire ham teas and the preparations her husband made for entertainment—a clean-swept barn for the factory lads and lasses to dance in on wet holidays, and swings and a donkey on a grassy plot nearby for fun and games on sunny days. "Ample accommodation for horses was always provided." How times have changed!

Until the 1830s the barn was used as a chapel when local Roman Catholics were prevented from crossing the river roaring in spate. They worshipped at Stonyhurst in those days, until the little St. Mary's Church, now abandoned, was erected. Today, Mrs. S. was preparing refreshments for an evening fellowship meeting; there was a delicious aroma from the kitchen.

In this same room Mistress Talbot tended the wounds of William Blundell, whose thigh had been smashed by a Roundhead musket ball at Lancaster. She nursed him a fortnight till he departed "in better sort". To this door came Cavaliers in flight from the Battle of Read Lane, breaking away because they knew quieter roads home, there to hide, whilst the main body headed for Salesbury and Preston. Stirring times once, and now as pleasant and peaceful a home as one could wish.

From 1678, when Dorothy Talbot as a bride brought her inheritance to Edward Warren, until 1801 their descendants lived here. The family was without doubt coming to an end, no male

144

child surviving. A grand-daughter as heiress married Thomas Viscount Bulkeley and their grand-daughter in turn succeeded, bringing Dinckley to the Fleming Leycesters. Two generations later came Lord De Tabley and tenant farmers. His heir, the second Lord De Tabley, sold all the Ribble valley manors—Talbot inheritance—in 1866, for £140,000. Full stop to one more old family story.

Talbot of Bashall, Holt and Audley

In Norman times when De Lacy took up his claim to the Honour of Clitheroe a De Tabley was with him. A descendant in 1250 was given demesne land of a later De Lacy at Bacshelf, where Bashall Brook waters the green hollow before running to the Ribble near Edisford. For faithful service Edward I gave Edmund Talbot a free warren for small game, being in a generous mood the day the first Prince of Wales was knighted.

Edmund Talbot was enriched by successful land-grabbing deals with neighbours, Coulthursts and Withgills, and, more valuable, acquired part of Rishton Manor and a hall called Holt. This he lost when outlawed for debt, but his grandson regained the manor and Henry VI allowed him to build an oratory at Holt, just ten years before Talbots were to betray him to his Yorkist enemies.

Talbot sons, all Edmund or Thomas, were bred for war and it was a sore disappointment if they were not knighted for warlike qualities. In peace they were equally ready for a fight, against neighbours if no better adversary cropped up, with their own retinue of armed retainers living at Bashall, kicking their heels if not employed.

They found an excuse after Singletons from the next farm at Withgill came over the rise with one hundred armed men, caught them unprepared, did great damage and went away rejoicing. The insult they repaid in full eight years later in 1464 when they knew that, being in Edward IV's good books they could get away with murder. An act of treachery which darkened the name of Talbot ever after was the capture of Henry VI and, with help of Salesbury cousins and Harrington their kinsman's encouragement, the safe delivery of the hapless king to the Yorkists and the Tower of London, a shameful chapter of local history.

After that they could do no wrong, so the time was opportune for revenge on the Singletons! Their first victim was the militant Alice Singleton. John Talbot struck her with a "mortal blow of a lance price 6d", Richard followed "with an arrow as far as the brain", and another "clubbed her with a stick which would have killed her had she not been dead already".

This incident prepares one for shocking deeds involving others, especially the Rishtons whose hackles rose every time they encountered a Talbot, takers-away of lands once theirs. Disputes were common. They did once attempt to heal the rift by marriages. One Rishton to John of Salesbury's daughter; and there was a later, less happy union.

Bashall Hall

When Edmund Talbot died, leaving a 3-year-old heir, his young widow moved into a higher social scale by marrying Sir James Stanley, brother of Lord Strange. Her second child, pretty Anne, was innocent cause of a feud. Lady Anne, again widowed, came with her children to live at Holt, her dower house. Young Ralph Rishton found his way into the family circle, winning the affections of young Anne. Not till she was three months pregnant did her mother find out what had happened. The girl was borne off protesting to Great Harwood Church for a midnight wedding, not to Ralph but John Rishton, son and heir of Dunkenhalgh. The sorry affair ended in divorce, John later marrying a Southworth daughter and Anne finding her way back to her first love; she bore him nine children.

Another hot-tempered Talbot was Anne's brother, Sir Thomas. He was a successful bidder for abbey property, buying the rectory lease of Blackburn, and making Audley Hall henceforth his home. Now his Livesey neighbours became antagonists—had he not occupied abbey glebeland? One night Dame Livesey headed an armed family foray and fired Talbot's place. The hay was consumed and they were about to fire the granary when some neighbours spying smoke ran to the rescue—otherwise, "Talbots might have been brent in their beddes". Such goings on!

Sir Thomas pursued Queen Mary's affairs in Scotland, his friend Sir Ralph Assheton with him and a young page, Ralph Rishton, born to trouble. As an 8-year-old he was married at Altham to Helen Towneley, aged 10. Naturally he went his own way a few years later, rejecting his wife so that she became deranged. He preferred his own choice, Elizabeth Parker of Horrocksford, who bore him six sons during his many periods of service in Scottish campaigns. He had meantime resumed his attachment to Anne Talbot, who joined him after her divorce— hence his tiring of faithful Elizabeth. One good point can be found for him. He kept out of the affrays wherein Rishtons and Talbots continued knocking each other about.

In Sir Thomas Talbot's will, made before setting out to war in 1557, young Anne was left his rights in Bashall and Audley, her brother Henry being heir, inherited the rest.

Now King Henry's curse was working. The king had pronounced that his betrayers would die out after nine generations, in each alternately a wise Talbot and an idiot. It came to pass that by the mid-seventeenth century none was left but two daughters, the survivor married to Colonel White of Bashall Hall inheriting a dwindled inheritance. The lordships of Rishton, Holt, Lower Darwen and Fearnhurst were sold in about 1600 to Sir Thomas Walmesley of Hacking and Dunkenhalgh.

There is much that the Whites knew left at Bashall—the central block with their arms over the fine door, gardens and summer houses. There is far less at The Holt, which Anne Stanley, 'Mistress Ralph Rishton', had described as "moated about with a drawbridge and attached to the Elizabethan hall a chapel and oratory". The present occupier had no idea The Holt had an historic past!

Sherburnes of Stonyhurst

On 29th August 1794 a band of weary travellers halted at their first sight of Stonyhurst. Two with more energy than the rest made a spurt, racing for the hall, making a wager as they ran. "I've won", shouted young George Lambert Clifford, climbing through a window whilst the other stared crestfallen at the locked and barred door. As the first in the new school Clifford's marble bust has pride of place in one of the present college corridors. On a wall nearby is the portrait of a handsome boy, the young Thomas Weld, who owned Stonyhurst but never lived there; in London he had arranged with the Jesuit fathers of his old school in Liège that if they ever found reason to leave Flanders they could have quarters in the vacant Hall of his mother's ancestors the Shireburnes, Sherburnes, an ancient family.

The need came with the French Revolution, when to stay in Liège was dangerous. Priests and students left without attracting notice, and travelled to Bruges where a boat carried them to Hull; then across Yorkshire by coach, on the new canal to Skipton and Shank's pony thereafter. Small wonder they sighed with relief when they stepped into the deserted house. "Just for the time being", they said. "Only temporarily", agreed the advance party, eight boys, ten priests. Their temporary exile became their permanent home.

The early Sherburnes were a Fylde family who came to the Ribble valley when Margaret, an heiress, married Richard of Bailey (Bayley). The bride already owned nearby manors, from cousins the De Mitton heiresses, so needed little persuasion to come to Bailey Hall; this old house was not far from Stonyhurst, a gift from his grandfather to her bridegroom. So the young couple were off to a good start. When their eldest son was old enough to carry on alone they passed Bailey to him and themselves moved to 'Stanihurst'.

De Baileys henceforth were 'Sherburnes'; and the eldest son was always Richard. The Tudor period brought them out on top among local families. They successfully trimmed their sails to the wind and, apt to time serving and conforming outwardly in public worship, earned the trust and gratitude of their sovereigns —which required skill in diplomacy and an easy conscience!

I have just returned from Stonyhurst—a short fifteen minutes by car from my home—where Father Macadam showed me the fine portraits of Sherburnes beginning with the bold Sir Richard. Hitherto they had been faceless, or as their tombs in Mitton Church showed them. All were handsome, and the women, as painted by Kneller and Lely and lesser-known seventeenth-century artists, able to stand with the Hampton Court beauties, their contemporaries. A descendant of Thomas Weld lent the College his ancestors' portraits during the war, when Leagram Hall was occupied, then

Stonyhurst

later made the loan a gift. One splendid room in the new part of the college has windows built to contain the heraldic glass from demolished Leagram showing all the families who held Leagram —beginning with the Earl of Leicester, from whom Sir Richard, being Master Forester of Bowland, was glad to buy it for his Lodge.

Sir Richard had his finger in many pies. He had an active part in the suppression of Whalley Abbey, as an appraiser of goods left by the brethren. Edward VI retained his valuable offices, and under Mary he was twice M.P. When the old chantry at Bailey was dissolved he set about collecting money for a new bridge to make the journey to Mitton Church easier—Lower Hodder bridge built in 1562 for £70. When his wife died he rebuilt the Sherburne chapel at Mitton to be a fitting resting place for himself and his heirs for generations to come.

The alabaster tomb whereon lie Sir Richard and Lady Maud in effigy, one of the most splendid of its kind in Lancashire, also carries a record of his titles and offices. This makes noble reading: "Master Forester of Bowland, Steward of the Manor of Slaidburn, Lieutenant of the Isle of Man, one of Her Majesty's Deputy Lieutenants". Close friendship with the Stanleys assured his allegiance to the Tudors. He was defender of the reformed church "against the contamination of Popery", loud in a declaration to fight all Papists who plotted against Elizabeth.

To Sir Richard also all praise is due for the frontage of Stonyhurst, the magnificent gateway with rows of Corinthian pillars, and a stone escutcheon over the arch which deserves closer scrutiny. The shield is slightly tilted away from the wall, half revealing a stone panel; over the shield is the knight's helmet with the visor raised—what better peephole?—whilst behind the panel is a small space where one could keep watch. To the right of the archway was the priest's room. The angle fireplace hides a narrow 'creep' with access to the look-out and secret hides, one on each side of the archway. In the thickness of the gatehouse walls are passages.

At the end of the Elizabethan frontage an unusual window, ecclesiastically decorated—the rest are transomed and square-headed, lights the family chapel which in Sir Richard's time had an arch "as high as Whalley Church chancel". When Bailey chantry was dissolved in Henry VIII's time masonry found its way to Stonyhurst—and here is the window.

So far, so good, Sir Richard leaving his mark in a wide field and on his own ground. His 'living portrait' at Stonyhurst, not the stillness of cold alabaster at Mitton, reveals something of his complicated character, something shared with other shrewd go-getting Elizabethans. Like them he could be a law unto himself in personal and family affairs. When he bought Leagram Lodge and Park he decided to increase the deer stock therein by leaving loopholes, gaps or 'sauters'. In leapt the free-ranging deer for his use and pleasure. Neighbours were incensed, poached ad lib, beat up his keepers—exactly as Sherburnes had done in the past when not in office. And Sir Richard retaliated. Also his tenants accused him of overtaxing them; and his constables who did not exert their authority in collecting reported that Sir Richard had threatened to hang them. Almost a feudal hangover!

To retain his offices he paid lip service to the reformed church, but during lapses it was noticed that "Sir Richard and his family do not go to church and if they do stop their ears with wool lest they should hear". The parishioners at Mitton commented that Lady Sherburne was never at church, and that she was a lady badly done by. Poor Maud Bold, knowing full well about mistresses sharing Sir Richard's attention and his favourite, Mistress Isabel Wood and her numerous children, fathered under her very roof. A not unusual state of affairs in old Lancashire families of that time.

The next Richard, his heir, had seen service under the Stanleys as captain when his father was Lieutenant of the Isle of Man, and he had married at Castletown one of the earl's 'natural' daughters. The very fine mural monument at Mitton shows the parents facing each other in stiff Tudor dress, and below nurses weeping by a cradle holding twins whose birth caused Catharine's death.

Richard II finished the building his father had begun, but no more. He conformed in 1600, proof being in his arrest, together with Thomas Hesketh, of a priest called Middleton. They handed him to the authorities but on his way to Lancaster four men on horses and one on foot attempted his rescue. They failed and the man on foot was captured. He was a priest in disguise, Hunt his name. He and Middleton were both condemned and executed as traitors.

His son Richard III never prevaricated. His wives, Molyneux and Walmesleys, were Papists and he was fined heavily for recusancy; building was at a standstill.

When Oliver Cromwell looked at 'Stanyares' in August 1648 he declared it was, in its unfinished state, "the best half house he had seen". His host Richard IV refused to welcome his undesirable visitor that night. His wife's kinswoman, the intrepid Lady Ingleby, at Ripley Castle had once confronted Cromwell with two loaded pistols! They say Cromwell slept uneasily at Stonyhurst, on the refectory table, pistols at his side, men on guard.

Stonyhurst remained a half house during the reigns of Charles II and James II. There was trouble when General Monk, honoured by the king, claimed Leagram and the Sherburnes forcibly denied it, encouraging their partisans to poach the deer. Once Monk's keepers caught three redhanded with a buck. Richard IV in 1667 recovered his forfeited estates on renouncing his religion, but ten years later Stonyhurst was again suspected and denounced as "centre of a damnable Jesuit Plot". After discovery of a list of infirm clergy helped by a common fund—but translated as names of plotters against William and the Protestant religion—Sherburnes again faced persecution. Richard IV died in Manchester jail for loyalty to his sovereign, James II.

Only his death prevented Richard from facing the Manchester Trial with others, his friends and old boys of St. Omers. His wife too had suffered for her "zeal in harbouring priests and missioners" at times when the peephole and 'creeps' must have been much used.

His second son Nicholas, knighted in the 'good time' of James II, succeeded his brother Richard V. Fortune augured well, for his bride, Katharine Charlton, brought great riches. The young couple avoided implication in family troubles by living in Northumberland out of harm's way, until 1693 when they and their small children returned to Stonyhurst and his old widowed mother, the indefatigable Isabel Ingleby.

Now work could start again. Plans were drawn up—I have seen them—for extensions to the left of the gate, a range to enclose the courtyard on the west and another to include the great hall on the north. Stone hewers again worked Kemple End quarries; artists, like the Stanton brothers who designed ornaments and John Nost who cast them in lead, were employed; and master craftsmen brought in to organize local labour. Directed by the agent Mason they formed a sizeable team. Work went on at a fine pace from the 1690s to 1717, not only on the house but also in the park.

During 1970 when Mr. Robin Bagot was searching Levens Hall records relating to the threatened avenue of trees and the landscaping of the park by Monsieur Beaumont, the royal gardener given a home here after James II's exile, he found a letter. Dated 1701, it was from Mr. Beaumont, then in Preston. He reported that work at Sir Nicholas Sherburne's was progressing very well. Is it proof that the same master mind which had worked on royal gardens and created the avenues and vistas at Levens—mercifully saved from motorway destruction—also wrought here? Standing by the gateway the two long canals, the drive and flanking grass, the side screens of trees and a great circle of limes sweeping over the landscape beyond, can be seen as part of a noble plan.

On Monday 8th June 1702 little Richard Sherburne, "a child extraordinary in all respects, both beautiful and forward", was carried in through the great gateway to die most tragically, poisoned by yew berries. Sir Nicholas tried to find words to express his sorrow, made attempts in his journal, discarded them, and left a bald statement of names and dates as epitaph. An artist who knew the child was left to design a fitting memorial. William Stanton told the story in marble in a wall monument at Mitton Church showing the boy in classic drapes "startled by the emblems of death", his young playmates as cherubs weeping marble tears, whilst a flight of small winged angels waits to carry him to the glory at Heaven's gates.

Plans for Stonyhurst were put aside now, or drastically curtailed. The great hall was finished already, the frieze dated 1699; the east range overlooking the gardens with their yew walks, bowling greens and summer houses, and Nost's statuary in place, all completed. Richard Ryding, master mason, was paid £50 for erecting the prominent lead cupolas "upon ye starecases to finish the battlement above the Tower, dress stone according to John Mason's direction". The Kemple End almshouses begun by his father were now finished too and occupied according to his wishes.

Enthusiasm had ebbed. Ten-year-old Mary was now heir, and she was a weakly child Sir Nicholas had taken to London five years earlier to be touched for the King's Evil. His travelling expenses amounted to £360. She survived, became Duchess of Norfolk and was last of her family to live at Stonyhurst, a woman of immense spirit and vitality. Her portrait shows her as a most attractive person, full of life and with signs of that strength of character which was to carry her through long and difficult times. She being the last was the proudest in recording, on marble, the achievements of the Sherburne's. In her own apartments, 'The Dutchess's Rooms', overlooking the formal gardens, she carefully drafted memorials to her well-beloved parents, and to her second husband, a marriage kept secret for reasons of safety.

In 1715 a supper party at Stonyhurst was presided over by old Sir Nicholas. What was the topic of conversation? One may guess, for from Widdrington kinsfolk word of the approaching Jacobite rebels must have arrived. All guests were of one mind; some had met to plan their participation in the coming rising at Dutton Lee and were later hunted by Hanoverian troops over the fells above Stonyhurst. That night Sir Nicholas and friends 'cast bullets', and when morning came four coachhorses laden with guns and pistols set out for Preston. Sir Nicholas was never charged as an accomplice, but less fortunate was 'cousin' Richard Sherburne of Bailey, outlawed the same year for treason, and the Hon. Peregrine Widdrington, who, according to the epitaph at Mitton, "was with his brother in the Preston affair where he lost his fortune with his health by long confinement in prison".

Sir Nicholas died in 1717 and his lady in 1727. Their like was never seen again. Their tenants mourned them. He was, in his daughter's words, "a man of great human sympathy and concern for the good of mankind and did many good and charitable things while he lived".

The central courtyard at Stonyhurst was Sir Nicholas's work, as his emblems and family arms, on carved stones and leaded rainheads show well. At ground level are several doors which opened into rooms occupied by Flemish or Huguenot weavers, refugees who here plied their craft. They probably gave Sir Nicholas the idea of making his tenants equally proficient.

Hurst Green was a small unremarkable community then, but after a 'training centre' had been set up in "empty rooms off one of the courtyards and a man set to teach how to prepare raw wool and a woman to explain the spinning of it", the local folk took to the idea. After spinning every day, or as long as they could spare from their families, until they were proficient "each was given wool ready for spinning and a wheel to start on their own, which did a vast deal of good on that north side of Ribble". So was the district embarked on the home spinning industry.

Lady Katharine, "a lady of excellent temper and fine sentiments, singular piety, virtue and charity, was constantly imployed in doing good". As Lady Bountiful she dealt out money on All Souls' Day, serving the poor with her own hands; and as local apothecary she kept salves, ointments and remedies to cure their ills. The "distressed, sick, poor and lame were constantly at her door".

The villagers came to Stonyhurst also to worship in the family chapel, entering at a small door just beyond the great gate and kneeling on the floor whilst the family watched from an upper room. This chapel is now divided in height by many floors, one lit by the Bailey window, a beautiful sun-filled room, having on its walls portraits of the Widdringtons, relatives, Papists, malignants, Jacobites. The Hon. Peregrine is among them, a pleasant, open-faced young man, "a fine gentleman, of so amiable a disposition, and so ingaging that he was beloved and esteemed by all who had the honor and happiness of his acquaintance".

Table-top tombs with their marble effigies of four generations of Sherburnes filled the floor space in the Mitton chapel, therefore Sir Nicholas decided to open a family vault beneath for his

154

generation and the next. His little son was first to lie there, then his wife's mother Lady Mary Charlton— who left him the Luttrell Psalter—followed by Sir Nicholas himself, Lady Katharine and the un-named husband of the 'Dutchess'. She was last to be brought here; and the last of the Sherburnes. I have seen the row of six trestles, each with the lead-sheathed, leather-covered coffin, and the two caskets, heart burials probably, of Sherburnes who died away from home.

The end of an era, 1754. The Duchess had no children, so the entire Sherburne inheritance came to her aunt Elizabeth's son, a Dorset Weld of Lulworth Castle, as remote from Stonyhurst as possible. Welds never lived here, and the house remained empty for forty years, until Thomas Weld handed it to the exiled Jesuits of Liège, who should hold their school's bicentenary in these 'temporary' quarters in 1994. In 1809 Thomas Weld signed a deed of gift conveying Stonyhurst to his old masters of Liège. Now the college looked forward to a permanency and planned accordingly. In August the next year new buildings had their official opening, an event marred by the death of Thomas Weld, who had arrived for the ceremony.

At Leagram Hall near Chipping a modern house stands on the site of the 1821 mansion built by Welds—it was demolished after the war—which had replaced the ancient H-shaped lodge of the Keepers of the royal park of pre-Tudor times. Sir Richard had made fast his claims by purchase in 1563, though Sherburnes had long been involved in the history of Lodge, Laund, and the Lordship of the Manor of Chipping, vigorously contesting their rights with de Hoghtons, vocal and rival claimants.

At one time the tenants never knew where they were, De Hoghton keeping his manorial courts at Black Hall near Thornley, the Sherburnes at the lonely, remote Wolf House, tucked away into the fells near the beginning of Chipping Brook. Lord Derby recognized Sherburnes as responsible for providing local bowmen as part of the old feudal tenure, in 1533 sending his messengers to Roger of Wolf House, commanding "XXij [24] tall men and good archers they being my Lds. tenants to be put in redynes as fotemen well haryssed after the manner of the cuntrie in whyt jacketts with my Badge of the Legges of Man of red clothe befor the brest or behynd on their backs", these to be sent "to my Ile for defence against the Ld. of the Owt Iles and summe Scottes".

From 1752 when Welds took Leagram there was no complication, a younger son usually being in occupation—until 1818 when the family head Thomas Weld of Lulworth Castle took holy orders and George of Leagram assumed responsibility for all the estates. Thomas Weld, Bishop of Amycla brought honour to his family when, as Cardinal Priest of St. Marcellus and called to the Papal Conclave, he was first Englishman since Clement IX to sit there as Cardinal.

George's younger brother also acquired great estates, from his kinsman Blundell of Ince—hence the many Weld-Blundells, all old boys of Stonyhurst. A distinguished cousin, John Weld of Leagram, a noted antiquarian, wrote with intimate detail fascinating memoirs of Chipping and district. He was in love with his subject and obviously more wrapped up with his Sherburne than his Weld forbears. Writers of family histories and recorders of old traditions are 'my kind'. John Weld had much to tell about the Teanleas, an ancient Chipping custom carried out on Hallow E'en. Families gathered in remote farms, to kneel and pray for souls released for a brief spell from Purgatory "as long as their lit torches, straw held on a pitch fork, showed a spark". Scores of lights blazed that night.

The Weld line today seems secure. Colonel J. W. Weld, O.B.E., of Lulworth Castle—once High Sheriff of Dorset—has six children and many grandchildren.

Parkers of Browsholme

 Colonel Robert Parker, D.S.O., J.P., F.S.A., of Browsholme Hall (pronounced 'Broosem'), Clitheroe, Lancashire, according to the postal address, can trace his 'mid-way' ancestors to Parkers, Royal Parkers of Radholme Laund who had a dwelling at Nether Brooksholme in the 1400s. In earlier times a thirteenth-century Peter of Alcancotes begat Adam, and Adam's grandson was Richard of Trawden—all Lancashire forbears. Richard begat Edmund who crossed west into Yorkshire.

Parkers have always had firm stakes in both counties, hence their right to be in this book. At Radholme—that intensely smooth and green limestone upland overlooking the Hodder gorge and traversed by the Cow Ark to Whitewell road, they supervised the royal Laund, therein fattening venison. In 1450 it was written:

> God bless Edmund Parker and all that wyth hym wonnes,
> His wyf, five daughters and his seven sonnes.

There were two sons when deputy Parkers leased a cow pasture and a vaccary at Lower Brooksholme, and Richard built a wattle and daub house there fixing the site for a future Browsholme Hall. His son and grandson retained the office, Edmund being "of Foulscales". This hoary old farm is still there, by a stream near the Marl Hill—Barney Brow high-level road from Cow Ark to Newton; it has lain snug in this hollow for over 500 years.

When Edmund's sister Elizabeth, married to another Edmund her cousin, became her father's heir, the Parkers, as tenants now, leased Nether Brooksholme from Henry VII. The King was eager to raise money, and up went rents in royal forests. Hence Edmund's eagerness to move to his own place. He enlarged in stone, adding an upper storey, long gallery and chapel to grandfather Richard's house.

A century passed, the Parkers weathered the changes of Tudor times most successfully with heads high, and were ready and able when James I (an acquisitive king, like Henry VII) offered more Bowland Forest property for sale, to acquire the Vaccary of Browsholme.

Thomas, 'Bowbearer of Bowland', called in Thomas Holt of York who had worked on the Bodleian and for Sherburnes at Stonyhurst. House building was rampant then, every family spurred on by hopes of peace and prosperity in the new reign.

Parkers living in their own outback were a tolerant family; each generation had Protestants and Papists. One heir as a Papist priest could not inherit. Two brothers of the builder, Thomas, were Dean of Lincoln (with a son a priest) and William Archdeacon of Cornwall, whose nephew for his convictions settled in Virginia, first of the American Parkers. The ladies of Browsholme worshipped as they chose.

I read a letter written by Roger Parker in 1639 saying, "Roger brother to Edward was one [Roman Catholic] from whom Parkers of Lickhurst [Little Bowland] were descended, and if living are still R.C. But Dunnow Parkers have been Protestants long."

Parkers of Greystoneley in Little Bowland had estates taken for Thomas Parker's delinquency in 1644; they were obviously Papists.

Arthur Parker of Lickhurst was buried at Chipping Church in 1614; he gave 6s. 8d. to repair Chipping bells, his chattels to the poor. And "to poore which shall fortune to be at my burial pence apiece and everyone bread and a piece of cheese, if cheese can be procured—for want of these a piece of fleshe". For all friends and neighbours at the funeral there was bread and milk.

Arthur and two Parkers of Chipping Lawn sound like poor relations. In 1718 James the Taller and James the Shorter gave evidence at Preston about the priest Penketh maintained by Sherburnes on land near Chipping. They said they had known him twenty years; "he was a reputed Romish priest and they had heard him say something in Latin which is called Mass but he hath not been there since the Rebellion".

An unlikely testimony from Papists!

This was a time of suspicion. Edward, who followed the builder of Browsholme who had died in 1634, had refused to be at Charles I's coronation, but in 1643 took the Oath of Allegiance. In 1652 he officially "abjured Popery."

There is no doubt, however, of this generation's sufferings for loyalty to the Stuarts throughout the Civil War period.

A young Parker student was sent down from Cambridge for drinking the King's health and eating a 'lobster'—'lobster' being a scurrilous term for a Roundhead.

A Cavalier Parker was killed at the Battle of Newbury—as were sons of Cliftons, Daltons, Bradylls and Rigbys. His buckskin jacket hangs in Browsholme entrance hall today. In a large batch of Cromwellian papers among the Parker archives in the County Record Office at Preston are letters of protection saying 'hands off' Edward Parker's property; these are signed by leaders of Parliament—Shuttleworth ("none shall plunder"), Lambert and Fairfax; there are also letters from Tyldesley in 1648, asking for forbearance from 'foreign troops' (Scots) under the Duke of Hamilton, who might stray over the Trough of Bowland road and, like raiding ancestors, be tempted to loot!

The gracious hall, rose-tinged in the sun, smiles today, serene in old age. Hard to imagine uproar and strife at this door? Yet time and time again Roundheads pounced, forced their way into the stables, ransacked the house. Once for ransom they carried off Edward Parker and at another time a 9-year-old son. Edward's release from prison at Bradford cost £200; the little boy's return from Thornton—£13. Losses of over £1,000 were endured in quartering troops and forcibly giving up stores for man and beast.

Isolated they were from centres of population but conveniently near the highway, York/Lancaster—Clitheroe/Lancaster, which bisected the lonely wilderness of Bowland. That way in August 1651 came a letter from Edward's kinsman, Lord Morley and

Monteagle (the same family which sent warning to Parliament of Gunpowder plotters) asking him to come over to Hornby for a commission with Mr. Leyburne of Cunswick. Plans were afoot to join young King Charles and his advancing Royalist supporters, and tragedy awaiting at the defeat in Wigan Lane. Lord Morley and Monteagle wrote the same month to thank Cousin Edward "for his love and entertainment" of his son—a bad lad banished to Browsholme for his own good!

Browsholme Hall in 1970

Edward survived Wigan Lane, endured the Commonwealth. He read warnings in a letter of 1658 that all was not well in Parliament—for Cromwell showed approval when addressed as 'Highness'! In 1659 there were more warning signs from George Monk (a ringleader in recalling Charles from exile) reporting from Edinburgh the conduct of Parliament and Army. Signs pointed to imminent Restoration—and Parker fingers were on the pulse.

Scores of letters were penned by Parkers at home and as many received by carrier 'in the Preston bag', folded and sealed, from sons at Cambridge, Jesus College; at Grays Inn, the Inns of Court —for many younger Parkers were lawyers—and from countless 'cousins' in many places, from men of importance named in English history with fingers in every pie, reporting rumour and news to Parkers.

Most were preserved, filed and later bound in several volumes —but haphazardly—and these were deposited with the County Records Office—what treasure for the patient student of social

159

history! What reading between the lines! I found many diverting side-tracks constantly luring me from the main path.

After the Restoration, Edward Parker wrote to his son: "On May 29th at our bone fyre att the top of our fields rejoicing for the birth and safe arrival of our sovereign". Was this an early Royal Oak Day? Did the bonfire flame out from Browsholme Spire, a family landmark?

But what was hid behind his petition to the Deputy Lieutenant of the West Riding in 1661? "It is fit for the King to do something extraordinary." Was he hoping for some reward for loyalty and compensation for over £2,000 losses?

I find this family correspondence fascinating. Anne Assheton sending congratulations from Middleton in January, "rejoicing to heare of yr good wife my cousin's safe delivery and wishing much joy of your new year's gift", willing to be godmother but "badness of wether with ye foulness of the way will not afforde me my desier. Sweet cousin Julian must be interested to stand proxy".

One long, tear-smudged letter penned by Jennet Parker to her "honerd brother Thomas" came with the carrier who had charge of her little baby, "the nurs being very yong and troubled to part with the child, unfit to perform this great charge". The little one travelled in one pannier, and his belongings (all listed on 'the backside of the paper') in another—all his needments to start life in the household of kind brother, Thomas, who had offered "to bring him up". How do these compare with a modern infant's requirements?

"Head bands, silk caps, pinirs, night caps, double crose cloths, cuffs, neckcloths, night and day blankets, woollen hippins, dimaty mantles", were all in his bag, as well as "one coral necklace, one silver corral without bells, a porringer and spoon, and a gill bottle of sackfifrody water"! Diet instructions added—the infant is "urged to eat 3 or 4 times a day of white bread and milk besides what he sucks".

Brother Thomas succeeded his father in 1667. He had a commission from Buckingham to raise a company of foot in Colonel Pudsay's regiment. In spite of loyalty to Charles II, like his father he waited long for financial reward. When it finally came Thomas used the money for re-panelling rooms. Letters of 1674 refer to this. The venerable Archdeacon of Cornwall, his uncle, brought the work of Grinling Gibbons to his notice "for altering and beautifying at Browsholme".

In a letter in shaky hand from old Uncle William to his "honerd" nephew Thomas: "I understand you have beautified your house and that your lot is fallen in a good ground." Being a venerable Churchman, he had in his piety to remind Thomas of the Kingdom of Heaven and Life to come.

Gifts came by carrier. "A little angelical" from a faithful servant, another Jennet Parker, in 1668, who writes, "My dearest wish is to see my mistress before I dy." She saw little hope of this but "as son Robert sent mee a lofe of suger and I have angelical in my garden", along came the angelica jelly.

Edward Parker, brother or son, who was "actually called to ye Barre" in 1684, wrote home from the 'Seven Stars', London. Interesting comment on recent events about "4 persons yt you have committed to Lancaster, sd. to be notorious villains, guilty of ill things. I am glad ye County has so well secured them." This was 1684, the last year of Charles II's reign, when the King, much troubled because of his son Monmouth's aspirations to the throne, forced exile upon him. Edward writes of "Thomas Armstrong one yt fled away from ye discovery of ye presbiterian plott," of death sentence for High Treason and his arrest at Leyden in Holland. Why did son Edward come home that summer by way of York, asking for horses to be provided for the journey to Browsholme by his family or Uncle Shuttleworth? "The Lord Chancellor Justice Jeffreys has been recommended by the King to the York July Assizes this year."

Parkers always kept letters from absent sons. From Jesus College one wrote of a Dr. Cook's death, "he who brought a gt. many students to this College and was splendidly buried. We had a very sickly College, many fellows sick but now all gotten well again." Some epidemic, and anxiety for Mistress Parker?

One young Thomas Parker in London, after a gay life at Cambridge, was endeavouring to live "as cheap and as little troublesome to my friends as possible". He occupied chambers, ready furnished by Mr. P. of Clitheroe, for £14 a year, but wonders if it is not "cheaper and more gentele to live in the inns of court? "My way of living here differs very much from Cambridge, but I hope to settle down very soon and keep within my allowance. P.S. Please desire my mother to send 2 pairs of shirts if I go into ye inn."

In the '15 Rising, Thomas Parker "of Brusom Junr," as captain was summoned by the Earl of Derby to join Sir Ralph Ashton Bt. and his regiment of foot and to quell the Stuart supporters. On the side of law and order. Daughters often thought differently.

Elizabeth Parker was a 'secret' Jacobite, who wore embroidered garters sent by her sweetheart and cousin Robert Parker, declaring her Stuart loyalties. On one pair—"God Bless P.C." and "Down With The Rump". On another "When This You See Remember Me". On one 'leg' of a third pair, "Our Prince Is Brave Our Cause Is Just" is completed on the other—"In God Above We Put Our Trust". She prized his gifts of Stuart tartan handkerchiefs and pincushions. They had an eleven-year courtship but their married life lasted only eight years. Her lovely flower-brocaded wedding dress is still in the house. Chests full of by-gone costumes made rainy days pleasant to generations of young Victorian and Edwardian Parkers 'dressing up', so I have been told.

During the eighteenth century Parker cousins of Extwistle Hall above Worsthorne, of New Hall on the flanks of Boulsworth Hill, and of Alkin-coats, exchanged visits and paid calls on and were visited by in-laws and kinsfolk of Giggleswick and Marsh House, Whitakers of Simonstone, Bouches of Ingleton, Flemings of Rydal, and the Listers of Westby and Gisburne Park. Their family circle was exceedingly large and close knit.

In 1750, when John Parker married Barbara Lister she added a strain of royal blood—which, alas, ended soon, for none of their children had sons. John Lister of Derby when marrying Isabel Clyderowe of Midhope near Twiston and Pendle, through an ancestor, Humphrey de Bohun who had for wife Elizabeth, of Edward I's line, introduced Plantagenet blood. This was passed down the long line of Listers.

One of their sons, William Vicar of Waddington, was Viscount Howe's chaplain. He wrote a history. Two brothers—seen elegantly posed in a Gardiner portrait, were pages to George III. Thomas Lister who succeeded in 1797 was friend of the Prince Regent, gentleman of the Court, Sergeant Trumpeter to George IV and William IV, and above all, a man of letters and antiquary. William Assheton of Downham was of like mind, and they travelled around together.

One day I perused Thomas Lister's sketch book of pen-and-wash drawings of the Hodder/Whitewell landscape in the 1830s, a present to brother William in 1839, the work delicate and detailed, lovingly drawn. It is most gratifying to handle the handsome first edition of his history of the family, in which are bound the original portrait drawings and landscapes by Buckler. It is a thing of beauty and great value.

He remained a bachelor and singleminded. He made of Browsholme a splendid place, enriched in so many ways, but was himself in such financial straits he had eventually to sell hall and estate to his heir and cousin, Thomas Parker of Alkincoates and Newton. When he did make this final decision he was 'in a bad way.'

Why did this come about? For a century his forbears had spent what they could on improving the Hall; and in each century before that. Soon after 1400 the wattle and daub first hall; in 1507 the stone 'replacement'; and in 1604 the whole re-fronted with the rose-tinged sandstone from Burholme Fell; in 1670's long-delayed compensation for war damage spent on the interior 'beautifying'. In 1704 the Tudor Hall, formerly screened off at the 'family' end, was now divided by a wall giving a breakfast parlour for more privacy, and a gracious Queen Anne staircase replaced Elizabethan spirals. A hundred years later young Thomas Lister Parker embarked on his ambitious schemes. He brought to Browsholme, Carr of York, who had built Gledstone Hall. Sir Jeffrey Wyatt remodelled the west wing, utilizing Tudor masonry. Chippendale and Sheraton designed interiors and furniture. Only the best satisfied him. The artist Northcote painted here; his portrait of Old Keeper was done with affectionate detail. William Mallord Turner, when commissioned to illustrate Dr. Whitaker's *History of Craven*, was a guest, Miss Parker a congenial companion on sketching expeditions.

He reduced the deer population, few escaping. Tree planting started by his father "for the war effort", he continued until 1813.

Money was poured out unstintingly. The gateway and arch from Ingleton Hall of his Bouch ancestors was erected at a new approach. A long decoy pond was contrived. Splendid gardenscapes swallowed over £100,000, whilst a fortune was spent on the house.

When all was as perfect as possible, he declared it Finished. The year was 1820. He paid his debts and retired. The Alkincoates Parkers moved in.

In Colonel Parker's life his fighting forbears have lived again. His D.S.O. was won leading a Pyatt mortar attack in North Africa; his F.S.A. places him beside his father and Thomas Lister and other family historians; as J.P. he has kept the peace like Parkers of every generation during many centuries.

A Peter of Alkincoates six centuries earlier was ancestor of the Bowland Parkers. A Peter Parker of Alkincoates, an East India merchant, was brother of John of Browsholme. Certain family friends of the East India merchant class kept the Parkers well provided with the best painted china from China—the splendid tea, coffee and chocolate set in the dining-room was a valued gift.

All this beauty Colonel Parker shares with visitors on 'open to the public' days.

Asshetons of Downham

 Lord Clitheroe has given me the freedom of his library at Downham Hall. The other day he took from the shelves volumes he thought I would find particularly interesting. One was very large and heavy, with a covering of green velvet, a family history compiled over the years by the Assheton historian, not for public perusal but to bring before young Asshetons of future generations cause for pride in their ancestry.

Perhaps this historian's name roused his early interest, as a boy in the 1840s. He was Richard Orme, Orm being name of early Norse and Anglo-Norse ancestors—Orme, Ormus Magnus, Orme Fitzward, the Ormes of Urmston and Ormskirk maybe. His father had considered Ralph Orme as a name for his first son, but rejected it as an embarrassing pun, being at the time opposed to the proposed Reform Bill! 'Orme' was saved for a second son.

These were the two talented brothers who a century ago beautified Downham Church, designing, staining the glass and assembling their own work in the east window. They were the first to enjoy this library, after their widowed father William II had made large-scale improvements at Downham Hall, remodelling the façade of which the library is part.

I like Richard Orme's way of tackling his tremendous subject—his ancestry which went back, recorded, for a thousand years.

He wrote, "I have no desire to penetrate beyond the Garden of Eden. Peering among the branches of the family tree . . . straight as a bee, true as a bell . . . there are Plantagenets galore, and crowned heads 4 a penny. . . ."

To trace his antecedents was a matter of "harmless pride and innocent conceit, along direct descents"—which he embellishes with crests, arms and badges. Through brides of good birth he traces unerringly Asshetons' claim to share the noble blood of

164

De Clares and Joanne Plantagenet in one pedigree; Boleyns, Howards, Mowbrays and Thomas Plantagenet in another; Nevilles, Earls of Westmorland, Beauforts and John of Gaunt in a third, these merging in the Edwards III, II, I, and bringing into the family tree very near its roots the Angevin and Norman kings, and the kings of France and Navarre.

The book is revealing in other ways. The writer in love with his subject speaks out from the pages. As a boy he was happiest when at Downham. Said their father, "One son would never ride if he could walk, and the other never walk if he could ride". Richard had a pony which threw him three times in a single ride. Ralph's pony once threw him and he suffered head injury which brought his father posting home from Florence in 1840. The young heir later had a fever which gave him a year's vacation from Eton, and, though he cared little for doing Latin and Greek with the minister of Chatburn, he acquired much skill in fishing from 'Old Smithies' and became an excellent shot. When an M.P., Ralph introduced a bill which was passed through Parliament, on the variation of the trout-fishing season.

Their father's strict time-table was sometimes irksome. Household prayers always came at 9 a.m. before breakfast—but before that William had been out riding for some hours, or had attended Gisburn or Clitheroe markets or fairs, "after partaking of cold tea and bread and butter left over from the previous evening's supper". The usual 6.30 dinner was an hour earlier on Sundays.

Downham Hall

Richard often climbed Pendle and back between dinner and bed-time, an energetic lad.

The brothers were young when William began to throw himself with vigour into improving estate and village. His wife was a Cockayne of Northants, through whom several streams of English and Norman and French royal blood ran to the present family. She died two months after Richard Orme's birth.

Three years later the eldest child, Fanny, grew pale and listless, victim of a rapid consumption. At once William prepared to take her to Italy. He bought "a big yellow chariot with dickey, imperials on top, boot boxes and sword case". They set out on a journey which took over eight weeks. Fanny and her governess, and little Richard between them on the floor sitting on his play box of bricks, travelled inside, Fanny's maid and Richard's nurse in the dickey. Ralph was left at school in England. Arriving in France a second carriage was bought, in which William rode with the courier. So they 'posted' with frequent change of horses to Rome, joined there not only by Aunt Armitage and her five small daughters, their governess, maid and courier, but by other cousins too. A full house for their apartments in the Piazza di Popola!

Fanny's health did not improve. They all left for a villa in Florence. Among those who bade them farewell was the sculptor who had done a marble head of Fanny—a lovely young face treated with much tenderness. She was 16 years old. The marble is now at the stairhead at Downham.

In 1840 news came of enormous treasure unearthed on Assheton's estate, the Cuerdale Hoard. It is not every day such a find is made—silver ingots, silver armlets, many pieces of silver weighing 70 ounces 10 pennyweights, and no less than six to seven thousand coins, English, French and Scandinavian, none minted after A.D. 928. William at once left Rome for England, excited at the find, but anxious about young Ralph's riding accident, news of which had arrived at the same time.

As soon as possible he was back in Italy. It was obvious his daughter would not live. With her governess she was taken to England by sea, but at Southampton she died and a sad cortege—all the family having returned in the yellow chariot—bore her home to Downham for burial.

The anxious father feared little Richard had the same symptoms and insisted the brothers spent their Christmases by the sea, at Brighton. They preferred summers at Downham. "We were happiest where there was a river." When Richard was 13 and Ralph at Trinity College a dreaded creeping paralysis struck their father. Later Ralph gave up his commission in the Royal Lancashire Militia and abandoned reading for the Bar, to devote himself to his father's affairs.

Like almost every Assheton squire, he was a magistrate. Three practising barristers then shared the work, Jonathan Peel of Knowlmere, Henry Littledale of Bolton Hall and Thomas Parker of Browsholme, "men who would never let themselves be bamboozled by the attorneys or unduly led by the clerks". Like twenty other Asshetons he became an M.P., from 1868 till 1880 when he was unseated by the Radical Richard Fort of Read Hall.

Richard Orme summed up the reasons why. The tide was turning against the Tory government. A strong local millowner with many workpeople behind him, supporters of Assheton, had closed his mill and the workers had left Clitheroe. Also there were too many missionary boxes. "It had become known that Fort's most active canvasser, his mother, had visited the cottagers assiduously on his behalf. On one mantelpiece she saw a missionary box and asked could she put in a small contribution? Allowing the glint of gold to be seen she dropped in a sovereign". After which every cottage mantelpiece as by magic had a similar box prominently positioned. Fort was elected!

Ralph married the fourth daughter of Joseph Feilden of Witton Park, and nine years later Richard Orme married the sixth.

Ralph's son was 'Old Mr. Assheton', who used to smile at us when we wandered around Downham as children. We often saw him leaning on the gate at the Rimington Road end, surveying his lands. He was made a baronet, a well-deserved recognition for a life-time of devotion to Lancashire. Lady Assheton also was tireless in public works, constantly alert and watchful when what she considered good was threatened. To preserve and protect an inheritance as perfect as this needs constant vigilance.

I remember much local talk when the amenities of electricity and sewerage were brought to the village. Electricity and no visible overhead cables or proliferation of poles! And Lady Assheton telling me how she had diverted the telephone engineers from carrying new lines across lovely vistas when far less conspicuous siting of poles was possible by other, shorter routes. In many ways Lady Assheton reminded me of Queen Mary, a lifelong friend from girlhood when they were neighbours.

Back to earlier generations. What was William II's upbringing?

Young Asshetons at a tender age were sent to school, William went at 8 to Fairfields Warrington, and thence when 14 to Drury's House, Harrow. Cricket was his game, and he was one of the scratch eleven which played the very first Eton-Harrow match at Lords in 1805. Lord Byron was also with these players collected from Harrovians in London at the time. Eton, victorious, produced an epigram.

> O foolish boys, of Harrow School
> Of cricket you've no knowledge,
> You played not cricket but the fool
> With men of Eton College.

The college bard reckoned without Byron.

> If 'twas not cricket but the fool,
> No wonder we were beaten
> For at that game no other school
> Could e'er compete with Eton.

William II was very young when his mother by an amicable agreement separated from his father, taking the one daughter with her to live at Bath. Two older brothers had died, so William, now the heir, was a lonely little boy.

William I, his father, travelled far and often, for long periods, neither Downham nor Cuerdale seeing him. Asshetons had scores of relations and many doors were open to them: at Cornwell near Chipping Norton, at Waterstock, Thorpe Arch, Beaconsfield, his mother's home, and Brandon, where he died.

His friend Thomas Lister Parker and he had interests in common, in antiques, books, estate improvements, modern architecture —and pictures. When Northcote was painting at Browsholme he completed the portrait of "Mr. Assheton and a friend with guns, grouse shooting in Bowland". William I looks down on me now in the Library, a pleasant young man, content with his day's sport.

He had already been painted by the famous Angelina Kauffman in Italy in 1783, and by Allen, the royal portrait painter, in 1801, against a Cuerdale background with Hoghton Tower in the distance. Like his friend William never travelled without notebook and pencil. Richard Orme found a paint and wash Italian sketch to put in his history.

During his travels his son and heir progressed from Harrow to Brasenose College Oxford as a Gentleman Commoner. He was too busy during his holidays to miss his father's company—

staying in Cheshire with his mother's family, riding with the Cheshire hounds, out with the harriers, looking at horses, at kennels, shooting, dancing till dawn, acting in masquerades and plays.

In 1809 he came of age and was encouraged by his Brooke uncles to join the Cheshire Militia as captain; then later he became major in the 1st Royal Lancashire Militia. In 1816 he married a co-heiress of Sir William Cockayne of Rushton in Northamptonshire—an ancient family with noble and royal ancestry. His bride brought with her the portrait of a lovely lady in black velvet and magnificent pearls, one the Earl of Leicester had sent to the Cockaynes for safe keeping when Queen Elizabeth was to be guest at Kenilworth. Mary Queen of Scots? The Cockaynes were not asked to return the picture to Kenilworth.

When William I died at Brandon House in 1833 William II and his wife lived there. Downham Hall had for several generations been only an occasional residence. Yet both shaped Downham village, Hall and park as we see them today.

Before them were two Ralphs, the first born in 1696 and his son in 1719. During their time landscaping and tree planting were completed at Downham, the avenue of noble beeches in 1721 not long before Ralph I's early death. His widow was Mary Lister of Arnoldsbiggin, Gisburn. His son, a child when he inherited, sought farther afield for his bride, heiress of the Hulls of Hatfield; theirs was a Westminster Abbey wedding. They rarely visited Downham, the Hall and land being let to a local farmer.

These two Ralphs were of the line of Richard Assheton of Cuerdale, who in 1678 inherited from his kinsman Sir Ralph Assheton of Whalley and Downham all the possessions of branches of the family which had no surviving male heirs—a great inheritance.

Richard Assheton was born at Cuerdale in 1642, soon after his father's death following the Battle of Edge Hill, fighting for Charles. His mother was Anne, the youngest Shuttleworth, her family all Parliamentarians; his grandfather, his father John, his Aunt Parker of Browsholme, Aunt Rawsthorne, wife of Colonel Edward who helped Lady Derby in defence of Lathom, and his grandmother Hyde's family—Lord Clarenden's—were all monarchists, Royalists, Cavaliers.

This branch was descended from Ralph Assheton of Middleton, who married the Lever heiress. He was a son of Ralph whose wife was Margery Barton, heiress of the Middleton estates. This Ralph was the 'Black Lad', youngest child of Sir John Assheton, K.B. and half-brother of Sir Thomas the Alchemist.

Lord Clitheroe is of this line, and of the fourteenth generation at Downham.

From 1558, when Richard, second son of Sir Ralph of Lever, Receiver General for Lancashire, purchased Whalley Abbey and Downham Manor, seven Asshetons were to own them, and none with sons to inherit. It seemed that Fate dogged them, or a curse which the superstitious believed was on all who had trafficked in monastic property.

Richard came to the Hall of the Dinelays, former lords of Downham, knowing he would have to 'look around' for his heir. He made few alterations. To his nephew, Ralph of Lever, all was to come, he and Margaret Hulton were so blessed with children the heritage seemed now in safe hands. But their eldest son Richard died a strange death and witchcraft was suspected—the Pendle witches feared by gentle and simple—and Nicholas, the second son was only 35 when he died. The young son of Nicholas, brought up by Sir Ralph of Lever and Whalley, saw little of Downham, living at the abbey and at his mother's home, Worston Hall. He died unmarried, last of the short-lived second line.

We know the Downham country in fascinating detail as it was in James I's reign through Nicholas Assheton's journals, as they appear in Dr. Whitaker's *History of Whalley*. The originals disappeared when the learned doctor borrowed and forgot to return them. Someday, maybe, the journal will turn up on neglected shelves of some forgotten library.

This is not the journal of a country squire, but of the son and heir, who lived at home with his parents, or with the Greenacres of Worston Hall, the heiress to this adjoining estate being his wife. He was 25 when he put pen to paper, sometimes in serious mood, very often the opposite.

He had little money to throw around but made the best of it. He was a very pleasant and popular hail-fellow-well-met kind of character, never missing a market or fair, a rush-bearing, summer game, or local happening. In hunting the fox he rode far, after hares too, and when otter hunting and digging out badgers. He enjoyed stag hunts in Bowland in the season—and on occasion poached on private preserves, as at Walloper Well.

Take June 1617. One can follow his sporting activities on the

Ordnance Survey map. He 'sported' over my favourite walking country, ranging from Pendle to Bowland.

June 17th. With Br. Greenacres to Portfield. Whalley, Fox hunting.

June 24th. To Worston Wood. Tried for a fox. Took a rabbit.

June 25th. Killed bitch fox in Warren (Worsa Hill), Had a badger on Salt Hill. Wrought him out & killed him.

June 26th. Fox in Worsa Wood. To Bolton by Bowland. To Slaidburn.

June 27th. At Slaidburn. With Coz Assheton, father, Br. Sherbourne. Fished with 2 wades up to ye bridge. Sent some fish to parsonage. (Coz Assheton-Vicar) Dined at parsonage.

June 28th. Easington Woods for a fox. Found nothing. To Brunghill to find a fox.

June 30th. Fox hunting with greyhounds to Harden. Up Scout Stones, lost him in the holds.

July 10th. Still at Slaidburn. Parson. Fished with great netts. Gott some 47 fishes and laid away.

July 11th. 2 little drafts with scamel [catch net] only above Newton. Gott about 65 fish but no samon.

Apart from outdoor sports, what were his activities?

In early June he set out through Wharfedale to lonely Raydale above Semerwater. Here Aunt Robinson with her three children had "been attacked by Sir Thomas Metcalfe with 40 men & with guns, ½ score bills, picks, & swords," and thrown out into the night "without stockings, headdressing or shoes to a towne called Buske [Stalling Busk] & thence afoot to Worton". She sent an S.O.S. to Nicholas who rode out to her aid. When he asked audience of the belligerent Sir Thomas for a peaceful settlement of an old mortgage dispute, he was attacked by men "with sword and pitchfork and horseman's staff".

The outcome? The Metcalfe ringleaders were taken into custody and Sir Thomas was tried for murder of a Raydale Hall defender, but won his case, the court being on Metcalfe's side. Nicholas was at the hearing in the Star Chamber to give evidence. Thomas Metcalfe was fined!

It is February and there are as I write this, drifts of snowdrops under the bare beeches. Nicholas's journal before me. How did he spend February in 1616?

Grafted stone fruit from Holker—Cousin Elizabeth Preston's.

Wife in chyldbirth. Delivery of much violence as the chyld died within half an hour . . . but God spared her a while longer to me and took the chyld to his mercy.

Divers met & went with us [from Worston Hall?] to Downham

and ther the chyld was buried. My mother with me laid the chyld in the grave.

Later gave to the pore of Twyston, Downham, Worston, Chadburn and Clitheroe according as their several needs required.

Snow. Traced fox from Harthill to Warren—Some wyves of Clitheroe heer this day. Fooled this day worse.

Being a Puritan Nicholas was very conscious of lapses from grace in drinking. He often confessed in his journal to being "merrie, very merrie, merrie as Robin Hood, tipplied and was too foolish, playing the baccharalians", and on many occasions "too busy with drink".

In March he set apple trees, grafted graffs, and was pleased to retire indoors to his new room. "Study over ye porch begun and finished this week. Teeth lanced. Tooth ache. Headache. Cold and rheum."

He rode to Portfield "to visit Millicent Bradyll delivered of a sonne and heir. Richard Shuttleworth came by and Cooz. Bradyll and I went with him to Whalley. Ther light at the abbey. Cooz. Assheton went with us. All to wyne. Then all to Lancaster . . . XI executed [after the March Assizes, Shuttleworth of Gawthorpe then High Sheriff]. Cooz. Ed. Bradyll the priest [a Papist] came to the Bar. Indicted for seducing the King's subjects."

In April religious differences crop up again. "John Greenacres to be godfather of Richard Sherbourne's child. Parson of Slaidburn (Cooz Assheton) asked to be the other, but by reason of my sister's Papish disposition would not. . . . So in want of one I was taken." Always accommodating!

He took his church going seriously, in nine months "hearing 40 sermons, 3 bishops, and taking 1 communion".

He was with the large company of gentry at the visit of James I to Hoghton Tower in August 1617.

16th. Accompanied the King stag hunting, visiting the alum mines, stag hunting again. . . .

17th. Dr. Morton, Bishop of Chester preached before the King. To dinner. 4 o'clock a rushbearing and pyping. To supp. 10 o'clock a maske of noblemen, knights, gentlemen & courtiers—in the garden. Some speeches. Of the rest, dancing the Huckler, Tom Bedloe.

Nicholas probably shared in the revels and must have been concerned in the petition handed to James, against the prohibition of "lawful recreations and honest exercises" on the Sabbath. James gave his authority in May 1618 permitting "dancing, archery, May games, Whitsun ales and May poles" to be enjoyed on Sunday evenings—after folk had been to church.

"The beginning of the end", cried bigoted Puritans. "The end of the English Sunday."

In the old days the parson of Downham, they say, kept the football in the pulpit till service was over; then he himself kicked off from the church gates, and "battle commenced", a free for all game with the top and bottom ends of the village instead of goal posts.

After Richard's death his second cousin, and nearest kinsman, the first Baronet Sir Ralph of Whalley (and of Great Lever, which he sold to raise the £1,095 to pay for his 1620 title) succeeded. He had many sorrows for he outlived all but one of his ten children. Ralph, the sole heir, married Lady Dorothy Tufton, who died tragically young. He was overwhelmed by sorrow—but more followed, for the one hope, their only son, died as a child and the dear-bought title lapsed. He married a second time but was to die without an heir. Downham Hall remained a modest house, stone walled, with mullioned windows and heavy roof. No one becomes an enthusiastic rebuilder unless his own flesh and blood are to succeed him.

Among the seventeenth-century Asshetons two had been outstanding. Civil war dividing the country divided families too, none more than the Asshetons. Both Ralphs, of Middleton, of Whalley, were in the Long Parliament when Civil War began. Both were Puritanically inclined. Such men were apprehensive at the influence Laud and Wentworth had over the King, heartily disliking their fierce episcopacy. In 1640 they had decided their loyalty was to Parliament.

Ralph of Middleton led his father's tenants, the Middleton Clubmen, against the Royalists defending Manchester at the outset. Before the war was over he was Major General of the Cromwellian troops with many victorious campaigns and successful sieges behind him.

Ralph of Whalley played an important part in the Blackburn Hundred. Had the 'judicial murder' of the King not been discussed by Parliament soon after the Battle of Preston in 1648 doubtless both would have continued behind Cromwell through the Commonwealth.

On 6th December 1648 Colonel Pride with two troops arrived at Westminster, proceeding to drive out those known to oppose the killing of Charles. Among the 140 thrown out of Parliament by Pride's Purge were the two Ralph Asshetons. The major general was 'banished', but with "thanks for his great services to Parliament and nation". He died within a short time, in 1650. Sir Ralph of Whalley lived through the Commonwealth—Downham Manor becoming his in 1657—and at the Restoration declared his allegiance to the monarchy, as did many who had been evicted in Pride's Purge.

At Whalley Abbey and at Downham Hall he kept detailed accounts. He made many journeys to London in fine style with carriage and a large company of servants. Surprisingly a Puritan, he enjoyed masques, mummings and such spectacles.

In the 1660s he ordered the demolition of Whalley Abbey, the monastic church and cloister walls. Masonry was built into the high wall along The Sands, with a broad walk on top. The herd of white cattle which had long grazed in the Abbey Park—below Clerk Hill, now the Whalley Golf Course, found a new home with his kinsman, in the Park at Gisburn. They ambled slowly along the highway following a fiddler who played sweet music. During the 1670s entries refer to outside contacts.

Arundlet (40 quarts) of sack, from 'Sister' Dorothy Bellingham of Levens.

From Dunkenhalgh: half a doe, pheasant and a pair of buck's horns in the velvet [a great delicacy]; 6s. 8d. to the bringer.

From the great Tarn of Mawmoor (Malham Tarn); "greate troute and tench got by his own fishing by the bringer"; 2s.

A present for Sir Ralph: a large Downham diamond which gained 5s. 6d. for the bringer. 'Diamonds' were large quartz crystals found in nearby limestone knolls.

From the tenants of Downham: "received 56 tithe geese"— therefore the goose population was 560!

To the Rossendale players at Christmas: 10s.

To the ringers for ringing late in the night, in 1676 on November 5th. For gunpowder Treason and Plot, in excess of loyalty during a no-Popery period?

To Cousin Betty Harrington: £2 10s. to buy her a good dulcimer.

To the Scrivener for teaching little Jack Clayton to write four weeks at 6d. a week.

Expenses for the now old and ailing Sir Ralph; for cassia, for white wine, and, as prescribed by the Haslingden Doctor, "crabbes' eyes" to be taken in it. These were hard round substances from inside cray fish.

Outlay on 109 books and papers—most of them now in the Downham Library.

From London: ordered 3½ yards brown broadcloth for a long day coat and broad black broadcloth for a pair of stocking legges —to be made into a comfortable coat for a housebound invalid, and gaiters or wrappings for swollen legs?

In 1678 he made a will. A deed conveyed the inheritance to his kinsman Richard of Cuerdale. He left £70 to raise £4 per annum for sermons to be said at Downham and Whalley "upon the day of the month it shall please God to call me from this transitory life". He died on 30th January 1679, in London most probably, for his burial in Downham's new vault was not till 3rd March. Journeys north were slow and difficult.

On 30th January 1971, I sat with Lord and Lady Clitheroe in the family pew, the heir, the Hon. Ralph John Assheton and his wife behind. It was a Sunday afternoon when Pendle was streaked with snow yet deceptive warmth of the sun had coaxed into activity a tortoiseshell butterfly. The preacher of the Assheton Sermon 1971 was the Reverend Ronald Brown of Ashton Parish Church—his forbears had been parish priests of the early Asshetons. Because Sir Ralph believed folk would come in larger numbers to hear a strange preacher rather than their own, "though no better", he gave instructions as to payment and choice of text which have been faithfully kept for almost 200 years. The preacher chose his text from Job.

In his life Sir Ralph had been generous, had distributed alms every Sunday to the poor at Downham or Whalley. Now £100 was to be set aside "for ye poore, though not to itinerant wanderers and vagabonds, but to the most indigent and impotent neighbourhood".

Also he expressed clearly in the following lines his affection for the wife he had lost so young.

> Tis my resolution when I die
> Under this place to bear thee company
> That both together when the trumpe shall sound
> Thy husband with thee may be found

Before the service we stood awhile looking over the lawns and the rooftops of the quiet village—half asleep it seemed in the hollow, towards Pendle. To Lord Clitheroe every field boundary, every enclosure wall on the hillside, every clump of old trees and nursery of new plantings meant something; and every acre had its own story, culled from four centuries of Assheton ownership.

I thought of Harrison Ainsworth's often quoted words put into Nicholas the Diarist's mouth, and which many an Assheton in truth would have endorsed. "I love Pendle Hill and whatever side I view it, whether from Whalley where I see it from end to end, from its lowest point to its highest; from Padiham where it frowns upon me; from Clitheroe where it smiles; or from Downham where it rises in full majesty before me—from all points and under all aspects, whether robed with mist or radiant with sunshine, I delight in it."

The family could have chosen from many estates on which to live; they chose this, and as squires they saw no need to withdraw from village life. This was the pleasant proximity of which in 1864 Trollope wrote, the old-time squire, father figure to his tenants, casting a paternal eye on all, "To be near the village . . . once seemed to be the wish of a gentleman when building . . . A solitude in the centre of a wide park is now the only site eligible. When the old Duke built he thought differently. There stood the church, there the village and pleased with such vicinity he sat himself down close to his God and his tenants". So did the Asshetons.

I remembered a dear old soul, enjoying some garden fête in the Hall grounds, who commented with deep feeling as she surveyed the pleasant surroundings, the enchanting prospects, "I think as Asshetons 'as their Heaven on earth". If they have, they have worked for generations to make it so and given others pleasure too.

In 1955 Ralph Assheton was created Baron Clitheroe; in 1971 he became Lord Lieutenant of Lancashire, an office he fills with dedication and zeal—as did so many of his ancestors, twenty of them as members of the King's Council and Parliament, fourteen High Sheriffs.

Among fourteenth-century Asshetons one was in Edward II's Great Council, Chancellor in Ireland and Admiral of the Coast West of Thames; one Edward III's Chancellor of the Exchequer and King's Chamberlain; one Richard II's Household Treasurer, Executor of the King's Will; another Chancellor to John o'Gaunt —generations have given devoted service to Crown, nation and Duchy. Above all Lord Clitheroe remembers with pride his part as Minister in Sir Winston Churchill's wartime government.

PART FOUR

North-East Lancashire and Calder Valley Families

Shuttleworths and Walmesleys of Hacking

When young people today find themselves as modern custodians of ancient houses they take their responsibilities seriously. Not like parents and grandparents who tore out old hearths to put in tiled fireplaces, papered over beams and applied paint over oak panelling. Old halls which are now farmhouses are fortunate when a young couple like the one at Hacking continue to appreciate the beauty age has brought, and endeavour to keep the old character.

I have known Hacking all my life. My first attempt at sketching was here, interrupted by the too-close approaches of a skittish and curious young horse. "When it comes too near, just chuck your 'at at it", counselled a farm lad.

I remember a Christmas Eve, after midnight communion, returning to the Hall with friends—all the landscape white with frost, silver in the moonlight, the sound of ice splintering in the cart

Hacking Hall Farm

179

ruts alone breaking the quiet. How enchanting all looked, the Hall dreaming of so many Christmas days.

A Norseman called Haakon possibly chose this spot and named it a thousand years ago. Del Hakkings were here in the eleventh century and a William del Hakking emulated his overlord, De Lacy, by granting land to the Cistercian abbot; Hughlockspighel was site for an abbey barn, Stanlaw's, then Whalley's, which still stands with its ancient beams and crucks on boulder footings, the shell many times renewed. Later a Hacking heiress married Henry Shuttleworth of Hapton. Sons became 'of Hacking', but Ughtred, given the task of protecting the royal war horse breeding farm up the Calder near Padiham, built a tower there and founded the Gawthorpe line.

After three centuries there were no sons at Hacking so the heiress was given in marriage to Thomas Walmesley of Showley, a Papist who chose to be a conformist, well trusted by Elizabeth.

The inn on the Billington side of Whalley Bridge is called the 'Judge Walmesley', a reminder of the upright Justice of Common Pleas who became Judge of the Northern Circuit; and a good judge too if his epitaph was to be believed.

> He never did for favour nor for awe
> Of great men's frowns quit or forsake the Law.

He remained in office as a professing Protestant whilst others were losing theirs, amassed great wealth and laid it out in property. Not only Billington but the Manors of Rishton and Lower Darwen —from the unfortunate Talbots, and half of Samlesbury from the equally impoverished Southworths. In 1607 he rebuilt most of Hacking Hall in keeping with his wealth, leaving the old west wing for stabling and shippons. The new many-gabled grey house looked across the northern scene, all its windows framing pastoral acres on both sides of the Ribble and to the distant fells beyond. At the same time he decided on rebuilding the Rishton's house in 'Dunkley' Park, but retaining the old battlements and gateways; and here he and his wife took up residence for the remaining years of his life. His arms and Anne's are coupled over the door. He planted a lime avenue and yew walks to enhance the approach to Dunkenhalgh.

Walmesleys of Dunkenhalgh—a notable local name in the generations following, but as Papists, Royalists, Jacobites, and that brought them a packet of troubles. Sons were sent abroad when young and came back to take their part in Stuart matters. Hacking, tenanted, could offer shelter and a quick getaway over the ferry to the woodland and secret places up the Hodder. In the long attic a tiny window, more like a peep-hole and now stuffed with sacking, looked towards the approach from Billington; none could draw near without being seen, and anyone sheltering in the Hall was warned and able to escape over the Ribble.

The Judge's parents were 'stubborn Papists', his own family and in-laws Protestant and Puritan, but the next generation married into families like the Sherburnes and Molyneux, and even Sir Thomas, his heir, reverted to the Old Faith. His son Sir Richard suffered much when Parliamentarians—thick in these parts—looted Dunkenhalgh. The worst damage occurred in 1659 when General Lambert's soldiers raided cellars and in drunken revelry destroyed valuable family documents.

His young son Bartholomew was safe, smuggled out of England, but old enough to get into trouble when he returned years later. One day he surveyed his Hacking lands, and nearby Langho Green, where in Marian times a church had been built from abbey masonry and was claimed by Walmesleys for court and manorial business. It seemed abandoned so Bartholomew obtained the key and took possession as Lord of the Manor, had Anglican fitments removed and preparations made for Romish worship. The community rose up in anger and reported this to the Vicar of Blackburn, who told the "King's most excellent majesty" that this chapel of ease "long used for clergy to pray, preach and solemnize communion, repaired, furnished and provided with a bell at the cost of the people themselves", had been illegally misappropriated. After much altercation Judge Jeffreys ordered the chapel should be restored for Protestant worship.

James II had eased restrictions against Papists, but in 1688 Bartholomew had gone too far—his acts were open to suspicion and Whig spies were on the look-out. Lunt, chief informer, swore in February 1691 that he delivered to Walmesley at Dunkenhalgh a commission from James II etc. But, swore his agent, his master had not been in England at that time. He was freed after the Manchester Trial in 1694 but died soon after, leaving the boy Francis as heir.

When he was 14 he died. Young Catherine his sister, as a rich heiress, married a bridegroom equally young, but when smallpox carried him off in 1713 his 15-year-old widow gave birth to the eighth Baron Petre. So Petres took the Walmesley lands between Ribble and Calder. I now own one piece of it.

181

Nowells of Read

The pleasant Regency mansion of Read Hall, which can be seen from the drive through Read Park, was not built in 1820 by the old family of Nowell but by Richard Fort, one of three local printers who bought their estate after the death of the last Nowell in 1772.

Poor Alexander, his fortunes brought low by an extravagant wife, had no way to recoup the losses. His experiments in home wine-making from sycamore juice never reached a commercial stage. (An Elizabethan namesake was credited with the discovery of bottled ale.) His death was unexpected, during alterations at Read when his bedroom being untenable he slept in a newly plastered drawing-room and caught a chill.

Read Hall

Nowells were an outstanding family, especially in late Tudor and early Stuart times, halfway through their history. They arrived with the Conqueror. "No ale, no ale", was their battlecry —or was it the call for refilling when their overlord's cup was empty? A rebus, a covered cup is their badge. A Peter Nowell came north with an early De Lacy to the Blackburn Hundred, and a later baron, John, handed Little Mearley to William Nowell. Other sons were lucky with heiresses, Adam winning Great Mearley with his bride, and Roger of that branch marrying the Fitton daughter, who was joint heiress of Great Harwood; so their influence widened. And kings thought well of them. Edward I, to reward Adam for good service in Scotland, granted him a weekly market at Nethertown Harwood 'for ever'.

A grandson became first 'of Read' in 1364 when a half share was given with his bride, a del Clough. His brother and he arranged a swop, Great Mearley for the other half of Read. So there were two branches: one for four centuries at Read and one for a shorter period at the two Mearleys, those farms with the incredibly green limestone pastures close against Pendle's western flanks.

Little Mearley Hall which fits so snugly into its wooded clough was added to by Christopher Nowell in 1590—as the handsome back door shows. The fine stone bay window with its mullions, transoms and little pinnacles was originally part of Sawley abbot's lodgings. Master Nowell's wife was a Walmesley of Cold Cotes, into which her father had incorporated carved stones—from Whalley Abbey. Their property later descended from their only daughter's husband to Prestons of Kirkby Malham, and so to Proctors of Malham and Bordley.

Great Mearley, linked to Little by a straight track between bent and writhen thorns and crab apple trees, is now a pleasant farmhouse overlooking green open pastures across which runs the new Clitheroe by pass.

Nowells departed, leaving little sign of their home—though a century ago, before demolition, it was described as "roofless in ruins, wind and weather playing havoc". Stairs were wrecked by fallen joists, fine oak panels broken and spoiled, but from gable wings still intact and from stone waterspouts and peaked gargoyles it was thought to be sixteenth century and a dwelling of well-to-do people. Relics? Stone gateposts too fine for a farmhouse and turf-covered mounds in crofts, foundations of the old hall.

The Read Nowells? My mother's forbears came from a Richard Read of Clerk Hill, who married Sarah Nowell of Read and moved from Calder to Clitheroe four centuries ago. Maybe kin of the Nowells: of the Roger who defined Nowell pew space before the chancel at Whalley Church in 1536; or of the next Roger of Gray's Inn, eldest brother of three distinguished Nowells, whose widowed mother married Charles Towneley on receiving papal dispensation.

They, the brothers, were pillars of Protestantism. Alexander was a famous divine who became Dean of St. Paul's in Elizabeth's reign, after enduring exile in Flanders during Mary's. He was first headmaster of Westminster School, close to the Thames and with

Little Mearley Hall today

good fishing—his major relaxation, in which he was harmlessly employed in 1550 when an old boy warned him of imminent arrest and at once carried him in one of his ships to safety in Flanders and Frankfurt. When Protestant religion was restored he was able to return. In Edward's time he was on the panel of churchmen who compiled and wrote the new Book of Common Prayer.

Brother Lawrence was Dean of Lichfield, whereas Robert made a competent fortune at the Bar in London whilst remaining very fond of his boyhood valley. He made a will of more than ordinary interest. His executors dispensed money to give poor brides dowries, and also black gowns and small sums to 'pore scholars'. Heading their lists in 1570 and '71 was Edmund Spenser of Merchant Taylor's School, now a sizar at 'Pembrock Haule' Cambridge—a lad of Calder valley origin, his father and uncle of Hurstwood above Burnley.

Alexander carried out all the arrangements for Robert's funeral in 1568 in Old St. Paul's, disbursing "threescore pounds upon a dyner and a supper . . . and upon the poore of the parrisshe where I shall fortune to be buried".

About £100 and more, by modern standards, were spent on sugar, and large amounts on "Ale, beir in barrels, wyne malmesey, white wyne, a rib of beyfe, muttons, calves loynes, breasts of veale". And on "maribones, suett, capons, does, hennes, patreges, feasants, woodcockes, 4 dowzon green plovers, 3 curleyeus, 26 dowsen and a half skylarks", plus blackbirds, seapies, 210 eggs, vinegar, 100 oranges and 101 pounds of butter, put down as £16 —in Tudor money.

It would seem all the staff of "the churche of pouls" were involved and paid well for their part in the "funerall, celebrating and burienge of the corpe in 'Sancta Sanctor' ".

Alexander was on the Pope's blacklist and, had the Armada invasion succeeded, it would have been thumbs down, hanging or burning for him. Instead he was "England's mouthpiece of thanks to the Almighty" in the great Defeat of the Armada thanksgiving in St. Paul's, the Queen and Parliament being present.

In the next generation another Roger, "a religious honest gent", tackled with great thoroughness the witchcraft menace in the Pendle area where he was J.P. He swore to rid the region of the plague and by Good Friday 1612 had succeeded, for he organized a round-up at a Witches' Sabbath held that day and caught the Demdike clan, the Chattoxes. The pack, nineteen in all, were carted off to Lancaster to await trial. Roger was convinced they were possessed of diabolical powers, and so were the jury and judge in condemning twelve of them to death.

During the Civil War another Roger, who tried and failed to avert the tragedy at the outset, was a Royalist surrounded by families like Bradylls, Starkies and Shuttleworths, old friends now enemies. Fighting came close to his home, the battle of Read Bridge being almost at his back door; and mass movements and small bands of Roundheads constantly passed by. In 1644 he stayed with Lady Derby during the siege of Lathom. Later he received the earl's, and royal, thanks. But the year after Marston Moor his estate was confiscated; his compounding to buy it back was £736 4s. 6d., which must have taken much borrowing and mortgaging, with help of friends. In 1660 a sign of the King's gratitude brought short-lived pleasure, for Charles had second thoughts about his new Order of the Royal Oak, in which he was named for knighthood. The king was afraid the old Parliamentarians who had now sworn loyalty would be angered and 'old wounds opened'.

The Nowells at Read, like their 'cousins' at Great and Little Mearley, were in two generations to disappear from the Calder valley, as had many other local landed gentry whose arms appear in the fine heraldic east window in Whalley Parish Church. The survivors in 1816 paid £8 if their arms were there displayed. Nowells 'cups' are thereon. But the large Read Pew, the Kage, is the most interesting relic of Nowells of several generations.

In a high-handed declaration Sir John Towneley in 1534 settled a long dispute involving 'sittings' and pews. "My man Shuttleworth of Hacking" had made a forme near the chancel and this said Towneley, "I will sit in when I come, and my cousin Nowell may make one behind if he please".

Roger did please; the large square 'cage' tells us so, Made by 'Rogerum Nowell Armigerum' in the same year. In 1610 a namesake added his work and suitable inscription. Another of the same name set skilled carpenters and wood carvers to produce the fine superstructure for him in 1697. It looks almost new!

Fyttons and Heskeths of Martholme and Rufford

Who were the Fyttons (Fittons) and Heskeths of Rufford and Harwood whose names crop up so often in the county's history? And the Fyttons in Cheshire too, of Gawsworth and Bolyn in the thirteenth century?

Hugh Fytton received the Manor of Harwode from the Earl of Lincoln, a De Lacy, and Richard Fytton held Rufford, then owned by St. Werburgha's abbey in Chester. From that beginning two brothers branched out, one becoming 'of Rufford and Harwood', the other staying on the Cheshire estates.

Martholme

Heskeths appeared much later, virtually landless, though they found a claim to kinship with 'Heskaythes of Ruffourd'. By marrying Maud Fytton in 1276 William was thrust into the landed gentry, for she and her two sisters had shares in Harwood and Rufford. William was quick to buy Amabel's third and with more land buying was to become a man of much property and influence.

The lands of Nowell of Read were separated from Hesketh's Martholme only by the intervening Calder. Because of lands Roger Nowell held through his wife, Elizabeth Fytton, every year 'for ever' he and his heirs had to kneel bareheaded before the overlord—a Hesketh. Before all gathered in Great Harwood Church they were required to swear on the book "to do loyally all the customs and services as Hesketh's man, doing homage and loyalty". Nowells deeply resented this, so friction was frequent.

One document in the County Record Office in medieval French, tells of John Nowell making his act of homage to Thomas Hesketh in May 1429 on Billinge Hill near Blackburn, a great crowd witnessing, one official the High Sheriff, Sir Robert Lawrence. Hesketh, seated on a great stone, hat on head, received the homage of Nowell bareheaded and kneeling, taking his hands between his own and saying: "Sir I will be your man from this day forward and faith will bear you for the lands which I hold of you in Harwood . . .", promising to perform the necessary military service owing to the king, an essential act when any land changed owners. Hesketh kissed Nowell, gave him the book on which he swore as above, "so help me God and all the saints".

Martholme was held by knight's service—that is, they provided a knight, or his value—£10, for the king's wars. This old hall named from the low-lying site by the river, near a Calder ford, had also the protection of a moat, which gave the Heskeths more peace of mind, leaving wives and children behind when they rode away to do their duty—in France, Wales, Scotland, at Crecy, Agincourt and Flodden. During lulls in war Heskeths sported in their own park, or rode out hawking, with birds from their own mews.

In Edward III's time Sir John came to own all the lands divided between the two branches—all by Calder and by Douglas—having married a kinswoman who possessed the missing piece. Their son Thomas who was heir at 10, was snapped up as husband for his guardian's little daughter, Sybil Lawrence of Ashton, all agreeable for she was an heiress too. Their heir, however, had so many sons there was little prospect for the younger end, so they became priests. Two grandsons did very well each reaching the top. Hugh son of Robert, with the Earl of Derby's patronage, became Bishop of Man, and Richard, Attorney General in Henry VIII's courts of law.

Their eldest brother Thomas had troubles with women. His first wife horrified all when she confessed she was married already. There was a divorce, but he did not readily repeat the experience. For some years he 'lived with' Mistress Alice Haworth but informed the visiting Herald she was his wife! Such an attachment could not be repeated with Grace Towneley; he married her. But he had great affection for his bastards, making the eldest, Robert, his heir and providing in his will for them all, and their mother.

One earlier Hesketh, loving his natural son, made provision for him by depositing 1,400 pounds weight of plate for safe keeping in Whalley Abbey vaults.

Robert did not get the lands without a fight, for angry heirs-at-law put in their claims. He won, and passed all to his son Thomas.

Sir Robert, knighted by Henry VIII in France, was a man of "valor, forwardness, activity and good service". His son, was also well thought of, knighted at Queen Mary's coronation and still in favour with Elizabeth, for he was High Sheriff in 1563. Being in the Protestant queen's service he must have conformed at some time. "A soldier most valiant" in campaigns against the Scots, he was "sore hurt in the siege of Leith, had his ensign strooken down, recovered again and won great commendations for his forwardness and service". Being fearful of not returning, before leaving home he made his will, bequeathing his hawks to Derby, his stoned horse and mare to his friend Sir Richard Sherburne, and to John Osbaldeston the keeping of his park.

In his latter days, returned alive and well from Scotland, he set to rebuilding Martholme. The stone gatehouse with court room above and flanking porters' lodges was erected in 1561. Now it has been restored—a hard task for the walls were cracking and roofing dangerous, but it is still scheduled with the hall as a building of architectural value.

They were true Elizabethans, these Heskeths, with a zest for all that was new in that flowering period. Sir Thomas dabbled in new sciences; both he and his son knew John Gerard, whose *Herbal* appeared in 1597. At Martholme in a damp place he located the Lancashire asphodel; he planted specimens "for the increase of his garden—a diligent searcher of simples and fervent lover of plants", said Gerard.

They had a love for music too, and play acting. Heskeths had a company of players at Rufford Hall, among them an actor called William Shakeshaft; this band toured the Lancashire halls.

One brother was caught up in serious intrigue when he joined Ferdinando Stanley's players in the 1590s. Men talking of Elizabeth's successor named the Earl of Derby's son, possessed of the blood of the Tudors and Plantagenets. Richard Hesketh was a Papist, suspect on this count; when caught with other friends of Ferdinando after the discovery of the plot he was executed at St. Alban's. Soon afterwards Thomas Hesketh Esquire of Rufford, finding this house too dangerous, came to his mother's home at Martholme; he informed the curate of the 'Chapel of Mooch Harwood' of his arrival. News followed of the strange unexplained death of Ferdinando, now the Earl of Derby. Poisoned? This was a second tragedy for the Heskeths, after Richard's execution, for Robert Hesketh of Rufford had a Stanley for first wife, and their son was heir. Dangerous days, but they came through.

They lived through the Civil War and managed to hold on to the family estates after Parliament sent men to sequester them— very remarkable because of their reputation as obstinate Papists for three generations, and malignant Royalists as well. The next Robert professed to have wholly agreed with Parliament "in their just and honourable undertakings". Most probably treatment was mild because Robert's wife was daughter of the Parliamentarian general, Alexander Rigby of Middleton, who naturally made sure his little grandson was to have a goodly inheritance.

Later generations grew too big for the old houses of Martholme and Rufford. Rufford Hall was vacated for a new Victorian Hall, and Martholme became a tenanted farm.

Now Martholme is owned by young people with a young family; they are taking great care and do not mind how many years it takes to restore it to something like its old pre-farmhouse state.

Rishtons and Althams

Among notable Calder and Hyndburn valley families the Rishtons of Antley, The Holt, Ponthalgh, Dunkenhalgh and Stanhill started well enough. They had a vaccary (a cow farm) in the Forest of Akarintun, a summer lodge for yearlings, according to De Lacy accounts 1296–1305. One branch was of Lower Antley for many generations after 1417.

Later they became 'notorious' rather than notable, being too highspirited and, abetted by neighbours, as quick at the draw— of bow or dagger.

From Henry VI's reign when a Rishton of Ponthalgh was outlawed and Talbots of Bashall tried to seize his manor, there was enmity between the two families. But far more frequent were frays and fights with their own kith and kin, a most bloodthirsty breed.

Take the repercussions after Rishton of Lower Antley rented the tithes and oblations (offerings) of Church Kirk from Abbot Paslew of Whalley—a family friend who had been present at the wedding of Ralph Rishton then aged 9, to Helen Towneley a 10-year-old bride.

Roger Rishton of Ponthalgh proceeding to church was attacked by the Lower Antley Rishtons. He retaliated with a backing of six armed men, destroying Dunkley bridge over the Hyndburn one day, and five days later took thirty men to waylay his wife's father on his way to church. Nicholas Rishton in defence threw in his armed men, complaining of damage to the church, breaking of images and such acts of sacrilege; his Antley pew had been smashed by Roger's gang and piled on a bonfire in the churchyard. Roger could brook no interference, so what did he do but ambush poor Nicholas, beat him up and leave him on the ground sore wounded.

Such happenings continued throughout 1536–7 when local feeling ran high, the period when Whalley Abbey was suppressed, Paslew hanged, the brethren dispersed. Obviously, Rishtons were a family divided—very much pro and anti the dissolution.

In Tudor and Stuart times the Rishtons were papists. One son arrived in England with Father Campion as a missioner—and after trial was shipped back to France, fortunate to avoid prison or death.

Of their houses, Holt after passing to Talbots fell on bad days; little remains. Ponthalgh was sold in 1659 to the Walmesleys who had also acquired Dunkenhalgh at the beginning of the century, much altered and enlarged by the famous judge.

Another Calderside family which only came to the fore in stormy periods lived in their 'manor place' behind Altham Church. They continued feuds with the Chews of 'Cho' near Hacking for generations, raiding and shedding blood. They seemed to enjoy it.

A daughter of John of Altham married one of the warlike

Banastres—and that, of course, plunged Althams into the Banastre Rebellion, for Edward II and opposed to Thomas, Earl of Lancaster. A great many families almost killed themselves off at that time and many were ruined. One hears little of the Althams after Edwardian days.

Starkies of Huntroyd

When I visited Huntroyd on a golden October day, I sauntered along the deserted drive from the West Lodge, savouring every minute. The mile-long avenue of beeches, oaks and chestnuts still holding on to their red-gold, orange and tawny foliage, cut out all signs of the outside world, The Calder valley and the belt of linked towns out of sight and out of mind. When the drive ended and the open prospect was of sunny parkland, fine old trees standing singly and muted blue-grey distances, this looked little different from an eighteenth-century drawing in a book on Lancashire country seats.

All this five centuries ago was hunting country of kings and dukes of Lancaster: 'hunt royd'—a clearing granted to Symond-stones. Starkies were later arrivals when Edward left Stretton and Barnton to marry the Symondstone heiress in the fifteenth century. Theirs must have been a modest 'lodge', but late-Tudor Starkies changed all that. One left his initials and date, 1576, over a door, and fifty years later John, High Sheriff in 1633, added his over an archway. They say Inigo Jones had a hand in the building. But this was not the elegant mansion drawn by Hunt-royd in Georgian times, set on a gentle rise with landscaped grounds as a fit setting. The first Starkie named Le Gendre planned this.

There have been many recent changes. Mr. Guy Starkie left his supervision of the building of new barns and farm buildings and Mrs. Starkie her motor mower, to show me the house. They have pulled down old sections, made modern improvements, so that Huntroyd can be run without a large staff, as a pleasant family house. Four-year-old Nicholas was expected home soon from his prep school, in the mini-bus.

Five centuries is a long time for one family to continue in possession of ancestral estates. One can always identify Starkie possessions by the dark-red paintwork on farms, cottages and gates, and by the inn sign 'Stork'. Their friends and near neigh-

191

bours were the Shuttleworths—both families committed to the cause of Parliament in the Civil War; one was Preston M.P. in eleven Parliaments during and after the Commonwealth. A son, Captain Nicholas, was killed with scores of his troops in an explosion after the surrender of Hoghton Tower in 1643. Colonel John had shared in the provision of Roundhead defences at Manchester and was co-leader with Sir Richard Shuttleworth of Parliamentary forces of Blackburn Hundred.

Huntroyd

I wondered why pride of place among the fine pictures on the walls—mostly of ancestors and their brides—was one splendid Van Dyck portrait of King Charles I. Obviously the Starkies, who captained Roundhead troops and held office—one as Sergeant of the Exchequer and High Sheriff—as supporters of Cromwell, changed their opinion at the Restoration. They held many posts of honour and trust in later years.

Le Gendre Nicholas Starkie—a most distinguished ancestor with an unusual name! The family tradition says he saved the life of a Frenchman or a Belgian and was asked to adopt the name. He had a stake in two counties—M.P. for Pontefract and Commissioner of Peace for the West Riding, and Deputy Lieutenant and Magistrate for Lancashire. His great work was, of course, the splendid restoration and additions to Huntroyd in 1777, making it the pride of the Calder valley.

Later generations spent less and less time in Lancashire, possessing other houses in London and on the south Devon coast, leaving the staff to care for Huntroyd and agents to manage their large estates.

I heard a tale from an old Padiham man who was invited, the master and family being absent, to see the greenhouses. He was a boy at the time and his friend a most enthusiastic garden lad eager to show off. Halfway through the tour they realized that a tall gentleman was at the door. The garden boy in alarm pushed his friend into a half-empty water butt. "It's Mister Starkie back home!" For a few minutes the master and very new employee talked of plants and their care. Then, suddenly, Mr. Starkie stopped in his progress and in a stern and loud voice commanded the boy, "Get your friend out of the water butt—and show him round like a gentleman, you young rascal!"

Later I wandered at will over the lawns, standing well away to enjoy the pleasant prospect the better. Huntroyd is a little-known, rarely-seen mansion wrapped in its own quiet seclusion.

Below the house the land drops into a small valley, watered by a hidden brook, shadowed by the dense foliage of a wild wood. Leaf drifts covered old paths, ivy mantled rustic footbridges.

In the woods, Mr. Starkie told me, are some trees five centuries old. On the front lawn stands in solitary state one venerable limbless broken-down hulk of an ancestral oak: a pity it can tell no tales.

Shuttleworths of Gawthorpe

It was at the shield hanging at Lancaster Castle—in May 1966 when I was writing *Portrait of Lancashire* —that I was inspired to dedicate the book to Rachel Kay-Shuttleworth. On the Shire Hall walls were the Shuttleworth arms appearing time and time again throughout the centuries whenever a member of the family held the office of High Sheriff, the king's deputy. Few families, thought I, have been more closely linked with the government of the county and its well-being. There was no woman I knew who had for so long identified herself with its life and history. Also I knew her as a dear friend.

When we met we talked always of Lancashire, the part her ancestors had played in peace and war. We probed into the branches of her family tree and turned the pages of the 'wide book' in which for many years she had built up a Shuttleworth history. As a young girl when her father realized her enthusiastic interest in genealogy and heraldry he made sure she started out on the right lines—a famous Victorian genealogist was to teach her.

Sometimes we made 'lucky dips' into the pages recording Shuttleworths and their family alliances, with copious marginal notes and insertions, letters, pictures, heraldic illustrations that were even more revealing and fascinating than the direct lines of research.

The roots of the tree were back in the Middle Ages with early Suttlewordes and Schutelsworths named; and Shuttleworth near Hapton, with land at Billington in A.D. 1200; and of Hacking when one married the de Hakking heiress; and of Gawkethorpe, Ughtred being the first to live at the great stone pele on Calder bank in Edward II's troubled times.

That the early English name Ughtred was often chosen for sons —'uhte-red' meaning 'early in counsel'—was always cause for pride. Many Shuttleworths were able counsellors of kings and parliaments. Their role for generations was to serve the cause of peace and good government. Rarely were Shuttleworths bred for war, but when war was inevitable their sons were at the forefront. There is a long list of those who were killed. . . . At the Hall were few weapons, only a long pike chest, which was the type of armoury used in the Second Crusade, of blackened oak, iron-barred. Shuttleworths fought then.

The Tudor period pages were more full of matter. Other names are linked with Shuttleworths, the branch at Hacking married to a Winckley Hall heiress, and Anne the heiress taking her inheritance to the great judge, Thomas Walmesley. At Gawthorpe sons had married daughters of old local families—Worsleys, Parkers, Grimshaws.

Hugh Shuttleworth and his Grimshaw wife had three sons who at the end of Elizabeth's reign made a decision. Gawthorpe Hall was old, neglected and ready for restoration as a family home once more. Sir Richard, Chief Justice of Chester—one of the many legal brains of the family—had for some years found Smithills Hall, left to his wife the Widow Barton during her sons' minority, a convenient home. There, as I have written in the Barton section of this book, he had a most conscientious clerk and household comptroller in his youngest brother Thomas who kept the accounts in such detail. Thomas married Anne Lever of Little Lever whilst at Smithills, and there his six children were born and there he

Gawthorpe Hall

died. Richard's wife also died and as the Barton sons were now more able to stand alone, time was ripe to return to Gawthorpe, with Anne Lever and her young brood.

The move came in 1599. The older boys had already started school at Burnley and were cared for in lodgings there, and doubtless Aunt Helen, wife of Roger Nowell at Read, kept an eye on them. The bachelor brother, the Reverend Laurence, B.D., Rector of Wickford, very interested in planning the new hall was also ready to travel to Padiham and he was to complete the rebuilding schemes. He outlived Sir Richard by seven years.

In February 1599 Mr. Laurence Shuttleworth began his accounts "touching his house at Gawthorpe".

Building material came rolling in, on wagons and carriages. Stone was quarried from the delphs close at hand, from Padiham Moor and Rycliffe for freestone. Timber came from Read Bank, from "Mr. Bradyll's wood at Whalley", timber trees from Mitton Wood from Thomas Sherburne, and great ashes from Nowell of Read.

Stonemasons heaved and shaped, slaters "squared and struck roddes of sclat at the pitte", wrights worked on timber whilst Roger Cockshutt, "fee-ed", levelled the ground, and John Baxenden set the new foundations.

Rearing day came in June 1602. A piper played on this day of rejoicing. Then the actual building was about to take place, all around the fourteenth-century stone pele with its massive walls. Within this, stairs were made "in the middest of the hall" and doors made within the old walls and 'flowers' built in. The 'Hall dower' was four days' work. A Burnley smith made its great lock and a smith from Billington the window casements, taking forty-four days.

During 1602–4 the new hall hummed with workmen, plastering, cleaving lathes and 'latting' the chambers, cutting plaster moulds, setting chimney pipes on the "hymost tower and battlements about the same".

Joiners were getting on apace with the ceilings, the gallery partition, furniture—tables and beds.

Stone carvers carved "my master's Arms in to stone" and cut the "fynyalls for ye starres".

In 1605 woodcarvers completed in the Great Hall gallery precepts of the brothers Richard and Laurence, Hugh their father and Thomas—in the door spandrels. A skilful artist set about with gusto carving 'images' of Sir Richard and Margaret, the Widow Barton, on the fine fireplace, and for cornice decoration three lions carrying Tudor badges, a man at arms and a woman with a distaff; all these in the withdrawing room which the family were to use as a private dining-room.

This was the period of elegant plaster work on ceilings, Italian artists excelling all others. So—teams of Italians arrived to create with beauty and detail the withdrawing room and long gallery ceilings.

The stone and wood work, the original window glass, leading bars and metal catches are still there. The plaster ceilings were once endangered, when surface coal mining and blasting during and after the war rocked the Hall. Miss Kay-Shuttleworth went around after each explosion sticking strips of Sellotape over the cracks the better to measure the extent of the damage.

Today the Hall looks permanent. New beauty was revealed by

Gawthorpe Hall, Tudor façade

winter floodlighting when the Hall was completed as the new college and centre for the study of arts and crafts, and had been formally handed over to the county in October 1970, an occasion in which the Shuttleworths took as much pleasure as the rest of the gathering.

"It is impossible for one family to keep such a great place as it should be. Far better it should be used for public good," one said, with no regrets for its past, only hopes for a useful future.

The new Gawthorpe really came to life when young Richard and his wife took it over in 1609.

Rachel Kay-Shuttleworth was always eager to talk of her Barton ancestors, the Bartons of Amounderness. One of Sir Richard's stepsons lived at Barton Hall and the little daughter, Fleetwood Barton, became his nephew's bride at the age of 14, after Richard Lord Molyneux repudiated a marriage contract (made when they were infants) "publicly solemnized but never consummated" and they were divorced.

I think she found a more 'compatible' type of husband. The young couple lived in London during the first years of the new Gawthorpe whilst Uncle Laurence lived. When, in May 1609, Richard as heir was needed in Lancashire, they returned north.

Travel was slow but completed with style. They rode through Barnet, Stony Stretford, Daintry, Coventry, Lichfield, Trent—so to Holmes Chapel, Budworth and Warrington, staying at roadside inns, tipping the maids, the men watering the mares, and those who mended damaged wheels, faulty pillions, the carouche, and "roped the bootes". Largesse was bestowed on fiddlers, musicians at their chamber door, "to the pore by the way". After a fortnight's journey—which cost £160 0s. 3d.—they came with relief into home ground. At Brindle they spent 12d. in ale, then refreshed continued by Blackburn to Padiham. An excited homecoming for Richard and Fleetwood, his mother Mistress Anne, brother Ughtred and his young sisters.

Gawthorpe was now a full house! What a merry time they had that Christmas! 'My Lorde of Darby's plaiers' played, and a succession of musicians, pipers and fiddlers. They all trooped to Towneley to be entertained and doubtless returned the hospitality. Everything went with a swing. Wedding bells began to ring. Sister Ellener (her marriage portion given to Mr. Assheton "£200 twice") was first to marry, then Sister Ann to Mr. Anderton of Clayton. Then babies began to arrive—twelve in all—and each a welcome addition. With careful consideration the parents chose precepts for each, with pious hopes. "Thus prays their Father that his children like Israel's offspring, learn ye the Lord to know, and His behests which never will decay and unto 1,000 generations grow.

"And this their Mother, that their inclinations to virtuous ways in perfect, pure religion, exceed their birth, excell their education, leading their lives in love."

The first birth at Gawthorpe caused great excitement: Dr. Jennion's fee for ten days was £5; William Wood and Cook wife had to go on horse back for the Wigan midwyfe—her payment 30s. Farrowe cowe milk cost 6d.—for the infant? A little boy brought posies for the mistress. A wench brought wimberries from Burnley Wood. All their neighbours' wives came to share their joy.

Once a midwife was called in "to help a cowe that could not calve" and given 2s. 6d.

Now Gawthorpe held three generations for the grandmother lived to a good age. In June 1611 the final break came with Smithills when "Beds were taken down and other work wrought".

In the accounts are now entries for expenses incurred by Old Mistress (£10 quarterly annuity) and by Young Mistress, who liked pretty things as much as when a young unmarried heiress. Her portrait shows her wearing a cute pointed hat with a feather perched upon elaborate hair style and a bright parakeet perched on her finger. Now, she received "comfits from London, sweet-meats from Manchester" and supplies of "Taffatie, saie [silk], goldwork, galloune lace, ribin, hooks and eyes, and dozens of silk and silver buttons".

At the same time 3s. 8d. was paid towards "powder and match for the beacons", and "To the Constable at Padiham ½ of 1/15 tax towards watching of the supposed wiches, 24d".

June 1612: "To Constable of Padiham towards taking Person his wife to Lancaster", 3s. 10d. She was Margaret Pearson, tried and acquitted but pilloried at Burnley and Clitheroe market crosses as a supposed witch.

In April 1613 6d. was paid for "bringing up of Bess Chattockes clothes"—Old Mother Chattox, second in precedence among the arrested Pendle Witches at Lancaster Castle. Richard was then a magistrate.

In 1617–18 he was Sheriff of Lancashire, so during the royal visit and stay at Hoghton Tower he was in the picture. In August 1617 moneys were collected by the Burnley Constable "for providing carts for the King's carriages". Richard, Fleetwood and company went to Colne to meet Sir Stephen Tempest and Sir

William Lister prior to their journey to meet James I. This was a busy year: expenses heavy, a third son born, and the need to borrow £200 from Mrs. Walmesley of Coldcotes, a relative. They had to show a proud front before the King, Mr. Sheriff and his house, and their three Assheton cousins who also accompanied them. The tradition that Richard burnt down his other house at Barton to avoid expense in entertaining James there, is probably without truth.

James was not loved locally. Ten years earlier he had thrown a bombshell at the Pendle Forest and Calder families declaring they had "unlawfully without right or title" entered and occupied royal lands. Advisors had been searching old records to find loopholes allowing James to make money. The old families like Shuttleworths and Towneleys, they discovered, occupied 'essart' lands, not copyholds. But the magnanimous king would allow them to perfect their titles—to lands their ancestors had occupied and improved for many generations—"on payment of 20 years ancient rent". This put £3,763 into the royal money pouch—finally twelve years ancient rents became acceptable to him. Lawyer Fanshawe settled the transaction for them in 1612.

Shuttleworths always had lawyers in the family. The brothers Nicholas and Ughtred were Barristers at Law in Grays Inn. Richard was to be M.P. for Preston during the Long Parliament, and little Richard, his firstborn, was M.P. for Clitheroe when civil war loomed ahead.

Rachel Kay-Shuttleworth was of the thirteenth generation from Richard and Fleetwood. The precept, she thought most apt of those written by Richard and Fleetwood, was that their twelve children should strive "to exceed their birth and excell their education". Lord Shuttleworth's children are of the fifteenth— "A long way off is the thousandth generation".

The growing up of the twelve children was in peaceful times and happiness was around them. In infancy the boys were sometimes parted from their parents. "Richard Stones wyf for nursing Mr. Richard for $3\frac{1}{4}$ years", and Mr. Barton (the third son) was nursed at Barton Hall when small. After this they were taught until 15 with sons of neighbours at Burnley Grammar School—or Clitheroe —naturally progressing to university, to Brasenose as Gentlemen Commoners, and to the inns of court.

The little girls stayed at their mother's side, with the company of neighbours' daughters as they acquired the skills every good gentlewoman should know. They plied their needles on silks and linens, and span fine threads on beautifully made wheels, chattering in the sunshine pouring through the windows of the long gallery. When visitors approached the Hall their eyes were first to see them and light feet ran down the many stairs to the great hall—to meet bands of actors: "My Lorde Monteagles Players", "the Players and Waits from Wakefield", "Waits from Carlill". Fiddlers and pipers played for the young girls to dance. On rare occasions came a Bearward, the antics of the lumbering patient bear making the little brothers laugh uproariously and loth to let him go, the man rewarded by 12d. from the Mistresses purse.

The youngest child Anne was 22 when Civil War began. The brothers and sisters had married into families both Protestant and Papist—Standish of Duxbury, Sherburne, Towneley— Margaret to Towneley of Royle and young Anne's second marriage to Towneley of Barnside, but her first husband was son of Radcliffe Assheton of Cuerdale. Ughtred's wife was daughter of Radcliffe, and Barton's wife Elizabeth Assheton of Cuerdale. Their aunt was also an Assheton wife, mother of the posthumous child who became heir of all the Assheton estates. All these Assheton alliances were with the Royalist branch. Yet from the outset of civil dissention Richard, their father, was in command of Parliamentary forces in the Blackburn Hundred, his neighbour, Starkie, a colonel with him; but their in-laws, Towneley, Nowell and Sherburnes and Cuerdale Asshetons now, in the divided nation, their enemies. Five sons were Roundhead captains, whilst many brothers-in-law and cousins were officers in the Royalist forces.

During the war Gawthorpe Hall was military headquarters, organizing defence of the vital cross-Pennine routes and from here troop movements were planned, and succeeded.

There were solemn occasions in 1642 when Shuttleworths, Nowells and Starkies believed Civil War could be avoided if men of goodwill got together, met in Bolton and talked things over. In October 1642 Roger Nowell and his friend and neighbour Richard Shuttleworth sent out invitations to six men inclined to the King's cause and six to Parliament's. But the Parliament forbade them to hold this peace conference.

At the same time Lord Strange despatched messengers to known supporters and to Parliament leaders, including Shuttleworth and Starkie, asking them to join with him at Warrington. No Parliament men turned up. He expected Shuttleworths to be on his side. Later in the year great multitudes of Papists and malignants rallied to the Royalist standard erected by Sir Gilbert de Hoghton on the Tower. From the Fylde, Leyland and Preston they "ran to Blackburn . . . disarming all and pillaging some . . . which Master Shuttleworth a Pt. man and Master Starkie hearing of presently had gotten together . . . about 8,000 men". The Royalists were bent on re-taking all arms and spoil seized by Parliament from East Lancashire Papists and stored in the arsenal, Whalley Abbey. They failed when Shuttleworth's forces stopped them at Enfield Moor, putting them to flight, attacked them the same night in full moonlight, took Blackburn—and retook all the arms from Whalley they had to leave behind.

From this victory Shuttleworth and Starkie troops, "with those sturdy churls in the two forests of Pendle and Rossendale have raised their spirits and have resolved to fight it out rather than their Beefe and fatt Bacon shall be taken from them".

Such was the quality of the men who marched in and out of Gawthorpe, some with young Captain Starkie's foot companies who attacked and took Hoghton Tower in February 1643 and were numbered among the killed in the explosion which followed. And others were with young Captain William Shuttleworth's Foot ten days later at the taking of Lancaster and formed the garrison under his command. Some returned in March with the body of 'Master William', killed on his way to the Castle with salvaged guns from a Spanish frigate beached at Wyre mouth.

In April, when the Earl of Derby with his 5,000 men surprised the Parliament leaders by 'invading' as far as Whalley, Gawthorpe was scene of great activity. Two troops of horse retreated from Dunkenhalgh to Padiham at Shuttleworth's direction. Caught ill-prepared Colonel Richard thought it best to retreat and live to fight another day; his captains agreed but not the soldiers; the musketeers, being resolute men, declared they would "have one bout with the enemy"—and at least see the colour of their faces. "God would fight for them".

The next morning they ambushed the earl's scouting party in Read Lane—a great victory after which "the Royalists never again looked up".

When William was killed early in the war, Ralph Assheton, the Cromwellian leader, brought back his body from Lancaster by Inglewhite and Chipping. Richard the eldest brother was so worn out he did not long survive the war. The elderly Colonel Richard was active through the Commonwealth as sequestrator of Royalist property—not popular among those who lost their possessions and whose money now provided pensions for Round-head soldiers. As a magistrate he bound couples in wedlock at Burnley. When he died his grandson Richard inherited.

Richard IV sat in ten Parliaments from 1705 to 1745, through years of great change. He was the 'Father' of the House of Commons.

The next heir James married the Aston heiress with extensive property in Derbyshire. There is a very attractive family group, now at Leck Hall Lord Shuttleworth's home, by a famous eight-eenth-century artist, Joseph Wright of Derby. Their eldest son took Gawthorpe, a younger son took over possession of Aston. Barton was still owned by the family until a Shuttleworth, whose patrimony it was, lost it by excessive spending and such untypical Shuttleworth indiscretion.

In the Georgian period the family were less in residence at Gawthorpe. London called the political and legal members; they also had a town house in Winckley Square, Preston, the centre of social life among Lancashire gentry of the time, especially in winter.

The tales of romantic entanglements of her ancestors during the reign of George III were highly diverting as I heard them from Rachel Kay-Shuttleworth, to whom each story seemed "as yester-day".

One precocious young student at Oxford fell head over heels in love with a ravishing beauty, the daughter of the Master of Magdalen; they called her The Infanta. They married, and he only 16. Both moved to the court where a Shuttleworth relative who knew of the marriage brought them to the notice of the King.

"A deucedly handsome young couple," said he. "Who are they?"

The Bishop told him, saying they already had a child.

"Then", exclaimed George, "I must knight him!"

George III had an equerry General Desgouliers, whose father was a notable refugee, the Reverend Theofilus Desgouliers who made a sensational escape from persecution as a Huguenot by floating in a barrel down the Garonne to the French coast, and then finding a boat to bring him to England and safety. He became Pastor of the Huguenots at Canterbury. Young Robert Shuttleworth made a runaway marriage with the grand-daughter, Ann, "She has the prettiest ankles", said her father-in-law when he first saw her stepping from a carriage. He gave them his blessing!

203

A later Robert, well loved as the people's magistrate, sought the hand of one of the Marjoribanks sisters. He went intending to court Rachel, but instead married Janet.

Their only offspring, Janet, was orphaned as a child. Her mother married a North as her second husband, this leading to friendship with successions of North women, most of them distinguished. One made a collection of very beautiful plant and flower studies for Kew, travelling in faraway places to paint them: an early and intrepid woman explorer.

Janet Shuttleworth, the heiress, was a lovely child, growing up to be a most beautiful woman, as fair as her portrait shows. I once saw this, the work of Grant, who declared his sitter, the dark-haired lady in the white dress, was the loveliest subject he had ever painted, and doubtless as gracious and good as she was beautiful.

Her mother was a Presbyterian, pious, a devout Bible reader, devoted to good works, concerned with the welfare of the tenants and people of Padiham. Her daughter was carefully guided by her into the role she was to fill. She was disturbed to find so many illiterates in the neighbourhood. On seeking advice from London friends they told her of the best man to help her: a pioneer in elementary education—Dr. James Kay. Janet and he met, found they were kindred spirits and married.

Rachel Kay-Shuttleworth often told me of her grandfather's early life in Rochdale. Born in 1804, the eldest of six children, he began work at 15 in his uncle's bank. A clerk's life was not for him, so he went to Edinburgh to study medicine. He thrived on study and hard work, a brilliant student.

Fever broke out among the deprived poor of the Royal Mile, occupants of those once noble halls of Scotland's great and courtly families degraded to slum tenements; his first contact with such disease and poverty. Even worse he found when he became physician at the Ardwick/Ancoats Hospital. Then he studied at first hand the appalling moral and physical conditions of Manchester's working population. They huddled in a rabbit warren of passages, flooded by the Medlock river, muddy water seeping into dark cellars where they lived. Smoke, filth and degradation of the worst kind were there, and he was not a man to stand aside and do nothing. When cholera broke out and galloped from family to family. Dr. Kay worked strenuously to stem the rampage. It was difficult, for ignorance and apathy thwarted him, the poor hardly lifted their dull, apathetic eyes.

There were, however, some gleams of hope. Women rose to meet him and put down stepping stones of bricks from door to bedside to keep his fine boots out of the muddy ooze. Among the children were boys who showed intelligence. Some had learnt the rudiments of the three Rs, hopeful material to build upon: Miss Janet was sharer of his plans to educate them.

Dr. James was kept busy for the rest of his life—always for the betterment of the poor, the paupers, the workhouse minded, and for education of the 'Little Oliver Twists' at the public expense. Of course he had his opponents and critics but they needed him on their committees; he was the only one who had first-hand information.

Miss Kay-Shuttleworth thoroughly enjoyed her visits to St. Mark's and St. John's College at Battersea, the very first teacher-training college started by her grandfather. And surely the students and staff were as pleased to have her to share their important occasions.

She inherited from him skill as an administrator in which he excelled. He was one of the great Victorians.

The Shuttleworth-Kay wedding took place in 1842. In 1849 he was created a baronet. The two names were linked and 'K' liberally used for decorative and commemorative purposes when the outstanding architect of the 1840s, Sir Charles Barry, was called to Gawthorpe to alter and add new building to the old.

During Janet's early days little repair work had been done and it was high time the Hall, now nearly 250 years old, had a face lift. Plans had long been in abeyance. When Padiham was caught in the terrible Cotton Famine the plans were brought out. Now work and pay could be found for all the out of work, able-bodied Padiham men, on the outdoor alterations. The Calder was given a new bed away from the house, a bastion raised from excavated earth, terraces constructed and garden landscaping undertaken. The men worked well, and for generations Padiham folk were allowed to enjoy the gardens and grounds their menfolk had worked on—only the war years, when no gardeners could be spared from war work, ending this happy state of things.

To the Hall was added the top storey to the pele, the 'K' motto devised by Sir James—"Kynd Kyn Knawen Keep" repeated—and, at high level, airy servants' quarters. Inside the great hall the dining-room (a lecture room today) was given a splendid ceiling with linked 'K' and 'S' to commemorate the marriage of true minds. The stone fireplace replaced the open Tudor-Jacobean hearth at which "my father was nursed on my grandmother's knee and up the great tall chimney stack would see stars in the sky in the daytime".

Barry moved forward the gallery—memories of Clitheroe waits, Durham fiddlers, and the visiting players of Lord Derby, Lord Monteagle and their like, not only during the Twelve Days of Christmas but on their summer wanderings too—so that Lady Kay-Shuttleworth "could keep an eye on the servants without coming down from her room". When exciting guests were at dinner the little Shuttleworths—Angela who was 14 when Rachel was born, and Nina, and later Rachel with two younger brothers Laurence and Edward, and baby Catherine, stole from their nurseries in the north wing and peeped through the balusters, until discovered and shoo-ed back to bed.

Here madrigal singers and local musicians perform to audiences today, in a perfect setting.

When I am present at some College evening I think of what formerly took place in the same room—rent-day dinners, family gatherings and banquets when Rachel, deputizing as hostess for her frail mother, entertained her father's guests, listening and remembering the conversation and table talk of the V.I.P.s present for later she must return to her mother's room and give a full account. Excellent memory training; and how she made her recollections live! She recalled tales heard from her parents, who remembered Sir James and Janet—who had passed down almost-legendary tales of eighteenth-century Shuttleworths.

Somehow the generations drew close together—blended, became as though there were no gaps in time: only Shuttleworths. She was not there, though it seemed so to hear her, when Cobden and Bright made public speeches to crowds in the garden, orating from the steps. Nor when little Mrs. Nicholls and her husband sat on the moss-green velvet sofa in the drawing-room and with regret decided they would not accept the living and vicarage at Habergham, a church newly built. Charlotte's father, Mr. Brontë, said Mr. Nicholls, would not be happy living away from Haworth and they must stay with him. Nor was she at the Shuttleworth's Lakeland home, the Briery near Ambleside, when the newly discovered Miss Brontë was their guest—and wishing, had they realized it, to be left on her own at times, to walk this enchanting region; carriages carried the Shuttleworths everywhere. It is sad to realize that Charlotte Brontë's last visit to Gawthorpe led to her early death; she did walk, along the avenues and garden paths on rainy days in thin slippers. The chill led to worse illness and her tragic end, her expected infant unborn.

For Rachel as a little girl, Sundays at home were very quiet. Each child was allowed choice of only one plaything: Rachel after careful thought picked a Noah's Ark—a hundred toys in one! She thought of the Ark borne away on flood tide—and longed to travel. Her first ambition was to be an explorer. Thanks to Sir Ughtred's work her desire for travel was often gratified; he was much abroad.

He was ambassador to the court of King Bomba of Naples, where a daughter was born. As a gift to his wife he found a beautiful Raphael "Mother and Child". This became Rachel's, and as a Gawthorpe Foundation Christmas Card raised money towards the £50,000 endowment neeeded before the gift of Gawthorpe Hall to Lancashire and the nation would be accepted.

He was a notable member of Gladstone's goverment, Under-Secretary for Indian Affairs, Chancellor of the Duchy of Lancaster and Parliamentary Secretary to the Admiralty. He and his children were often with the Gladstones. The G.O.M., a formidable character, nevertheless had his softer moments when he took time off to relax. He would tell tales and whistle tunes to little Rachel and her brother, one on each knee, whilst his flashing eyes fascinated them at such close quarters.

Rachel's education included art training in Paris and lectures at the Louvre, visits to the Victoria and Albert—with a chaperone—and, when her passion for embroidery developed, lectures given by herself at the National Gallery—after some practice on the village women at Barbon, the family summer home near Kirkby Lonsdale.

Her father was Victoria's Privy Councillor. In the year of Edward VII's coronation he became the first Lord Shuttleworth— and Rachel 'came out'.

Now her travels began in earnest for, as she and her sisters were Lord Shuttleworth's companions and he was a Chairman of a royal commission on canals, they visited Holland, France and Germany. She visited her sister, whose husband was Military Attache to the British Embassy in Washington. With another sister she travelled through Italy—for which she had a lifelong love— enthusiastically taking photographs with a heavy camera and cumbersome equipment and themselves developing the plates, visiting churches and art collections—and watching and learning from craftsmen and artists at work.

The two sisters, in order to watch Tunisian women lace makers and embroidresses, once penetrated a closely guarded harem. The small girl who practised stiches along the straight lines of bed ticking, under her mother's watchful eye, was on the way to becoming an outstanding embroideress of her time and an authority on needlecrafts, gathering all she could of every century from the four corners of the world, the nucleus of her priceless collection.

The First World War showed her as organizer and launcher of new and necessary projects—local national relief funds, maternity, infant and child welfare committees—and in 1915 she took up Girl Guide work with enthusiasm: for thirty years she was County Commissioner for North-east Lancashire. She was a founder-member of the Civic Arts Association. She was the unmarried daughter who cared for her delicate mother, stood at her father's side wherever he went as Lord Lieutenant. When Death struck twice—one brother the heir killed in action in March 1917, and the next heir her younger brother in July—she worked all the harder in public. She devoted her private hours to her stricken parents and the three young orphan nephews. She also occupied her fingers on the embroidered counterpane for an ancestor's 1650 four-poster bed, then the curtains and the valance, putting the final flourish and finishing stitches to a nine years' labour of love, on the day the war ended, 11th November 1918. "Palm leaves for victory", she would say, showing off the final details of the embroidery. I thought of the monkish missal illuminators and their garden flowers entwined round letters and margins; and of the young ladies of the seventeenth century up in the long gallery working on their embroidery frames. Here were all the leaves and flowers of England embroidered into the Tree of Life design.

This bed and the embroideries, with furniture of the same century, now adorn the beautiful Period Room of the college. The Reverend Laurence's bedroom where the bed formerly stood is now a small lecture room, adjoining the Gawthorpe and Shuttleworth Documents Room.

Changes? But for over sixty years the Hon. Rachel Kay-Shuttleworth worked to achieve all this; and she refused to die before all was completed.

I think she would approve what is being done in the 1970s. And welcome the crowds of young students and smaller groups who come to learn more of chosen subjects—a surprising variety.

I watched a pageant put on in the old dining hall and enjoyed refreshments, 'Lancashire Fare', prepared by local students of cookery and served in the spacious new refectory where the old kitchens were. I could hear from the past her voice telling with much humour of King George V's visit. Lunch was served, the table spread like a coloured plate from Mrs. Beeton's book, pride of place a pyramid of strawberries carefully piled one by one into a luscious creation by the helpful bishop and her two brothers; temptation was too strong and one by one hands reached out and the pyramid dwindled long before the royal guests arrived! The king, however, was off colour that day: all he asked for was simple rice pudding!

Those were happy days, with seasonal movements of the family to other homes. Each move involved enormous preparations. The butler spent a full day packing the silver in a large baize-lined chest which was lifted into one of the carriages of a cavalcade taking family and household along the drive to the station where a special railway coach was reserved for them. They travelled in style in pre-war days.

The baize-lined chest—discovered a few years ago and at once utilized to hold some of the many treasures that came pouring in every week to augment 'Miss Rachel's' collection (which has now been handed over to the National Trust). From the priceless collection chosen articles are now fittingly displayed in a new exhibition gallery, made by removing the partition walls of the Victorian nurseries.

I once was told that there were 100 first cousins living. What impressed me most was an injunction firmly enforced by Sir Ughtred on his young daughter:

"My father told me one day, 'Treat every visitor who comes to the door, saying he is a Shuttleworth—and there'll be hundreds from all over the world—as if he were your first cousin'."

She went farther than that. Everyone who came to talk to her was listened to as if all they spoke of was important, and they were the only people who mattered. That made everyone feel good.

One day we were discussing Lancashire folk and outstanding characteristics: their friendliness, neighbourliness, hospitality, their forthrightness—on these we agreed. Brusqueness sometimes, verging on rudeness? "That I have never come across," she said.

Of course not. With her all without realizing it were at their best, their niceness brought out by her interest, kindness, grace and natural gentility.

If these words describe the typical Edwardian lady—tall, elegant, graceful, gracious, with an inner strength, "steel true, blade straight"—then Rachel Kay-Shuttleworth was one.

"And they don't make 'em any more like that—the mould's been broken", as a workman once remarked with deep thought and feeling.

I wonder what the 'people down the drive' think?

One day in 1966 she said she thought it was right that she should show neighbourly feeling to those "nice new people and their children who wave to me from their back gardens". Land in a long strip had been developed by a private builder along the drive within the park. Curiously they watched the comings and goings of the lady who lived alone in the big house.

"I'll invite them all to tea", she decided, "in three parties." They arrived—scores of them.

"We all enjoyed it enormously", she told me, "but none of them seemed eager to go home."

Within a year there was no great lady in the big house; the last Shuttleworth at Gawthorpe had died, and the last chapter written of the first book. Everyone is happy about the opening chapter of the new book of Gawthorpe, especially the Shuttleworths themselves who have good hope that the old hall—which was too large for any modern family and upkeep well nigh impossible—will have as long a life and one more useful to many more people.

Lord Shuttleworth had to make the decision in 1953 forced upon him by ill health and war injuries, and the needs of his growing family. Here was an inheritance cruelly cut by crippling death duties three times in as many years. When Lord Shuttleworth died in 1939 he was 95, last of Queen Victoria's Privy Counsellors. Two of his sons were killed in the 1914–18 war, and two young grandsons, Richard shot down in the R.A.F. the second Baron, and Ronald the third Baron killed in the same year, 1942.

No family could recoup such losses. The fourth Lord Shuttleworth chose Leck Hall as the family seat, not many miles from Barbon Manor for which all Shuttleworths have had deepest affection.

Though it is seventy years since the last Towneley lived at the Hall the family has not lost interest in the place. One day I talked with Simon Towneley in the long gallery. After a long session with the family tree in the 'Towneley Room' I reckoned about twenty-six generations divided the mother of Simon Towneley and his brother Peregrine Worsthorne, the well-known editor and broadcaster, from Geoffrey, the first of Tunley. He built a hunting lodge near the Brun on land granted by his father-in-law, Roger de Lacy, early in the thirteenth century. Geoffrey's forbears, the hereditary Deans of Whalley had long ranged the same countryside enjoying good hunting.

From this stock, English from the days of Alfred, plus Norman baronial, came Towneleys brave and good, brave and bad; and faceless ones in between who lived and died remembered by nothing remarkable. They adopted their name De Tunley when the Deans gave way to the celibate Abbots of Whalley in the 1290s and the family came to live here. In a short time their lands increased, by good fortune or marriages with heiresses. One of William and Cecilia's three daughters who wed John of the Leigh —the others married two Hargreaves sons—began a long line. Their son when he died held Towneley and Hapton, both coming in course of time to Richard de Towneley, whose shield, the first of five Towneley shields, you will find among the High Sheriffs' in Lancaster Castle, and whose good counsel as Knight of the Shire was sought by kings.

His grandson Richard was a small boy on the death of his father, John, whereupon the Duke of Lancaster as his guardian put him in the care of William de Rigmaden. In 1415 when "there was glory for England on Agincourt's plain", his Towneley followers were with the Billmen of Bowland where they "the palm bore away", victorious. That same eventful year was born his heir, John, who married a Sherburne and produced in good time many sons, five of them founding the separate branches of Towneleys of Hurstwood, Hapton, Barnside, Royle and Dutton, the heir of course being 'of Towneley Hall'. So their influence widened, their sons gained renown in war, and the more peaceably inclined, credit in the Law.

Richard of Towneley soon after he succeeded was away to Scotland, fought well at Hutton Field, was knighted there but did not long survive. The small boy who inherited at 9 years old lived long and his memory longer still. Generations talked of 'Wicked Sir John'.

John Towneley began well enough. The bride found for him was heir of the Pilkingtons, the last male dying in 1485. When he was 17 Henry VII licensed him to impark Towneley as preserve for small game. Like his forbears, hunting meant a great deal to him, but property even more as the years advanced. At Hapton was a hunting tower with a fine view over the countryside ad-

Towneley Hall

joining Towneley Park. To have them both, one extensive demesne, that would be worth something! He was 31 when the King granted him leave to enclose these lands, whereupon he set to with great enthusiasm evicting the tenants, driving off stock which had long grazed the Hapton pastures, demolishing cottages and riding rough-shod over the helpless folk. Naturally they objected, and thereafter dearly hated him. After the ruthless 'laying out' the tower was to be more of a refuge than a hunting lodge. If looks could have killed!

Legend says he never again had peace of mind, and his unquiet ghost haunted the lands he had enclosed, warning Towneleys:

> Be warned! Lay out! Lay out! Be warned!
> Around Horelaw and Hollinghey Clough;

To her children give back the widow's cot,
For you and yours there's still enough!

The bad he did lived after him, the good was interred with his bones, according to folk memory. At Towneley, they say, he thrust poachers and all who dared oppose him into the deep dungeons below the oldest part of the Hall. But he built the beautiful family chapel at the new courtyard frontage of the Hall —now rebuilt behind the north wing, and the Towneley Chantry in Burnley Parish Church was his foundation. He was a very valiant fighter, receiving knighthood like many of his ancestors on the field of battle. In 1531 he served as High Sheriff, respected as the King's deputy. A pity he blotted his copybook among his own people.

The next two generations were fated to be cut off in their youth. A 13-year-old granddaughter whose three little brothers had died was only survivor. Naturally great care was taken over her marriage, final choice being her cousin John, lawyer of Gray's Inn, after a papal dispensation.

John Towneley the Papist throughout the very worst religious persecution obeyed the family motto, "Tenez le Vraye" (hold to the truth). Towneley was 'blacklisted', on Burleigh's map his name marked with the X of greatest obstinacy. Aided and abetted by his wife and thirteen children he allowed secret masses to be held and priests to be harboured. He was more often in prison than at Towneley, as writing on a family portrait tells—"at Chester Castle, the Marshalsea, York Castle, the Blockhouses at Hull, to Manchester, to Broughton in Oxford, twice to Ely in Cambridgeshire"; by which time aged 73, blind and frail he was allowed to return to Towneley, "on a 5 mile chain". In 1601 he had already paid £5,000 and more to the Exchequer in monthly fines.

At this time the Towneleys' path crossed the Blundells and Southworths, but they succeeded, as the others did not, in holding their estates intact, partly through the intervention of Ralph Assheton, whose daughter married Richard the heir. He bought their forfeited property, holding it for the next generation. Equally useful had been the friendship of John's half-brother, Alexander Nowell.

How lonely Towneley Hall was in those days, close against the Pennine slopes, on the ancient ways which linked Lancashire with Yorkshire, along which men could come and few note their passing. So in penal times it was an admirable reception centre

213

for 'travellers'—in John's lifetime many being seminaries in disguise, in his son's and grandson's days Royalists and Stuart loyalists on equally dangerous missions.

According to a secret list of hides compiled by Ursula Towneley in 1680, the Hall was then riddled with them. Especially near the chapel door where "loose board opens to another hide" and "alter table draws out and upper steps for hiding the guilding". Over the Green Parlour, garret steps led to one secret room. In the library were cunning openings, a "middle panel by the closet door, backside of the door wainscot", sliding panels which gave access to space for hiding incriminating books, and a "hole by the door into which an iron hook is put and opens to a large place". One, 18 feet by 15 feet, was soundproofed by a daub, clay and rush floor: it provided reception for many at one time.

Some hides were occupied as late as the '45 rebellion. Of all their kinsfolk only Asshetons, Bradylls and Nowells were Protestant, the rest being up to the neck in Stuart plots and conspiracies.

Richard Towneley had a philosophical turn of mind, developed like that of William Blundell the Cavalier, during spells in prison. He began the transcribing and annotating of Towneley deeds and documents, which his younger son Christopher, one of Lancashire's early historians, continued, and from which Dr. Whitaker borrowed freely. He was a scientist too and must have been gratified to find his young nephew with the same inquiring mind, student of mathematics, chemistry and Greek geometry. They compared notes on expansion of gases. Young Richard began rain-recording at Towneley, an innocent diversion, during the waiting years of the Commonwealth.

Richard was orphaned when his father was slain fighting for the King. Charles Towneley the Cavalier when the Civil War began at once joined Lord Strange and his Lancashire forces, was in the fighting at Preston and escaped with his life into hiding. He had many near escapes when Towneley, in spite of the secret rooms, was too dangerous, hiding with tenants on their lonely farms. His wife and other Royalist ladies who followed their menfolk were carried off as prisoners of Parliament. When Charles had recruited more tenants' sons for the defence of the Pennine routes his task was an onerous one, for they were beset by Roundhead troops, and most of the countryfolk, "the sturdy churls of Calder and Pendle" fought for Parliament.

Prince Rupert's successes of 1644 buoyed Royalists with new

hope. Charles gathered his men together and off they rode over the tops to Yorkshire. They were with the Prince outside York; and were numbered among the thousands slain by Cromwell's army. Tradition says Charles' wife journeyed from Knaresborough to Marston Moor to seek for his body and was helped in her search by Oliver Cromwell himself. His men found the body among piles of slain. Was it carried back to Towneley for burial, or was his grave on that battlefield with his men?

One young soldier who did not return had bade farewell to his sweetheart on the Long Causeway above Mereclough, by the ancient waymark stone; she waited his coming, and when all hope was lost died of grief at the 'Maiden's Cross'; so says a local legend.

His young heir Richard held to the Towneley faith and Stuart loyalties, enduring confiscation of part of Towneley by Parliament and the restrictions of the Commonwealth. Being able to share his uncle Richard's interests at Carr Hall Nelson, and to follow his own quiet pursuits at Towneley helped him endure the tedious years before the Restoration.

Nothing could be done to improve Towneley during the next two generations; the family were compelled to stay quiet to avoid trouble. Richard was 61 when a warrant arrived for his arrest. He was accused with Walmesley, Blundell, Clifton and so many other Papists of conspiring against William III's life, with the evidence of Whig spies that he had enlisted troops for James II, had sent "cartloads of swords, pistols, carbines, jackboots and kettledrums to Hertfordshire "to be used against William. Instead of staying to meet his trial like the other Lancashire plotters, he must have decided there was no hope for him. He fled the country before arrest; no clemency for him when many Papists were pardoned by the king. Of the few names excluded Richard Towneley was one. He died in exile in 1707, and his heir five years later. Which was so timed that grandson Richard returned to Towneley when Stuart loyalists were waiting events, and the '15 rising not far off. He must have known what was afoot, his wife Mary being sister of the Widdringtons, so deeply involved in preparations for rebellion. And he must have realized the implications when he set off in a coach with a following of tenants, to reach Preston before the Earl of Derwentwater arrived that fateful November day.

When the rebels, betrayed by their leaders, were taken prisoners by the Hanoverian troops, so was Richard Towneley. He was despatched with Jacobites of notable family to prison and trial in London—his companions including Tyldesley, Dalton and Butler from the Fylde. Did he really believe his defence, that he was merely visiting Preston and caught up against his will with the rebel throng, was good enough? He was fortunate to be tried among the last prisoners when the court was sick and tired of condemning so many, the public weary of executions. He was acquitted, in spite of the judge's objection. A miraculous escape! But not for three Towneley servants caught with him; brutal execution at Manchester for them.

What was happening back at Towneley during those anxious days? The family priest recorded the masses said that November.

Nov. 3. For our King James III.
Nov. 15. For the soldiers—remembering the absent Richard and his Burnley servants.
Nov. 17. For patience and resignation—after the surrender at Preston.
Nov. 18. For resignation—when the worst was known.
Nov. 19. For James III—in flight to the continent.

There was much sorrow at Towneley during that period. Five infant sons died, leaving Richard's two brothers to continue the tradition of loyalty to the Stuarts. Francis was only 7 when Richard escaped the execution block; the little boy was sent to France to school, and stayed on to learn the skills of war under the King of France, training in a wide field of battles and sieges which experience he naturally, placed at the service of Prince Charles Edward. In 1745 Colonel Towneley was 36, gallant and bold, a fearless leader. His older brother Sir John had also served the French king whilst in exile. For chivalry and nobility he earned the title, Knight of St. Louis of France. He was a great scholar too, returning to his literary occupations in 1746; he was a fortunate one who escaped the butchery after Culloden. He had travelled north with Bonnie Prince Charlie when his invasion of England had failed, and passed over the border in the melancholy retreat, whereas Colonel Francis was left behind to hold Carlisle against advancing troops and the main force with the Duke of Cumberland at their head.

Surrender was forced upon him. His trial in London was in the early hearings, his execution the first of many.

There are many stories told of Colonel Francis. John Byron the Manchester Jacobite poet met him at Didsbury during a meeting of Stuart supporters. Willing to admire his military attributes his matching language shocked Byron.

216

Oh that the Muse might call without offence
The gallant soldier back to his good sense!
Soldier so tender of thy prince's fame,
Why so profuse of a superior's name?
For the king's sake the brunt of battles bear,
But—for the King of king's sake—do not SWEAR!

At Towneley Hall, on the top floor, is The Barracks, a secret place large enough to conceal many men—those waiting for Francis's leadership when time was ripe.

At Gawthorpe Hall carpenters a century ago, renewing window frames, found treasure—about £150 in gold coins and none later than 1745, mostly Spanish pieces. Was it Francis who hid them, believing here in this Shuttleworth house was the safest conceal-ment; Francis who thrust his dagger into the panel, lifted and dropped in the money, then carefully tapped it down with the pommel leaving dints in the wood? This has seemed the best solution of the mystery.

A story was told of Towneley's daredevilry when following the Prince on the retreat through Lancaster. In the priory church was a beautiful organ on which he played, no hymn but a stirring 'lilibulero' tune much favoured by anti-Hanoverians.

When the king shall come to his own again
And the Whigs shall run away.

That King George's men were entering Lancaster and this jingle was as a red rag to them, worried him not at all. He repeated the song, then out of the church, mounted and away! That organ is now in Whalley Parish Church, very fine in a Grinling Gibbon's period casing.

He led his Manchester Regiment over the execrable Shap road, fought at Clifton, continued north to Carlisle where his Lancashire men were loath to go farther. Therefore they were left to garrison the town, whilst the Duke of Perth's companies under Hamilton held the castle. After disastrous battering by Cumberland's 18-pounders Hamilton was eager to give in. Said Towneley, "Better die by the sword than fall into the hands of the damned Hanoverians".

He pleaded in vain at his trial that as a commissioned officer of France he should be returned to France. The death sentence he met with composure, "nor did his countenance undergo any change of colour". After execution friends begged his head should be given them, to spare the final degradation. So is there no truth

217

in the tale of his head being stolen by night from a spike on Temple Bar; to rest in the Towneley chapel?

The Towneley story in the following years is a happier one. Sons could now pursue peaceful arts unmolested, and continue long interrupted work on Towneley Hall.

Early Tudor Towneleys dwelt in a house foursquare round a court-yard, with a gatehouse entrance with flanking towers and a sacristy completed about 1500. Charles Towneley decided to open out the courtyard frontage by removing this 1500 work, carefully marking each piece of masonry for rebuilding, to the north-west, behind the great hall. The family chapel also became part of the new wing, in 1700.

Charles' son in 1725 found it possible to alter the entrance hall, removing a floor to open it out to the present roofline. He must have raised considerable revenue to call in so famous an Italian as Vassili, a master at plaster mouldings; the result was very beautiful, in white and terra cotta which modern decorating has tried to reproduce; a most attractive entrance now to the great house. What must it have looked like when it was background for some of Charles Towneley's Greek and Roman marbles?

When Francis and John Towneley were fighting for the Young Pretender, William of Towneley, who died young, had been succeeded by a little son, Charles. A marriage to Cecilia, Ralph Standish's heiress, brought valuable property to the Towneleys, Standish becoming the second son's inheritance. The young heir of Towneley sent to France for his education, the family tradition, had the guidance of his uncle Sir John and through him met the most learned men. Antiquities were to become an overpowering interest, making him one of Europe's leading connoisseurs, and the Pope himself sought his help in collecting treasures for the Vatican. So his exile was put to excellent use, and when he returned to England all the greatest scholars and antiquaries were among his friends. The Towneley Collection was eventually bought for the newly-founded British Museum, for £20,000.

He visited Towneley each summer, and walked and talked with his friends—like Blundell of Ince, and his brother Edward of Standish who became his heir and robbed Standish Hall of its front door to add dignity to Towneley's during the short time he was owner. Changes were too frequent. An uncle succeeded Edward, and six years later the new head of the Towneleys was his son Peregrine. The peregrine falcon was the family badge; one is carved on the Towneley pew in Whalley Church, and others wherever the family owned land.

Burnley folk used to comment when Charles the Collector, a rich man they thought, chose to live so frugally when 'at home', refusing to take a carriage when visiting his tenants, and appearing to be quite happy in his simple life.

In 1828 Catholic Emancipation allowed Towneleys for the first time for centuries to take their part in local affairs. Peregrine was first High Sheriff since Tudor times, an office held 1971/2 by Simon Towneley. What a number of new outlets now waited for members of old families whose skills could not be used for the public good during penal times.

Towneley estates around Whitewell and Dunsop covered thousands of acres and Peregrine was anxious to obtain more when offered for sale at the Whitewell Inn. Among the first arrivals at the auction was a shabby tramp, so out of place the rest made fun of him. The bidding could not start, said the auctioneer, until Mr. Towneley arrived, but to pass the time he ran a mock auction. The tramp made the highest bid and amid great hilarity the property was 'knocked down' to him, dirt cheap. Then he made himself known. He enjoyed the joke—as well he might!

Charles Towneley followed in his father's footsteps in county affairs but is best remembered as trainer of the 1861 Derby winner Kettledrum, a horse he and his friend Mr. Gillow of Leighton Hall bought in Ireland, for £5!

In the 1870s came the beginning of the end. Peregrine's first son was thirty years at Towneley, his brother only two, more tragic as his only son died the year before in Italy. Six daughters, now heiresses of the two brothers, as a result of an Act of Parliament each received fair shares. Towneley came to Alice Mary, wife of Lord O'Hagan, Lord Chancellor of Ireland; and here she lived for seventeen years before enormous upkeep costs compelled her to relinquish house and park—offering all to Burnley.

Towneley Hall is one of the best under public corporation ownership. Burnley does nothing by halves. They keep up, restore, add to what is there, and let the public enjoy all of it.

The other day a chattering, delighted and disorganized flock of toddlers from a nursery school were kicking up the dry autumn leaves along the avenue, near Boggart Bridge. Not a sign of any malevolent creature nowadays. They say the boggart who made such a nuisance of himself was exorcized by bell, book and candle, and made to promise never to return "whilst green leaf grew in the clough". To make sure they planted hollies!

The gardens were a joy, the one in front with the large pond most faithfully mirroring the whole of the house, central block and flanking creeper-clad towers; the one behind gay with flowers and admirable background to the high walls of the gracious Georgian entrance hall.

The entrance hall, neo-classic and the best work of Vassili who was called in to do interior decor in some of the most stately homes of Georgian England, is magnificent, a foretaste of more good things in store. Upstairs is the long gallery, panelled from end to end, nearly 90 feet of it; a pity none of the hundred family portraits remain. The period rooms off, once guest bedrooms, are each complete with period furniture, a useful source book for "Going for a Song" addicts, as are other rooms, full of antiques and choice pieces. The family dining-room is a peep into Jacobean richness and dignity. The restored servants' dining hall, flag-floored and still with original table and benches looks ready for henchmen and kitchen maids to take their places.

For meditation there is always the chapel, once the heart of the house.

Whitakers of Holme

 The gorge of Cliviger, "a long and solitary pass through the English Appennine, where eagles long ago clung to overhanging rocky spurs and instinctively the traveller struck spurs into his horse and accelerated his pace" (fearing what awful dangers?).

Probably the eighteenth-century wayfarer in his trepidation never noticed the house called Holme, tucked away safely in a sheltered nook a little distance from the old Burnley-Halifax road.

In the 1330s the successor of the Earls of Lincoln granted land to Richard de Whitaker—who arrived here from High Whiteacre near Padiham. Their kinsmen were the de la Leighs near Hapton linked by marriage with the Towneleys.

In time they married Nowells too. Thomas Whitaker married Elizabeth, sister of Alexander, Laurence and Roger Nowell of Read, which placed them on visiting terms with their more highly placed kinsfolk—Harringtons, Sherburnes, and Stanleys as well. Their son William was taken under Uncle Alexander's wing at

St. Paul's School, and went thence to Cambridge where his brilliance led to his election as professor at a very early age. In dispute few could master him, though the most vocal Papists pitted their wits against his, and Father Campion attacked him in his finest rhetoric. His death came too soon, through excess of study when Master of St. John's College. In his weakened state he set off for Holme but *en route* fever struck him down on 5th December 1595.

"The most learned heretic that I have ever read," wrote a Papist.

Elizabeth gave him the Chancellorship of St. Paul's; Lord Burleigh chose him as his chaplain.

"Champion of the Reformation", his friends called him.

When I first visited Holme some years ago I did not know why Alexander Nowell's portrait hung in the Hall—as kinsman and patron—nor that Elizabeth's portrait as a young queen had long been treasured by Whitakers who reached prominence in her reign.

Then the Tudor hall was timber-built, this being enlarged by two wings in 1603. More changes were made in 1717, after which the house of Holme was unaltered till the learned Dr. Whitaker, churchman and historian of Whalley, Craven and Richmondshire, began laudable estate planning. Dodd commented forty years later on the plantations along the road: "larch, mountain ash and birch trees at every step". Some of the 422,000 trees were planted between 1784 and 1799, when the Doctor was also

Holme

cutting out miles of paths "several miles in circuit" the better to enjoy interesting views, both romantic and dramatic.

Holme seemed a very pleasant oasis of calm in earlier days when Eagles Crag *was* haunt of eagles, and natives believed evil spirits lurked under the hanging rocks and that round every dark corner a witch was waiting.

Dr. Whitaker accounted for the disappearance of witches "to manufactures which had invaded the seclusion and liberated society from old distressing illusions, and commerce working towards disenchantment". Perhaps his own civilizing work had been a contributory factor?

In Dr. Whitaker's study, the morning sun pouring in through the windows, I once sat awhile, looking through the heavy leather-strapped earlier editions of his works, into which he had bound documents and letters received by his compilers. These histories were team work, his secretaries doing a great deal of searching through archives for him. The letters were interesting—each with additional material or corrections suggested by knowledgable readers.

But Nicholas Assheton's original journal was not bound within the covers! The Doctor borrowed, used—and often did not return! This diary was mislaid and lost. It might turn up some day.

Mrs. Macnamara who showed me the Hall was of Whitaker connection. Since then there have been several changes of ownership. Recently the Halsteads showed me their home.

No one could call Cliviger "notorious haunt of evil spirits" now. The horrors are banished. Express coaches, Leeds and Bradford to Blackpool, career by; Todmorden-Burnley buses, streams of passing traffic. If there were eagles, or carrion crows, none could hear them—except at quiet times, out of the holiday season.

Cunliffes of Wycoller

The badge of the Cunliffes is the coney, as it appears in the heraldic glass in Whalley Church east window. According to rather far-fetched tradition they came west over the Pennines ahead of massacring Danes, by Rossendale and Cliviger, but had a bad time when the Normans ruthlessly cleared up pockets of resistance in 1067, being forced west again, this time to the moors between Whalley and Wilpshire. They must have lived hereabouts for generations for Whalley Abbey documents and feudal records

222

Wycoller Hall in ruins

name them as owning "meadows, pasturelands, woodlands and turbary".

The Cunliffes, the eldest sons a succession of Roberts, entered deep waters during the York-Lancaster strife, and in 1500 one unfortunate Robert was outlawed, for "felony against the wife of Eli Wood". By the end of Tudor times the family had moved out of Billington township—whilst Judge Walmesley occupied lands bought from them. Now they settled down at Hollins, Accrington, identified themselves with Parliament and their sons as firm Cromwellians were in the thick of fighting locally with their father-in-law, General Lambert's, forces.

John Cunliffe married the daughter of a Chetham. Her uncle Humphrey, having sold sequestered Royalist property, was wealthy enough to buy the old manor house of Manchester and turn it into Chetham's School. John was a trustee.

One would hardly guess that Hollins saw so much movement and action during the Civil War. Accrington was on a route from Yorkshire towards Manchester, so here was a good half-way house for their friend General Lambert; in 1651 he arrived with a great following *en route* for Cheshire, there to intercept leaders of a planned Booth rising.

Where do the Cunliffes of Wycoller come in? When a son wed the daughter of the owner, and thereafter Hartleys gave way to Cunliffes. About this time there must have been a change

223

of heart if another tale be true, that Cunliffes "lost all for loyalty to the Stuarts" and retreated to the hidden nook within the Forest of Trawden for sanctuary. No Cunliffes are on the list of families who lost possessions as Jacobites.

A rocky eminence, called Foster's Leap—after a dare-devil Cunliffe of that name leapt it on his way home, looks towards wild moorland much enjoyed by the hunting-mad family. Foster was a great horseman and gambler, a trait shared by many before and after. One with horse and hounds gave chase to a fox over the old bridge opposite the Hall, into the rooms and upstairs to Mistress Cunliffe's bedchamber, where to the accompaniment of her screams and entreaties they made the kill. The pack of ghostly hounds driven by a ghostly horseman through the deserted hamlet on stormy nights could be his, and their howling and baying, as if the hounds of hell were let loose, heard in the winds.

They layed wagers on cocks too—very popular among local squires. A dying Cunliffe ordered his friends to a main of cocks fought out at his bedside to make the long wait less tedious. Full blooded they all were, and needed to be to weather the hard conditions of life in this moorland region. Wuthering Heights is not many miles away eastwards over the watershed. The Brontë sisters knew Wycoller and Charlotte heard here a tale of a mad-woman who burnt down a house—and made this the Ferndean of *Jane Eyre*. Henry Owen Cunliffe had died childless some years before and the Hall was abandoned.

PART FIVE

Fylde of Amounderness Families

Cliftons of Salwick, Clifton and Lytham

Since Osbert, early lord of Clifton and Salwick, came into the Fylde nearly a thousand years ago the Cliftons were top dogs, sharing the scene—more or less—with lesser families, Tyldesleys, Butlers, Rigbys, Bartons, Gerrards. The best of them were sheriffs, seneschals of baronial castles, wise men called into the council of kings, whilst the worst, their colourful deeds long remembered, were bad lads in their youth and a law unto themselves in maturity.

The Fylde, cut off from the world by Ribble, Lune and impassable mosslands, was always opposed to change and outside intervention, the folk all 'little Englanders' and the Cliftons more so. Take William in King John's reign, waging a private feud against foreign abbeys, man-handling Vale Royal abbot's agents, spearing one inoffensive monk, his tenants cheering on the sidelines, appropriating the abbot's mare for his own purposes, allowing the abbey tithe corn to rot in his fields, and threatening death to any who "touches my stock, my calves, my game, huntings and hawkings". His tenants shared in the beating up of a non-English priest in Preston, in broad daylight—knowing full well they must later crave pardon and do penance.

With neighbours they had trouble too. Robert Clifton, at the right hand of John Stanley in Irish campaigns and close to Edward I in Wales as chamberlain and receiver at the new stronghold and palace of Caernarvon, rode roughshod at home over Bartons and others who claimed rights of wreck of the sea, using force against them. And one unfortunate tenant of Little Singleton whose corn and goods he took from him he cast later into Westby prison as an escaped villein!

Fighting came naturally to Clifton men; honours were won at Agincourt, Harfleur, in Wales and Scotland, during their absences lesser lords in Amounderness coping with their children and nurses 'for the duration'. Bartons, Singletons, Hoghtons, whose ancestors had signed an agreement of 1304 that they and "their heirs for ever" would take charge of Clifton's offspring during their periods in the kings' service, deeply resented the imposition but had to obey, supplying also "all needful for Cliftons' sumpter horses, colts, for their hounds, goshawks, falcons and sparrow-hawks and men in charge". Another unpopular demand was the provision of thrice-yearly feasts "with free use of wine cellars" for Cliftons and their serving men.

Cliftons were fortunate to survive wars and win amnesties after civil strife. Henry VII pardoned them, maybe because of their friendship with the Stanleys. In the dangerous Tudor reigns during religious troubles, as minors were head of the house they were not implicated, though all were reared in Papist homes and betrothed to young Osbaldestons, Kirkbys, Molyneux and Hoghtons, often Papist in private if not in public. One 3-year-old heir was handed into Norris guardianship at Speke when Queen Elizabeth deemed the family trustworthy. His great uncle William had given his friend Alexander Osbaldeston the custody of his large brood, "to be a fader to my chylder as my trust is in him".

All were involved more or less in the trials of penal times when they took over their estates, but none thought fit to change their faith, nor did the rank and file of Fylde folk. They were fortunate to avoid penalties others suffered. Sir Cuthbert Clifton was able to buy Lytham Manor from the impoverished, penalized Molyneux, the old priory site becoming the new Tudor Hall of his heir Thomas and his young bride Ann Halsall.

In Stuart times, with Charles I's free pardon to Papists, they were ringleaders for King against Parliament. The spokesman for Fylde loyalists, Roman Catholics most of them, was Thomas of Lytham Hall. He mustered in the first year of the Civil War with "antique armor, corselettes, pikes, muskets, calivers, pistils, saddles" and obsolete "furnitures of war", last worn by warring ancestors fighting against the Scots, and won the king's permission for arms of more modern type to be provided for all Royalists, irrespective of their religion. Three young brothers fought and were killed, another doing dangerous secret work as a Jesuit priest. Another son with Prince Rupert outside York in 1644 was captured, with his friend Richard Butler, and both clapped into Manchester jail, where he died. When the war was over Thomas, surviving so many of his family, had all his estates sequestered and the money given to the navy. He did not live to see the Restoration but his son and heir Thomas was there to welcome

Charles II. The king created him a baronet but gave no money to help him buy back some family lands.

Some Cliftons were marked out by misfortune, none more than Sir Thomas, destined to see seven children die one by one, the only surviving son "A virgin masculine, whom sacred love did much refine", an old student of the school at St. Omers, living only to the age of 20. Apart from family tragedy old Sir Thomas, frail and infirm, had to face suspicion of complicity against William III in 1694 when a band of 'Dutch troopers' dragged him from Lytham to be questioned before the deputy lieutenant at Preston. Such a "peaceful and quiet old man, who often praised the Government and said the Catholics should be satisfied with the equality they now had with others" was the Deputy Lieutenant's defence spoken before the Jury in Manchester.

Though the old Sir Thomas was doubtless unfit to take part in any of the plots his neighbours were accused of, his forbears had always been foremost in Papist, Stuart and later in Jacobite conspiracies, and he must have voiced his pleasure with that of the old landed families of Fylde when all rejoiced and Kirkham bells pealed "On thanksgiving day when news came that James II's queen was enceinte" and even greater joy was shown at the birth of a prince. In fact Fylde gentry were quick to send from Garstang a congratulatory message to the royal parents: "Great Sir, the Happy News of the Birth of the Illustrious Prince of Wales has doubled both our duty and our diligence to return again with Joy and Satisfaction to your Sacred Feet, humbly to congratulate Yr. Majesty and these kingdoms on fixing the throne. . . ."

The countryfolk, less enthusiastic, were soon to ring the bells after James' defeat and the victory of the Boyne, and for discovery of the Popish Plot, no longer seeing eye to eye with the Cliftons.

The old Sir Thomas died soon after his release, leaving Thomas his nephew, as heir, and his brother to face Jacobite trials. They decided it wise to hide away in the wilds of Bleasdale. Three uncles, all had been political prisoners and had emigrated to Maryland, to the Potomac banks, but the brothers thought it best to stay in England, keeping on the right side of the law.

The Clifton Account Books of this period give no hint of implication in anti-government movements, unless frequent visits to Preston and Inglewhite fairs, or journeys over the Ribble at low tide to friends' homes at Bank Hall or Wrightington, to cockings or bowling matches, were cover for Jacobite conspiracy which was rife. Entries are innocent enough: costs of buying stirks, bulls, corn and hay—or selling them, amounts of fish caught in the meres, or the harvest of the tides, payments to folk who spun, twisted and twined hemp and who knitted and corded fishing nets (a 50-fathom net for 4s.). One might read between the lines and find clues in large loans, the Cliftons, being short of ready money, borrowing from Mr. Brockholes £100, from Mr. Eccleston £60, from Robert Osbaldeston £106—and why a loan of £2,500 from Dicconson of Wrightington unless for large building schemes being carried out at Kirkham Church?

Trying times were ahead. Who would the dying Queen Anne name as next sovereign, her Papist exiled half-brother, or German but Protestant George of Hanover? George it was, not a king to whom Cliftons could swear loyalty. So, "The family of Thomas Clifton were deeply engaged in the late rebellion, George his brother outlawed, and so many depositions made against Thomas and his steward, with proper encouragement clouds of witnesses could be produced to pin guilt on them". Small wonder that after the '15 rising—which ended the fortunes of many neighbours and kinsfolk—Thomas Clifton's 19-year-old heir with his Molyneux bride and her £6,000 dowry had absconded to France, there to become parents of one small son—who died young—and five daughters. The grandfather died at Lytham in 1720, the heir remaining in exile. His second son, born in 1728, became the next heir when 7 years old, and was 17 when the second Jacobite rising involved those Stuart loyalists who had survived the '15. He was the lucky one, with sufficient wealth to marry three times, support two daughters of the first wife, three daughters of the second, and leave a goodly heritage to his only son, born to his third wife.

This young man, born in happier times and faced by a more settled future, decided to rebuild the Old Hall at Lytham calling in Robert Carr of York to design a new mansion. This pleasant well timbered house within a spacious landscaped park was home of succeeding generations who added their work to the Lytham and local scene, draining and reclaiming extensive marshlands, grazing cattle on once flooded acres, growing crops, establishing rich farms. This reclamation made improvements possible, and new roads were built to open out long-isolated coastal villages. The Clifton-Kirkham-Wrea Green highway to the coast in the 1780s brought about a new era. The outside world, kept out by impassable swamps and meres since the days when Agmundr named the Scandinavian Amounderness and the Anglian settlers farmed the pockets of good land in the Fylde, discovered the seaside.

Naturally succeeding generations of Cliftons shared the more prosperous period but all insisted that Lytham should keep its green almost rural and village atmosphere—that the green with its windmill should not be touched—and no one ever thought the almost sacred park precincts would ever be invaded.

Now the family appears to have relinquished its hold. The Clifton Estates use the Hall for office work and the like. Plot by plot the park is about to dwindle as modern housing creeps in.

Cliftons had a good innings. They long kept their grip when neighbours fell on bad times, outlasting the Butlers, Rigbys, Daltons, Bartons and Tyldesleys whose fortunes were so often linked with theirs.

Tyldesleys of Myerscough and Fox Hall

 The Fylde Tyldesleys were fourteenth-century transplants from the place from which they took their name, just north of Chat Moss, about the time 'three wicked landlords' of the family had blotted their reputations and perpetuated their memories on the black list of south Lancashire traditions. Their Salford Hundred roots were not competely severed, for other Tyldesleys were of Wardleys and Worsley, and their dead were buried in Leigh Church—as was the brave Cavalier slain in Wigan Lane in 1651 fighting for Charles II.

Early ancestors' fortunes were tied up with Butlers when Lords of Warrington, but later Tyldesleys rose in the world by attachment to the Derbys, a loyalty surviving the centuries. One was Receiver General to the Stanleys when Lords of Man and others served the Tudor sovereigns, as did Thurstan, M.P. in 1547. His heir was 'of Wardleys' whilst a younger brother's bride augmented their old and long-held Fylde lands by bringing him Myrescough and Morleys.

The Receiver General of the Isle of Man and his successors saw to it that sons had good legal training, which served in good stead throughout the Elizabethan period when astute lawyers and attorneys feathered their family nests. Sir Thomas was James I's Attorney General, and sat in the Parliament of the North at York. He offered the king a warm welcome and good sport if he graced

Myrescough Lodge with his presence on his royal progress of 1617. James accepted and went hunting on Sollum Hill, on the breezy heights east of Garstang.

In the next generation died the last Tyldesley of Tyldesley. All their possessions passed to the Fylde 'cousins' in 1635.

Before long Thomas Tyldesley, a very 'firm Papist', as friend of the Stanleys was playing an active part in the Civil War.

The Fylde 'group', Clifton's, Gerrards, Layton Rigbys and the Tyldesleys, were early volunteers for the King's cause and issued with weapons. As soon as Thomas received his commission he raised companies of men from his neighbourhood, "every Captain a Papist". Ripe for fight they joined the Fylde freeholders and behind their leader marched to Warrington, and with Lancashire Royalists shared in the Battle of Edge Hill. Few returned. New fighting men were trained, 3,000 clubmen from the tenants and countrymen of Amounderness Hundred, to join forces with the Earl's 1,000 foot and horse, to protect and keep secure from the Parliament Lancashire and the north-west approaches. Which they did, until the King decided otherwise. "Take all your troops to join the Queen in Yorkshire", he ordered.

On that fatal April morning of 1643 Tyldesley left Whalley Abbey with the Royalist scouts to spy out the land, totally unaware of the ambush prepared by the stout churls of Pendle and Calder in Read Lane beyond Sabden Water bridge. After the shock of musket fire and confusion in the narrow way, he turned his horse around, leapt the gates and walls of Easterly Farm scattering the cows and barnyard fowl, and by roundabout route succeeded in warning the earl and the main army leaving Whalley what had happened. Little could be done to recoup the losses; the soldiers scattered and many made for home.

Whilst the earl starting from scratch, raised funds in the Isle of Man, Tyldesley did all he could to whip up enthusiasm for Charles' cause among his own tenantry once more. He trained the raw lads and led them over the Ribble to meet Molyneux and his men near Ormskirk. Major Richard Ashton and his very active troops intercepted them and a great chase began, back over the Ribble fords at low tide, across Tyldesley's home ground, left recently with such high hopes. They had been cheered by successes such as the capture of a Spanish frigate, its guns, its crew and a bevy of flashing-eyed Spanish ladies from under the very noses of Parliamentary troops set to guard it on the Rossall shore. That had given the young Cavaliers encouragement; escorting the señoras to Lathom was active service to their liking. Now—this humiliating flight over their own territory and no chance to call on wives and parents. Ashton kept up his chase to Cockerham, Lancaster and Royalist-held castles on the Lune. In spite of their opposition, before the summer was over Ashton had taken Hornby, and Thurland Castle too, last refuge for the wives and children of Royalist leaders.

Tyldesley was kept busy. He was put in command of Liverpool and Lichfield and made many sorties with Fylde soldiers when the Roundheads made ready for attack. He was among the last to retire from conflict. Parliament's sequestrators were very happy to lay hands on his property and enthusiastically appropriated its revenues, Fulwood tithes, moneys from Poulton rectory and Greenhalgh—£50 a year of this was used to "maintain a preaching minister and St. Lawrence Chapel, Barton".

In 1646 the Tyldesleys were stripped of their possessions; 1649, the execution of the King; 1651, the gates of Myrescough opened to young Charles II and his army. The next day Tyldesleys were behind him on the long journey south—but for Thomas only to Wigan Lane. As his roadside monument tells, "He followed the fortune of the Crown through the three kingdoms, and never compounded with the rebels—on the 25th of August 1651 was here slain commanding as major-general under the Earl of Derby".

Meagre years followed, during which Tyldesleys held on to their loyalty and their faith, harbouring priests and Royalists on the run, living at the loneliest of their houses, Fox Hall near the seashore—where is now the Fox Hall Hotel at Blackpool Central! A fox was chained to the door to deter too-curious visitors, so says a tradition; though the sea before and the impassable mosses behind were enough to deter undesirable strangers.

Like their Cavalier neighbours the family hoped for better times when the king came back. Edward went so far as to enclose common land at Layton, intending—with royal approval anticipated—to improve it for cultivation. Over the front door at Fox Hall he placed a fine new escutcheon. Charles was to inaugurate the Order of the Royal Oak to honour families most loyal to his father's cause, and Tyldesleys surely qualified. Their hopes faded soon, for the king anxious to prevent friction between the old Royalists and the new families who had now come out for the monarchy, so recently firm for Parliament, abandoned the order.

Edward received no title, no grant of common or waste, nothing to leave to his heir Thomas save his blessing, Myrescough and

Fox Hall; and also a legacy of heavy debts, £1,000 to be repaid to creditors who had helped to buy back lost estates.

Thomas was a diarist, so we can read how he faced the quiet life of a country gentleman in reduced circumstances. He was not alone; a strong bond of friendship existed among those who had shared the same losses, loyalties and suffering. Thomas, in public and among boon companions, was a gay, accommodating, hail-fellow-well-met, popular among Protestants and Papists. In private none more deeply religious, nor more ardent for the Stuarts.

Only the journals of his last three years have survived—those lost probably dealt with visits and journeys to Papist friends, to Jacobite meetings where King James II's fortunes were talked of. In secret they prepared for James' arrival by boat from Ireland; after his defeat by William on the banks of the Boyne he did not cross to this coast. At home during Anne's reign the family priest was told to pray for "our Master, the Pretender". At Walton-le-dale near Preston he was listed among the members of the Mock Corporations, a cover for Jacobite activities. Always the members toasted "the King over the water", fervently hoping for his return.

Tyldesleys could hardly avoid implication in the Lancashire Plot of 1689. Thomas was a close friend of Cuthbert Threlfall who lived at Ashes near Beacon Fell. Lunt, the paid informer, swore in June he had seen Threlfall at Cockerham with commissions from the exiled James, and had actually watched as they were handed to Cliftons at Lytham and to Tyldesleys at Myrescough. No smoke without fire?

After the anxious times of the plot and the Manchester Trial Thomas settled down as a peaceable countryman engrossed in family and country matters. His diary records hunting the fox, horse racing at Ormskirk, drinking with cronies at the Holly Inn, enjoying the cocks at Conder Green, a-fowling on the common, sea-pye hunting at Rossall; and paying calls on 'Brother Dalton' at Thurnham—in spite of the danger, especially after dark, of being robbed on Myrescough Plank, a cord causeway over the swamps. Very occasionally Mistress Tyldesley shared his jaunts. She was the dedicated housewife, much concerned with herbs and simples. Thomas was often 'physicked', submitting with lamblike docility.

Cures at Myrescough were not so nasty as those inflicted on the Blundells at Crosby. Pleasant by comparison was the blood purgative of scurvy grass pounded and strained with beer; beer boiled with licorice, good for the kidneys; manna as a laxative; cream of tartar and manna for gout fever; tobacco and oil of turpentine for lameness; warm cabbage leaves as cure for aches and pains. Less pleasant was the cure for the sufferer from fever, whose feet were placed inside live pigeons, cut open!

The last months of Thomas' life coincided with Queen Anne's. Had he lived, doubtless he would have been with his friends. Gabriel Hesketh, Ned Winckley, Richard Butler and Dick Shuttleworth, Brother Dalton and Cousin Wadsworth, answering the call when the Old Pretender's Jacobite adherents came along the Lancaster-Garstang-Preston road. His son and heir Edward represented the family.

With other Jacobites they converged upon Preston. Many had town houses there and, the winter season having begun, were already preparing entertainment for the Jacobite officers, whilst their excited wives and daughters thought how best to beguile the expected guests. Meanwhile the Duke of Marlborough, in charge of the Hanoverian army, had guessed Preston would be gathering place for rebels and that there he could round them up. When the rebel forces were wining, dining and courting from Wednesday till Saturday and Preston was agog, crowded with curious countryfolk in to see the excitement, Marlborough drew near.

On the eve of the rising the Preston clergyman Peploe spoke in the pulpit of the dangers ahead. "The Pretender is indeed of disputed family. While the Bishop of Rome has disciples in England expect designs against our religion and liberty. It is to our well-being to watch all Papist movements with care . . . allow them no power. Separate they are too weak. Now is the chance to end the threatening danger." Loyalties within Preston were divided.

Little did the gay crowds enjoying a rare social occasion know that as night fell on Friday 11th November eight regiments were massing across the Ribble and east of the town. The rebels had barricaded all approaches, six captured ships' guns had been dragged in on improvised carriages—Mr. Hoghtons coach wheels! Would these precautions suffice? The best marksmen as snipers had taken up vantage points on roof tops in Church Street and on the church tower. There was firing, elation among the rebels. Meanwhile the king's redcoats—General Carpenter having now joined General Wills—and some eager and valiant nailmakers from Chowbent under their minister James Woods—armed, with antique weapons from the Civil War and makeshift pikes hammered overnight on their forges, made ready to surround and take Preston with all the rebels in it.

To the rebel officers the situation now looked serious; the Northumberland rebels under Derwentwater, the highlanders under MacIntosh, the lowland Scots, were given their stations to defend. Before that Saturday was over the English troops had found their way over the fords, by side alleys to Church Street, and had fought for and taken and fired town houses. The fire and smoke forced the defenders from the barricades near the church, then in Friargate. Darkness only stopped the fighting. Where then were the Lancashire Jacobites from Fylde and south-east Lancashire, from Burnley and points east? Hiding, watching or actively engaged?

By Sunday morning Carpenter's dragoons had arrived to hem in the Jacobites. The Scots were still battling on, but the leaders with Colonel Oxburgh as their spokesman were for seeking terms. He was passed secretly out of the town to treat with General Wills!

Anger, confusion and despair seized the Jacobites when they realized their leaders had 'sold them'. On Monday morning outside the Mitre Inn the officers put down their swords, whilst the rank and file silently piled up their weapons in a great heap in the market place, and as silently allowed themselves to be herded into the parish church, in their hundreds. Among them were some who claimed wrongful arrest; they had merely been bystanders.

What Tyldesley and his friends did whilst they were in Preston is hazy. They were among the 1,550 rebels taken out of town to prison and trial. The main body of rebels, after bread and water and such cold comfort in the church that they had torn up pew linings for warmth, were herded and taken off to fill the jails of Lancaster, Liverpool and Chester. The Scottish officers were carried away from three Preston inns used to contain them and began their long journey south. The English officers and gentlemen had been guarded in Mr. Winckley's town house; they also were taken to London jails.

Among the fortunate who convinced a jury, growing weary of the whole sordid business of condemning so many men to death, that they had raised no weapons against King George, that they had been forced into the rebels' company in the excitement of fighting and borne along with them willy-nilly, was Richard Towneley who had arrived with a coachload of servants and been forced to mingle with the rebels. He and Standish and young Edward Tyldesley the jury would not convict. Other friends were freed also. 'Brother Dalton' after conviction was reprieved and returned home after long imprisonment. Richard Butler died before they had chance to carry out the death sentence. George Clifton was outlawed.

For the Tyldesleys it had been a lucky escape; to have been accused of raising troops, marching with sword drawn, dining with the rebels, drinking James III's health—and to be acquitted! The family henceforward did not meddle in dangerous politics. Fortune had knocked them. All their resources were needed to keep heads above water. Few had any enthusiasm for the second Jacobite rebellion which was something of a damp squib in these parts.

In course of time no Tyldesleys remained, their acres were absorbed in Duchy of Lancaster farms. In 1969 H.M. Queen Elizabeth opened a new College of Agriculture at Myrescough Hall.

Stanleys of Greenhalgh Castle

It is not obvious to passing travellers that Garstang has a castle. Now Greenhalgh Castle is but a hollow tower and fragments of crumbling walls, M6 to the east crossing 'the Park of Greenhall' which the first Earl of Derby had royal licence to enclose "for free warren and chase, and fine any who trespassed therein". Thomas Stanley was granted by his stepson, "as an act of gratitude for his loyalty and support" at Bosworth Field, the power to

Greenhalgh Castle Farm in 1971

237

"embattle, turrelate, crenallate, machionlate and fortify his new castle". This Stanley raised for his own security when given the Fylde estates.

Then many tall towers with linking walls rose proud and fair on the low green mound, a spacious courtyard within.

These lands, and others at Treales, Roseacre, Weeton, Prees, Elswick and Inskip—mostly added by a fortunate marriage with a Butler heiress—made the Earls of Derby powerful landlords in Amounderness; and a strong restraining Protestant influence. Fylde Papists, however, respected Stanley well enough to put themselves under his leadership during the Civil War.

Greenhalgh Castle was fortified and garrisoned for Charles, and when its small Royalist defence under Sir Christopher Anderton was forced to surrender it was the last which had stood for the King. Roundhead attempts to starve them out, dig them out, "undermine and blow them up", failed. Sickness and death among the garrison made them seek terms. Soon Roundhead batteries demolished the castle.

In 1870 Atticus wrote, "nearly every inch hereabouts is Derby's —the earthly deities are Lord Derby and his Agent . . . the people believe a lot of things but regard for Derby eclipses all—and would vote any day for the sun standing still if His Lordship said it might be so!"

Cardinal Allen of Rossall

At Rossall, between Blackpool and Fleetwood, the Fylde makes a sharp turn which receives the full battering of the waves. When rough seas thundered folk said, "That's Rossall's wife churning". Once high seas flung a Spanish ship on the shore, to be seized by Cromwell's men then captured from them by Lord Derby's Cavaliers, the Spanish crew and their Spanish ladies escorted in triumph to Lathom.

A ship of the Armada fired a cannon ball at Rossall, so they say. Spain and the Armada were often on the lips of the Allens, who lived here in Tudor times. William Allen came to be known throughout western Europe as King Philip's "devoted servant and subject", when the Spanish king was the hope of Papist Europe in reconverting England. When the invasion was complete William Allen, now Cardinal, was to be the Papal Legate who would organize the English Papists—half the population he reckoned— in destroying the Protestant church. His friends in Lancashire knew him as "a gentle, patient man, a good husband and father". To Roman Catholics like Philip "his Cardinal's hat was dyed on the blood of the martyrs he had educated".

Who was this man who had he stayed in the Fylde might have shared with the Cliftons, Butlers, Tyldesleys, the trials of Elizabethan times and survived as they did? In 1565 he resigned as Principal of St. Mary's Hall Oxford for exile in Flanders, founding a school for sons of English Papists, later moving to Rheims. There he received young men for training for the 'mission field' at home, to return as priests, inducing lapsed Papists back into the fold, and persuading Protestants to give up their new religion and be saved from everlasting Purgatory. His next move was to Rome and the English School, from which a flow of seminaries trained by him began to reach these shores.

He believed he had his finger on the religious pulse of the English. The Pope trusted his judgement but his ill-timed Papal Bull of Excommunication of Elizabeth "the pretended queen . . . binding under the same curse all who gave her duty, fidelity and obedience", had the opposite effect of unifying the English. The Bull meant that no man could continue to pay lip service to the new Faith, conforming in public but worshipping at home as he wished—as many did, finding Elizabeth's Anglicanism tolerable. Those who were "quiet and not manifestly repugnant and obstinate to the laws of the realm established for frequenting divine service in ordinary churches" were not persecuted. The Vatican was worried that so many now conformed.

Poor Mary Queen of Scots also believed, like Allen, that the rising of northern Roman Catholic families would free her. She would then be Queen of England and mass would once more be said in all churches. The Rising of the North failed; it was necessary, said Elizabeth's advisors, she should die to win peace for England. Then did Cardinal Allen pin his hopes on Philip of Spain. Papists had to make their choice: was their first loyalty as Englishmen to the Church, or the Queen? A wave of loyalty drove many to the Protestant Church. "God gave us Elizabeth and with her peace, and as long a peace as England has seldom seen before".

For those whose allegiance was for the Pope a very dark period was ahead. And for the priests, if arrested, there was the 'Bloody Question'. "In the event of an invasion sponsored by the Pope to dethrone Elizabeth would you fight on her side?" As simple as that! Life or death followed. For the many laymen coercion to the Old Faith was not to be countenanced, nor aid for an invasion from Spain, nor was the Infanta Isabella thinkable as substitute for Elizabeth.

The winds of God and the men in the little ships brought the Invincible Armada to nought. It was said that when news of its defeat reached the young students of the English College in Rome, many threw up their hats and cheered!

At Rossall the Allen family were in danger of arrest by the High Sheriff, but this was prevented by friends who hid them across the Wyre until the search was over. One hears little of the family after this, though one lady was in Queen Elizabeth's household!

Strange that centuries later the site of the Allen's home became Rossall School for sons of Anglican clergy and gentry.

Its Fylde roots were too firm for the Old Faith to be destroyed. It persisted long, partly because of a studied tolerance exerted by the Earls of Derby, landlords, neighbours, and often in-laws. There were Papists who came from counties where persecution was bitter to the 'Stanley country', where conditions were more tolerable.

Friends and associates of the Allens were Rigbys of Layton to the south, Butlers with lands by Wyre, and Daltons of Thurnham by the Cocker.

Butlers and other Wyreside Families

 The Richard Butler of Out Rawcliffe who died in prison before execution in 1716 ended the main branch of an old family, for he was last of the royal 'botelers' of Bewsey and Rawcliffe, Lords of Warrington, powerful landholders 'from time immemorial' in the Fylde. Once they held fishing rights in the Wyre—yet poached other men's salmon—and took tolls from two ferryboats making the river passage. Their church was St. Michael's, their chantry—for generations their burial place—there named St. Katharine's. When the church tower was rebuilt by them in 1611 the Butler arms, a shield with three cups, was carved thereon.

They also, as Papists, Royalists and Jacobites, sealed their own fate. Captain Richard was captured when fighting with Rupert at Liverpool in 1644, and possibly died in prison—or got away to fight and die at Brindle in 1651. Richard the Jacobite died in prison and his kinsman of Kirkland Hall might have met the same fate but for a timely rescue.

After the 1715 rebellion the Vicar of St. Michael's and others quickly bought up the Butlers' Rawcliffe forfeited estates, and after them the Ffrances'. Butlers retained Kirkland for another generation. In 1745 the Hanoverian troops, returning from Carlisle, made surprise visits on homes of known Jacobite sympathisers. They arrived at Kirkland Hall to take away Mr. Butler to Preston. The coachman did his best to thwart them by hiding the stable keys. This failing he begged to accompany his aged master. At the point where the highway at Barton Hall dips to a bridge he made a desperate bid at rescue by hamstringing Mr. Butler's mount. The old man fell to the ground, so badly hurt the soldiers left them behind. Later he recovered, thanks to the coachman's care.

Kirkland, a gracious Georgian hall, was to have another Butler as owner, the eccentric Butler Cole who according to his fulsome epitaph in St. Helen's Churchtown, "Courted no preferment or distinction but content with his ample patrimony chose an elegant retirement".

Rigmadens, another ancient family have their memorials in the same church. Wedacre Hall, between Garstang and the fells, was their home, near the forests of Wyresdale and Quernmore of which their menfolk were often Master Foresters. Elizabeth discharged one from this office because of "disorder and destroying of deer".

Fyfes became later owners of Wedacre and, as one of the few Parliamentary Fylde families John Fyfe commanded a company of soldiers. He was a casualty at Bolton in 1644, killed in Prince Rupert's attack. The Gerrards and Dukes of Hamilton later added Wedacre to their estates. The popular 'Dutchess' lived here as her Dower House in the days of George I. M6 cuts through the farm fields nearby, between bluebell woods and lambing pastures.

Across the Wyre from St. Helens, over a swing bridge, is Catterall Hall where in the thirteenth century lived Alan Catterall, whose wife was Loretta Pontchardon, an heiress who gave him the Manor of Little Mitton on Ribble banks, near Whalley, where later generations worshipped. There is a fascinating brass of 1515 in the north chapel once theirs, showing Ralph Catterall and his wife with a very large attendance of nine sons and eleven daughters—more fortunate than a grandson Thomas left with no less than seven, all daughters. What estate can survive division into seven parts? Robert Sherburne's wife Dorothy Catterall brought him Little Mitton, but their heir Thomas Sherburne, Papist and delinquent, faced hard times, and his son worse, for Parliament seized the lot, selling Catterall and Little Mitton in 1652. No hope remained of borrowing money; they were far too deep in debt.

In time Catterall Hall became a farmhouse, but Little Mitton Hall, one of the outstanding early Tudor houses in the Ribble valley had a succession of owners, and now, as a residential hotel, has quite a lot of its old dignity intact. It stands well back from the road, lovely gardens sloping to the river bank.

Land by Wyre was always worth having, about the richest in the Fylde until long-established landowners added to their acres by reclaiming the marshes. Heskeths had early claims on the Wyre bank at Mains, earlier called Monks Hall, buying it from the widowed Countess Derby in 1602. They were Roman Catholics like their kinsmen at Meols Hall on the edge of the Ribble estuary, at Rufford and Martholme. One son of the house married the young widow, Mrs. Edward Weld of Dorset, who in her second widowhood at 25 as the reluctant Mrs. Fitzherbert caught the amorous eye of George Prince of Wales, who wooed and finally won her. Perhaps she visited her late husband's home with him. They say she returned here when as his morganatic wife she was replaced by a royal bride.

When Earl of Mortain King John was generous in doling out land to his supporters. Geoffrey the Arblaster received Preesall and Hackinsall in that sunny neck of land over the Wyre toll bridge at Shard, his sons taking the name Hackinsall. Their end came in 1495—four daughters and no son.

One daughter with her fourth part was accepted as a Butler bride—as though Butlers were not already well endowed with acres—but this line ended in an heiress after a long period. A young Butler wife came from the lonely pastures of Wedacre, daughter of the Fyfe who succeeded unfortunate Rigmadens. Their great-grand-daughter Katharine—whose father had been court physician of Charles II—became John Elletson's wife, and their descendants have been at Parrox Hall in Preesall ever since. Their Hall, one of the most pleasant in setting and appearance in north Fylde, I visited one summer day when skies were unbroken blue, the gardens drenched in warm sun.

The Elletsons were accustomed to bluer skies and warmer sun in the West Indies, where they were among the first settlers and land holders, they and the Hopes into which family they married. Roger Hope Elletson was Governor of Jamaica in 1760 to 1768. There is an Elletson Road leading from the Kingston Harbour wharf.

The Hall is a perfect setting for splendid heirlooms of these days. One set of chairs covered in tooled Portuguese leather was a gift from the King of Portugal. Every lovely object has a tale to tell, relics of Elletsons at home and in hotter climes. This is one of the Fylde's pleasant surprises, a pocket of rural peace—not many miles from the coastal resorts and their milling throngs. In fact all the old places linked with Fylde history are come upon when least expected. And must remain so, unadvertised, uncommercialized, if their atmosphere and charm are to stay unspoilt.

The most interesting of the old Fylde families did not leave behind the most imposing halls. Radcliffes, Gerrards and the Dukes of Hamilton certainly lived in almost baronial style at Ashton Hall, set in a park north of the Conder which is now the very excellent Lancaster City golf course. The medieval hall, the Jacobean central block plus Mr. Starkie's Gothic battlements of 1856, form a most imposing mass—about the most impressive in Amounderness.

Tyldesley's houses have gone, Myrescough Lodge opened by H.M. the Queen in 1969 as an agricultural college on her Duchy of Lancaster land. Shuttleworth's Barton Hall is now H.Q. of the Board of Trade—giving us up-to-date weather forecasts. Fitzherbert-Brockholes' mansion at Claughton-with-Brock was demolished and a smaller house built for the family today. Lytham Hall of the Cliftons is intact—but one fears the age of modern building may overcome—some day.

Less important homes of less important families have fared better.

Ashes is a much more modest house in a remote setting, near the foot of Beacon Fell at Whitechapel, was home of the Threlfalls, with a family history which has in it almost every ingredient shared by all the others.

They held their land from Bartons of Barton, who claimed theirs at Goosnargh by payment of a pound of cummin yearly to the Catteralls. In the seventeenth century troubles began to pile thick and fast. Edward for non-attendance at church etc. was deprived of two-thirds of his land. Cuthbert his younger son, a Royalist, lost all by forfeiture as a delinquent early in the Commonwealth. How these unfortunates the Fylde 'squires', must have commiserated with others in the same boat. They stuck without faltering to their Jacobite allegiance, especially in danger periods following James II's flight and exile. One was the go-between who delivered to the Lancashire Jacobites their commissions from the king in exile, spied upon by arch informers—and whose name recurs in the stories of many local families who took part in the plot and came to trial at Manchester in 1694.

One day visiting Ashes farm I was told a Threlfall had been killed there "because he was a Catholic"—in fact Edward was slain by the militia in attempting to avoid arrest when they came for him, an accomplice of the Lancashire plotters (in 1690?). After his brother Cuthbert, Tyldesley's crony 'Cuddy Threlfall', took over Ashes a bad patch was ahead, for he too was a Jacobite in the '15. Was he the son of the house who sniped at King George's redcoats from the window? His sister Jane's husband, a farmer from Bleasdale, went with the rebels to Preston and was taken prisoner.

It is an interesting house where I have heard of ghosts and hauntings—usual where secret hides are contrived within walls, here beneath the attic's clay floor and bedroom ceilings. They tell of a chapel in the house, and that "once it was a convent", all pointing to its being a centre of Roman Catholicism.

Around the house, gardens and orchard was an encircling moat designed to safeguard the occupants back in the early Tudor times when it was new. Unexpected discoveries at a little-known house!

Another old house near Goosnargh has remains of a moat, its approach a stone bridge where once was the drawbridge. Chingle Hall was built by a Singleton in 1260, thereafter held by younger sons, whilst the heirs occupied Broughton Tower. The tower as such has gone, the hall remains, with its haunted room and monkish ghost, the headless ghost of a martyred priest? Or of John Wall the Franciscan born here, so it is thought, and executed in 1679? Secret rooms have been discovered, and a praying cross.

Brockholes of Brockhall and Claughton

 Brockholes took their name from the badger holts on Ribble valley estates bordering Dinckley Brook; their brock badge is found wherever the family held property, near Whalley and at Claughton-with-Brock near Garstang where they were living in

Elizabethan times. In the 1580s two marriages welded Brockholes with Bradyll neighbours: Thomas with Jennet Bradyll and her brother John with Elizabeth Brockholes, crossing the boundaries of religious differences. The Brockholes of Claughton became an important Amounderness family within the Roman Catholic community. One married his daughter to the Duke of Norfolk. Another married William Hesketh of Mains Hall on Wyre banks.

Their son married a Hampshire girl, convent bred Maria Smythe. He was her second husband. Mrs. Fitzherbert—"no beauty but fresh as an English white rose"—in her second widowhood at 25 was destined to attract the roving eye of 'Prinny'. The wooing, which began after the young Prince of Wales first saw her at the theatre in her black widow's veil, continued stormily for four years. It was interrupted by the widow's flight to France and Holland, "a virtuous religious woman", seeking sanctuary from his amorous advances; and the prince's threats to kill himself for love of her, to banish himself to America, to renounce the Crown if she would become his wife.

Mrs. F. eventually surrendered to his importuning when she was 29 and he but 23, vowing she would wed none other. She finally agreed to a secret ceremony performed by a clergyman, in Fleet prison for debt, who was willing to comply for £500. Prinny swore everlasting fidelity, provided his bride with a fine house near his own in Pall Mall, and carried her off to Brighton when his creditors grew too pressing. Yet in public he denied vehemently any marriage, especially to Fox who defended him in Parliament. In 1794 when the old king offered to pay his debts if he married his cousin, the unprepossessing Caroline of Brunswick, he agreed to a Treaty of Separation. Poor Mrs. Fitzherbert! George married Caroline, too drunk to care what happened, and in due course England had an heir. Three days after the child was born he made a will in favour of Mrs. Fitzherbert and "care of his spirit after death". The Pope had declared their marriage valid and the royal alliance bigamous. The two resumed relations for a while—until a new influence began to come between them, the comfortable, motherly Lady Hertford.

Mrs. Fitzherbert, it is said, sought the quiet of Mains Hall, her former husband's old home, in her forlorn state. When the Brockholes were without a direct heir to Claughton, her brother-in-law William Fitzherbert inherited, hence the name Fitzherbert-Brockholes for the squires of Claughton to this day. In their chapel in the village the priest once showed me in the baptismal register the signatures of George Prince of Wales and Mrs. Fitzherbert, as sponsors at the christening of an infant Brockholes.

Like the Bradylls, who remained in the Calder valley, this family had its ups and downs, troubles falling thick and fast because of their Roman Catholicism; they were fined and imprisoned, and in King James' reign forced to see their estates taken over by Scots, David Stuart and another court hanger-on. But they survived. Everyone around Garstang knows of their part in the modern life of the community.

Gerrards and Dukes of Hamilton

 When a fellow traveller on the bus near Garstang told me in all seriousness, "Lady Hamilton—Nelson's Lady Hamilton, once lived near here," I knew she was wrong. But how?

There was the Hamilton Arms with its splendid shield over the portico—we passed it a little later —and the Lancaster Golf House at Ashton Hall which everyone said was once the Duke of Hamilton's.

The truth was this. At Wedacre Hall, now a farmhouse close against M6, the Duchess of Hamilton often lived quietly in her widowhood—until 1744. Her Grace, the 'Dutchess', whose arrivals caused such a stir in Garstang—they spent lavishly on treating her—was the Gerrard heiress whose marriage to the young earl, soon to be Duke of Hamilton, came to a tragic end in a famous duel with Lord Mohun. In *Henry Esmond* Thackeray introduced the notorious case, and its political consequences.

Gerards or Gerrards only came into Amounderness in Elizabethan times. Their forbears were of Bryn near Wigan soon after the Conquest, a succession of soldiers, squires, and knights high in esteem. When Peter a younger son found an Ince heiress for his bride, that started the branch line 'Gerrards of Ince', which moved rapidly ahead in Tudor times. It was a good thing then to have a lawyer in the family, almost essential for preferment.

Gilbert Gerrard of Ince was a courtier who became Sergeant at Law in the 1550s, received knighthood from Elizabeth in the 1560s and became Attorney General and Master of the Rolls. This was good progress indeed, opening doors and the chance of a wealthy match with William Radcliffe's sister Anne on whom he had settled rich manors and mesne lands. This gave Sir Gilbert Gerrard manorial lands in Winmarleigh, Astley, Clitheroe, Balderstone, Showley Hall and estates in Mellor, Little Harwood, Pleasington, etc., etc. His 'good and grave office' was asked for in the foundation of the Queen Elizabeth Grammar School at Blackburn. His wife's kin had far-flung interests across Lancashire for Radcliffes were of Ordsall Hall, Radcliffe Tower, Smithills Hall, and had been Lords of Blackburn, Witton, Tockholes and Balderstone.

Sir Gilbert was always 'on the ball' in legal affairs and on the look-out for further improvements, in real estate especially.

His kinsmen, Gerrards of Bryn the senior line, were marked as dangerous Papists, their actions always highly suspect. Sir Gilbert's line had conformed and gained preferment, but Sir Thomas of Bryn, for his suspected part in the northern conspiracy to put Mary Stuart on Elizabeth's throne, was captured, imprisoned—and his estates confiscated for treason. Sir Gilbert bought up some of his Staffordshire estates. The Queen considering him 'trusty' gave him the wardship of Richard Hoghton, heir of wide estates from Hoghton to Walton and Lea after his father's killing by Baron Langton in 1589. Just the match for Gilbert's daughter Katharine!

His sons, Thomas and Radcliffe, became great names, founders of Lords Gerrard of Bromley, and Lords Gerrard of Brandon later Earls of Macclesfield.

In the Civil War Gerrards Papist and Protestant were Royalists all, eight sons colonels or officers and early in the fray fighting side by side with Cliftons, Butlers, Tyldesleys and Hoghtons, and fined as ferociously when Cromwell had overcome King, and the Commonwealth replaced monarchy.

The submerged Gerrards of Bryn recouped their losses with the Restoration, and built a new Hall at Ince. Members of the same family carried Stuart loyalties through Jacobite times. Sir William Gerrard of Bryn was tried at Manchester in 1694, with his friends the Andertons, Dicconsons, Standishes and Blundells, for participating in the 'Lancashire Plot' and like all the accused was acquitted with a caution.

At Ashton Hall changes had come in the 1670s. Viscount Brandon Earl of Macclesfield had no heir but his sister who had married Digby a distant Gerrard kinsman, fifth Baron Gerrard of Gerrards Bromley. All these high-sounding titles lapsed. The sole heiress kept the estates and won eventually a more noble title as Duchess of Hamilton, often at Queen Anne's court where her husband was Queen's Privy Counsellor. He was Lord Lieutenant of Lancashire and Admiral of the Sea Coast. And all ended in the 1712 duel with Lord Mohun, the sensation of the year.

In the next eighty years the succeeding Dukes enjoyed but short tenures, the Duchess's husband, son, two grandsons and a great-great-nephew—all of Ashton Hall. In 1799 the uncle of the seventh duke, Lord Archibald Hamilton, became eighth Duke of Hamilton.

Ashton Hall in 1850

The Hamiltons did a great deal for the Fylde, for the land, large areas of mossland were reclaimed; they set up their own tile works and produced miles of drainage material. Improved agricultural methods were introduced and Agricultural Shows established at Cabus. Last century was a period which changed the face of the Fylde, thanks to the Duke—and the Heskeths, Cliftons and Hoghtons.

In 1793 when Lord Archibald gave readily a site at Scorton for a British School "the appointment of a master was invested in his Lordship and his Lordship's heirs for ever".

'For ever' is a long time. Gerrards and Hamiltons were mortal. Lawrences, Butlers, Radcliffes too—only memories on the Ashton landscape.

Apart from Lancaster townsfolk and golf enthusiasts surprisingly few know of the existence of Ashton Hall, the fortified house of medieval times altered at different periods, now the Lancaster Golf

Club house. It stands in the old park, a formidable sight as one approaches, Green Court in front, the Edwardian pele on one side, its massive shell with 6-feet-thick walls, a seventeenth-century central block with the great door entered up a stone stairway, and numerous Victorian Gothic additions of the Victorian Starkies who owned it.

Once it was a stumbling block to Scots who came so far south of the border, and chance of shelter to families surrounding, warned of danger. In those days the moat gave a greater feeling of security.

Now, landscape with old Hall, it is very pleasant. In the twilight, and moonlight it all looks authentic, "as in the days of yore". But no longer as 'in days of yore' with an air of waiting for sudden onslaught death or disaster. The only weapons now are golf clubs!

So much of Lancashire looks so peaceful, so commonplace, it stretches the imagination to fill it with stormy scenes and warlike happenings. Ancient houses have an aura of calm belying their histories. The bearers of old family names are very pleasant people, as I have known them and enjoyed their unstinted help and hospitality. Often I wonder how the black sheep and skeletons in their cupboards can possibly have places on the family tree. Always I derive deep pleasure in discovering in what divers and diverse ways generations of the good, the wise and noble have made their mark on our history and Lancashire's landscape.

Index

251

252

Shakespeare [Shakeshaft], 52, 97,
115, 189
Sherburnes, 51, 147–55
Shuttleworths, 36, 54, 121, 180,
193–210
Singletons, 120, 145, 227, 244
Smithills Hall, 34–39, 194, 199
Southworths, 51, 129–35, 180
Speke Hall, 74, 87–91, 228
Spensers, 52, 184
Standishes, 98–100, 101, 109
Stanleys, 45–61, 62f, 72, 85, 91,
93, 96, 108, 133, 137, 151, 189,
237f
Starkies, 116, 191–93, 201, 202
Stonyhurst, 147–55

T

Talbots of Bashall, 51, 139, 145f,
180, 190
Talbots of Dinckley, 143f
Talbots of Salesbury, 139–43
Tempests, 140
Test Act, 66, 76
Thomas of Lancaster, 86, 92f, 107
Threlfalls, 243
Titus Oates Plot, 76
Towneley Hall, 198, 211–20
Towneleys, 76, 138, 211–19
Turton Tower, 39–41
Tyldesleys, 231–37

U

Upholland priory, 92f

W

Walmesley, Judge, 147, 180, 194
Walmesleys, 180f, 190
Walton Hall, 117, 119f
Warrington, 49, 86
Wars of Roses, 18, 40, 63, 92,
139
Wedacre Hall, 241
Weld-Blundells, 84, 104, 156
Welds, 82, 148, 155f
Welsh Wars, 24, 92, 118
West Derby, 62, 70
Whalley Abbey, 17, 114, 170, 172,
174, 190
Whalley Church, 183, 185f, 188,
217, 232
Whitaker, Doctor, 170, 221
Whitakers, 220
Widdringtons, 81, 153, 215
Wigan, 54, 56, 79, 94, 99, 102,
120, 199
Wigan Lane Battle, 56, 159, 231,
233
William I, King, 27
William II (Rufus), King, 31
William III, King, 58, 67, 76, 118
Witton Park, 124
Worsley Hall, 31–33
Worsleys, 31f
Worston Hall, 170
Wycoller Hall, 222f

Y

York, 55, 161, 215
Yorkists, 25, 47, 92, 108, 145